White-Collar Crime: An Agenda for Research

The Battelle Human Affairs Research Centers Series

The White-Collar Challenge to Nuclear Safeguards
by Herbert Edelhertz and *Marilyn Walsh*

Government Requirements of Small Business
by Roland J. Cole and *Philip D. Tegeler*

Third-World Poverty
edited by William Paul McGreevey

National Strategy for Containing White-Collar Crime
edited by Herbert Edelhertz and *Charles Rogovin*

Nuclear Power and the Public
by Stanley Nealey

Evacuation Planning in Emergency Management
by Ronald W. Perry, Michael K. Lindell, and *Marjorie R. Green*

White-Collar Crime: An Agenda for Research
edited by Herbert Edelhertz and *Thomas D. Overcast*

White-Collar Crime: An Agenda for Research

Edited by
Herbert Edelhertz
Thomas D. Overcast
Battelle Human Affairs
Research Centers

LexingtonBooks
D.C. Heath and Company
Lexington, Massachusetts
Toronto

This study and text were supported by and prepared under Grant No. 79-N1-AX-0130 of the National Institute of Justice, Law Enforcement Assistance Administration, U.S. Department of Justice, awarded pursuant to the Omnibus Safe Streets and Crime Control Act of 1968 as amended. Points of view or opinions stated in this document are those of the authors and do not necessarily represent the official position or policies of the U.S. Department of Justice.

Library of Congress Cataloging in Publication Data

Main entry under title:
  White-collar crime.

  Bibliography: p.
  Includes index.
  Contents: The consequences of white-collar crime / Robert F. Meier and James F. Short, Jr.—Corporate violations of the corrupt practices act . . . / M. David Ermann and Richard J. Lundman—The role of law enforcement in the fight against white-collar crime / Ezra Stotland—[etc.]
    1. White collar crimes—United States—Addresses, essays, lectures. 2. Corporations—United States—Corrupt practices—Addresses, essays, lectures. I. Edelhertz, Herbert. II. Overcast, Thomas D.
HV6769.W48   364.1'68'0973   81-47541
ISBN 0-669-04649-3   AACR2

Copyright © 1982 by D.C. Heath and Company

Published simultaneously in Canada

Printed in the United States of America

International Standard Book Number: 0-669-04649-3

Library of Congress Catalog Card Number: 81-47541

Contents

Preface and Acknowledgments

The public, government agencies, and the research community have become increasingly aware of white-collar crime in recent years. The special challenges of white-collar crime are perceived by the public and government in terms of economic losses, inflated costs, and threats to the integrity of marketplace and government activities. The research community shares these perspectives but must also face the many complexities involved in any scholarly response, such as definition of the problem, the absence of methodological approaches of proven use in this field, difficulties of data collection, and data uniquely lacking in comprehensiveness because of the essentially covert nature of white-collar crime. This work was commissioned by the National Institute of Justice to assist the efforts of researchers from all disciplines who seek to contribute to our knowledge of white-collar crime.

Acknowledgments

Many individuals contributed to this work. We hope that we may be forgiven for any we have inadvertently overlooked. First, we recognize the support of those who prepared the papers that are the major part of this book, reviewed and critiqued all aspects of this work, and gave so much of themselves to the colloquium that was the center of this effort. Professor Gilbert Geis of the University of California at Irvine and Professor Simon Dinitz of Ohio State University merit special mention among the authors of these chapters for their guidance and advice on the organization and agenda of the colloquium. The colloquium owed much to the presence of those who participated in its deliberations, who are listed in the appendix, and whose observations were of great value to us. Thomas Clay, a graduate student at the University of California at Irvine, prepared the initial draft for the bibliography of recent literature that appears at the end of this book.

We are particularly grateful to Bernard Auchter and Dr. Fred Heinzelmann of the Community Crime Prevention Division of the National Institute of Justice. Mr. Auchter, the National Institute's project monitor, and Dr. Heinzelmann, who is the division's director, gave unstintingly of their time and effort to ensure the success of this project. We particularly acknowledge their many substantive contributions to this book.

Finally, we express our gratitude to the many members of the staff of the Battelle Human Affairs Research Centers in Seattle, Washington, who assisted us. Research scientists Frederic M. Morris and Bert H. Hoff reviewed this work and made valuable suggestions for its improvement. Jacquie Moore, Battelle procurement specialist, smoothed our path in all matters involving business relationships with consultants, suppliers, and the facility that housed our colloquium deliberations—an essential function too often overlooked when making acknowledgments. Barbara Keen, librarian in the Battelle Science and Government Study Center, reviewed and supplemented this report's bibliography and verified the report's citations. Finally, we thank the secretarial staffs of the Battelle Science and Government Study Center and the Battelle Law and Justice Study Center, and particularly Charleen Duitsman, Ingrid McCormack, Patricia Davis, Cheryl Osborn, and Kathy Feaster, who typed our manuscripts, kept our files, and did all those things without which this project could not have succeeded.

White-Collar Crime: An Agenda for Research

1

Introduction

Herbert Edelhertz

Issues

Problems of Research

The study of white-collar crime presents unique challenges to those who undertake it. There are problems both of definition and of data availability and interpretation. Compared with other areas of criminological inquiry, this is a new field, which only began to be seriously cultivated after Sutherland captured researcher attention through the force of his presentation and analysis of the issues in 1940.[1] There was a long period of dead time between 1940 and the early 1970s, during which only limited, though in some instances significant, attention was given to white-collar crime by the criminological community.[2]

Another complicating factor has been, and continues to be, that different disciplines and interest groups examine white-collar-crime issues through their own lenses, with little or no awareness of the relevance and importance of other perspectives. Legal scholars have analyzed white-collar-crime issues as part of their studies of criminal law, administrative law, government regulation, and consumer law. The accounting profession has studied these issues in narrow terms of internal auditing and investigative-accounting theory and practice, although the recent vulnerability of accountants to civil and criminal liability for the manner in which they conduct their practices has now caused them to adopt broader perspectives.[3] Policy analysis, as an emerging discipline, is only now making its presence felt in this field.[4] Enforcement agencies have engaged in applied research, including studies of patterns of violations as bases for deterring potential violators or zeroing in on likely candidates for audit or investigation by the Internal Revenue Service (IRS), and analyses by the U.S. Department of Health, Education and Welfare (HEW) of payments to Medicaid providers as a guide to targeting of fraud violators.

Research on white-collar-crime issues has proved resistant to organization in a clear conceptual framework because those who work in the field have been unable to agree on the character and nature of behavior to be studied.[5] Political and ideological currents have broad and deep influences here.[6] There is strong disagreement, for example, as to whether wrongful behavior is to be defined in terms of the status of the offender, the

1

characteristics of his or her behavior, or the harm (actual or potential) inflicted on the victims.[7]

White-Collar-Crime Data

There is a paucity of reliable information on the impact or costs of white-collar crime, even with respect to specific and narrowly defined crimes, although there is great demand for such information.[8] The National Institute of Justice has taken a first step toward filling this gap through its support of a study of federal-level sources of data on white-collar criminal lawbreaking, which was recently completed under a grant to the Bureau of Social Science Research.[9] The Battelle Law and Justice Study Center, under a grant from the National District Attorneys Association, is currently collecting and analyzing data on investigations and prosecutions of such crime in a number of local prosecutors' offices.[10] The Federal Justice Research Program of the U.S. Department of Justice is now preparing to commission a study to gather information on the incidence and impact of white-collar crime.[11]

Until recently, researchers have failed to tap many sources of data that could shed light on the numerous issues posed by white-collar criminal behavior. There have been specific case studies—for example, Herling's study of the electrical price-fixing conspiracy; Susan Shapiro's study of enforcement by the U.S. Securities and Exchange Commission; and Clinard's recently completed study of corporate crime—many supported by the National Institute of Law Enforcement and Criminal Justice.[12] In addition, some of the most-significant work in this field has been done by journalists and investigative reporters.[13]

It is noteworthy that until very recently there were few links between the research and action communities (the latter including police, investigators, prosecutors, regulators, compliance staffs, and so forth). This is in sharp contrast to other areas of criminological inquiry, such as corrections and juvenile delinquency, where data have been consistently collected, analyzed, and reported back to user communities, and where knowledge acquired could be specifically organized for use in the training of professional staffs and in the implementation of their day-to-day working tasks. Those engaged in white-collar-crime containment efforts, such as prevention, detection, investigation, prosecution, and regulation, have only within the past few years become aware of the existence of consistent research interest in their endeavors.

Growth of Research Interest

Opportunities for research have expanded with the growth of strong media and public interest in white-collar crime. This was fueled originally by the consumer movement and by reaction to the Watergate scandal. Momentum was maintained and even increased thereafter. In part, this increase is due to some sense of the inequity reflected by the existence of different standards for prosecution and punishment of "common" and of white-collar criminals. But perhaps more significant have been new concerns with the integrity of costly government benefit and subsidy programs afflicted with patterns of fraud, waste, and abuse; with public corruption; with the abuses of power inherent in looting of pension funds; with patterns of commercial bribery, which raise widespread questions as the ethics of the business community; with recognition of links between white-collar and organized crime; with disclosures of fraud and corruption in the procurement of goods and services by public agencies; with media attention to conflicts of interest by those in positions of power in the corporate world and in public agencies; with public consciousness of tax frauds that have unfairly shifted economic burdens; with (justified or unjustified) concern that shortages of energy were being fraudulently exploited; with growing sensitivity to hidden taxes imposed on the public by monopolistic and price-fixing activities; with white-collar criminal behavior used to circumvent public programs to protect our health and environment; with threats to the health of urban environments posed by the phenomenon of arson for profit; and with crimes arising out of new technologies, such as electronic fund transfers and computer applications.

The Need for White-Collar-Crime Research

Government and private-sector planning and decision making, in order to contain white-collar crime in these and related areas, will require firmer bases of knowledge than now exist. Who are the perpetrators and who are the victims? What are the dimensions in dollar terms of harm inflicted? What harm is done indirectly through undercutting the integrity of our institutions, and by use of the techniques of white-collar crime to facilitate damage to our environment and to affect our individual health and well-being?

Are the resources marshaled to deal with white-collar crime appropriate to the challenge it presents, and are personnel and money deployed in a manner rationally calculated to achieve maximum containment of such crime? Do public agencies have the information they need to demonstrate that the benefits of white-collar-crime containment efforts justify the cost? As we plan for future public action in this area, decisions must be made as to whether government will respond with criminal, civil, or regulatory remedies, or with some mix of these. Even now, as public programs are designed and legislation enacted to implement them, there is intense debate over the appropriateness of particular remedies—arguments that are conducted without any respectable base of knowledge to illuminate the debate. Enforcement activities, similarly, lack any comprehensive grounding in systematically developed information and, instead, rely largely on impressionistic data. There are ongoing moves to develop and implement a rational approach to white-collar-crime containment involving federal, state, and local steps toward a "national strategy," as well as congressional interest in providing support to a vigorous national enforcement program; but progress along such lines is badly hampered by the absence of an adequate base of knowledge.[14]

Transnational White-Collar Crime

Our national economy is more and more interwined with those of other nations, and hence it is not surprising that there is heightened consciousness of white-collar crime in the world community. White-collar-crime issues were addressed as one aspect of abuse of power at the United Nations Congress on Criminology, held in Caracas, Venezuela, in August 1980; this followed earlier work done for the United Nations by di Gennaro and Vetere and a preliminary meeting of persons working in the subject area held at U.N. headquarters in New York in July 1979.[15]

At U.N. meetings major attention was given to the wielding of economic power by large transnational enterprises. It is perhaps more important that criminological and policy-planning researchers address problems arising out of the structure and increasing magnitude of international trade; the vulnerability of domestic institutions to white-collar crimes managed from abroad; and the dilemmas posed by conflicting national laws, interests, and mores.[16] In adopting this broader view of transnational white-collar crime, it must be recognized that these conflicting laws, interests, and mores are unique cultural features, which must be respected.

White-Collar-Crime Remedies

Finally, any effort to deal with white-collar crime comprehensively must consider the interrelated issues of equity and sentencing. There is a widespread impression that white-collar offenders are rarely charged with criminal violations, and that the entire weight of the criminal-justice system is directed with bias against the crimes of the poor and disadvantaged.[17] Recent observations by those active in enforcement indicate that prosecutors have become more willing to prosecute white-collar offenses and our courts more willing to impose prison terms on those convicted of such offenses.

Nevertheless, there exist numerous alternative remedies, in the form of regulatory and civil penalties, which provide law-enforcement agencies with a rationale for not proceeding criminally, especially where agencies are overworked, where cases are complex and time consuming, where offenders are powerful, or where there are conflicting interests.[18] There does appear to be greater willingness to impose prison sentences if there is a criminal conviction, but dilemmas still exist. Can we apply conventional sentencing and correctional standards that are geared to violent or other common crimes to white-collar offenders who are usually in court for the first time? How do we deal with the fact that a white-collar felon who is not a career con man can walk the streets without endangering the public? Are prison sentences justified in white-collar-crime cases on the theory of general deterrence alone, as many believe, where there is clearly no need specifically to deter the individual offender? How is probation to be monitored? How are publicly held corporations to be punished and deterred?

Conclusion

For those who study white-collar crime or who commission or use studies in this field, these are only some of the issues they must consider. It is an illustrative rather than a comprehensive list. Even those who would agree with the relevance of each of the parts of the list hold different views about how the questions should be structured, and about their differing weight and importance. This book describes how these and related issues were considered during a colloquium designed to contribute to the development of a research agenda on white-collar crime.

**Planning for a Research Agenda
on White-Collar Crime**

This book is not and was not planned to be a research agenda on white-collar crime, but is, rather, meant as a contribution to the development of such an agenda. The plan was a simple one—to base this contribution on a preliminary weighing of what appeared to be central-core issues in the field; to commission a series of papers to respond to these issues; and then to hold a colloquium at which the authors and others would use the papers as a springboard for wider-ranging examination of research needs in this field. The original plan, which in large part was implemented, was to seek insights both from those who have conducted research on white-collar crime in the past and from others within and outide the research community. It was also planned to expose the work of the individual authors to examination by colloquium participants—the authors of commissioned papers and other researchers, potential users of research on white-collar crime, and the professional staffs of the National Institute of Justice and the U.S. Department of Justice who would be responsible for implementing plans for research in this field. To tie all this together, Professor Gilbert Geis of the University of California at Irvine was chosen to sum up the colloquium proceedings in closing remarks, and then to follow up with a paper that would both represent in itself a contribution to this effort, and reflect his consideration of the discussions that had taken place.

Developing a Candidate List of Issues

The task of selecting topics to be addressed in colloquium papers was, we believe, a constructive exercise. It required an inventory not only of prospective issues, but also of all disciplines that might be brought together to provide the broadest possible perspectives. The result of this selection process (which involved the Battelle staff and its consultant, Professor Gilbert Geis, members of the staff of the Community Crime Prevention Division of the National Institute of Justice, and comments from the staff of the Criminal Division of the U.S. Department of Justice) was the commissioning of six papers in five general areas. This was done with the understanding that those selected to prepare the papers would have their own appreciation of the subject matter and would be quite likely to see the selected topic in a very different light. In most instances, in fact, this is just what happened.

The overall rationale for final selection of papers was that any research agenda must demonstrate the importance of the subject, consider the role of government in containing white-collar-crime research, discuss characteristics of offenders, determine who can make research contributions, weigh possible remedies for wrongful behavior with which we were concerned, and undertake a comprehensive review of possible research contributors. The topics selected and the authors who agreed to address them are discussed in the following section of this chapter.

Background Issues

There were a number of significant topics that were not selected as a basis for papers to be commissioned. In the minds of those who were part of the selection process, some were as important as any topics selected; but they were not chosen because an appropriate author could not be identified, or because the subject matter overlapped another, or simply because choices had to be made. In many instances omitted topics were reintroduced as part of the colloquium discussions. Some brief consideration of these topics is in order here so that they may be kept in mind as we go on to review the colloquium proceedings themselves.

Two suggested topics were somewhat outside the usual lists for discussion, but are nonetheless of long-range importance. The first is *the role of ideology in white-collar-crime research.* It is noteworthy that the main focus of most research on white-collar crime, and of most conceptualizations of the problem, is on the crimes of the powerful, or at least of those in positions of trust and authority. This surfaces first and most powerfully with the work of Sutherland and is still the dominating theme in the work of white-collar-crime researchers. This can be seen in most of the papers that were presented at this colloquium. Even Geis, who has most critically dissected Sutherland's biases,[19] follows this path when, in chapter 8, he unhesitatingly characterizes antitrust violations and physician-Medicaid fraud as white-collar crime, but goes on to say that "cheating on applications for food stamps or welfare payments by persons in the lower socioeconomic strata also is not a clear contender for classification as white-collar crime."[20] Do we lose something, as researchers, when we make distinctions of this kind? Can we take the same crime—embezzlement—and call it "white-collar" when it is committed by the bank president but not when the teller is the perpetrator? Where do we draw the line hierarchically between gradations of power and control? The standard of trust abused, so rightly cited by many of the authors of these chapters as of crucial importance, can be applied at many levels. It is not the presumption of honesty in applications for food stamps that makes it possible for there to be as little red tape as there is? And when government's trust in the applicant is abused, do not the poor suffer even more from new controls that are imposed as a result? Where are the studies of recipient welfare fraud, of frauds by community groups entrusted with the dispensation of benefits? In large part, they appear to be left to auditors, journalists, and legislative committees.

A second suggestion outside the usual list was most intriguing—that we should address the *philosophical aspects of white-collar crime: ethics, harm, and justice.* Some white-collar crimes are *malum in se,* regarded as wrong in and of themselves. These are largely crimes at common law. Other white-collar crimes are punishable by imprisonment because laws have been enacted to channel behavior in certain ways, or because it is felt that certain harmful or undesirable behavior warrants such remedies. But do not underlying perceptions of ethics, harm, and justice in fact determine how our laws are enacted and enforced in the area of white-collar crime? It is illegal to issue and sell securities under the Securities Act of 1933 without filing a registration statement with the U.S. Securities and Exchange Commission (SEC). A violation may be referred to the U.S. Department of Justice for prosecution, or the SEC may seek other remedies. As a practical matter, no one will be criminally indicted solely for his violation *unless* there was a wrongful intent to defraud or hurt the investing public. Most such charges are joined with fraud allegations, or stand alone when fraud was probably intended but the intent cannot be proved beyond a reasonable doubt. Just as many students in this field have considered the political or ideological bases for differential law-enforcement policies,[21] we might understand far more about how laws proscribing white-collar crime are enacted or not enacted, or vigorously enforced or not, if we would address underlying ethical issues. Studies of public attitudes, as suggested by Meier and Short in chapter 2, could contribute valuable data for such research; but it is also intriguing to consider new and valuable insights that might come from philosophers and even from theologians.

Another subject that should rank high on any agenda is *the role and responsibility of the business community in containing white-collar crime.* We hear much today about corporate codes of ethics—thou shalt not pay bribes, nor use corporate money for political contributions, nor talk with thy competitor about what to charge the customer, nor collude with thy competitor to determine who will win a particular contract. These codes are printed in fancy booklets. The fact remains that crimes are committed both *by* business and against business, as is noted in every chapter in this book and in innumerable past studies. Yet those white-collar criminal violations often are not reported by officials of the businesses involved, even where crimes are committed against them by their officers or employees. One can only speculate as to the reasons for coverups; no empirical evidence is available. The disclosure of a white-collar crime may be embarrassing and hurt the reputation of the company. Higher-level management may appear negligent to stockholders and directors, and may lose their jobs or at least their bonuses. Perhaps worse, the directors and officers may become defendants in stockholder derivative actions and may suffer losses if their negligence is proved. Last but not least, based on a simple cost analysis, management may determine that the expense of dealing with prosecutors and the time in court will make this a red-ink effort. How many corporate scoundrels have been allowed to resign and leave with honor?

The situation is far more complex where white-collar criminal activities are mounted on behalf of the employer, as in the case of antitrust, price-fixing, or environmental violations. What is the rationale for such activity? Corporate patriotism? The conception that it is the only way to do business? Another question for research by the philosopher-ethicist is how one distinguishes between "illegal" activities that are wrong and those that are not wrong.

In chapter 8, Geis refers to a meeting sponsored by accountants to consider white-collar-crime issues.[22] The thrust of that meeting was how accountants could comport themselves and be protected against client fraud (which has resulted in accountant's convictions and substantial civil judgments against their firms). One federal law-enforcement-agency representative who was present, and was in a particularly good position to know, was not aware of a single client white-collar crime ever reported by accountants or auditors; another former federal official knew of only one.

White-collar crime is in large part crime by, within, among, or against businesses. Although it is vital that the research community study business criminality, as so often suggested in the colloquium papers and the discussions triggered by them, it is of equal or greater importance that we find ways to consider what businesses should do, and how they can meet their responsibilities in this field. What incentives and disincentives will best promote assumptions of responsibility to control white-collar crime in the business community? This may be a field to which lawyers contribute by considering crime-reporting statutes that have more teeth than existing misprision or compounding statutes.[23] It is also a major area for policy research. Further, in considering the ways in which businessmen comport themselves, we should not overlook the roles of the supporting professions, such as accounting and law.

Evaluation of white-collar enforcement efforts received surprisingly little attention during this colloquium, although it was given serious consideration as a possible separate colloquium subject. Evaluation issues in the field of criminal justice are difficult at best. They are even more complex in an area in which concealment is an essential element of the crime, where victims do not know they are victims in most instances, and where the line between the licit and the illicit is exceedingly hard to draw. These considerations may raise currently unbreachable barriers to the development of baseline data on the incidence of white-collar crime, data that are so important in evaluation research. But there may be more room for constructive evaluative studies of law-enforcement activities in this field. The area is admittedly a murky one. Numbers of investigations or prosecutions are not the key because large numbers may mean that only easy cases are taken up, and that more significant matters are avoided. Other measures should be considered by evaluation researchers, such as demonstrations of deterrent effect—for example, changes in industry practices. Major SEC actions, not even prosecuted criminally, such as the *Texas Gulf Sulphur* case, resulted in hundreds of conferences throughout the United States in which corporate attorneys sought to learn how to advise their clients to avoid violations involving use of insider information for their own profit.[24] Recent prosecutions of partners in some of the most prominent and prestigious accounting firms in the United States led to much reexamination of the firms' responsibility to the public. A study of improved means to weigh the difficulty of specific kinds of cases, and to determine the personnel and other resources needed, could do much to assist investigative and prosecutive agencies to set priorities and make decisions as to where they can best employ such resources. There would be many benefits from longitudinal tracking of investigations and cases, by subject matter, to shed light on the resources such cases consume; on the likelihood that an investigation will result in restitution or provide prosecution or some other remedy; on the likelihood that if a case is prosecuted, a conviction and a particular sentence will result; on the likelihood that court-ordered restitution or fines will in fact be paid; and on the time each step is likely to take.[25] Evaluation researchers, working with policy analysts, may also find better ways to assist policymakers and thereby to influence agency performance. For example, if prosecution of those who have inflicted the greatest harm to victims is allowed to become a dominant measurement standard, this will certainly not be an incentive for a proactive policy of moving as quickly as possible to protect potential victims.

Among other topics considered but not selected for special attention at the colloquium were the general and specific deterrence of white-collar offenders, public-corruption crimes arising out of developing technologies, the relationship between white-collar and other sophisticated crime, and government-program fraud. As noted previously, many of these subjects were subsumed within the topics selected for special attention.

The Colloquium

The greater part of this book consists of the papers prepared for the colloquium, which was held in Sterling, Virginia, on 21-22 August 1980. The list of participants at that meeting is included as the appendix to this book.

The overall rationale for the selection of topics was, as noted earlier, that any research agenda must demonstrate the importance of the subject, the role of government in containing white-collar-crime research, the characteristics of offenders, who can make research contributions, and remedies for behavior that falls under the general rubric of white-collar crime and related abuses. Since the chapters speak for themselves and they are also discussed in the summary in chapter 8 by Gilbert Geis, they will not be reviewed at length in this section. However, they will be briefly considered here with respect to issues dealt with in the colloquium.

The Importance of White-Collar-Crime Research

To focus most directly on the importance of white-collar crime as a subject for research, Robert F. Meier and James F. Short, Jr., were asked to prepare their paper on "The Consequences of White-Collar Crime" (chapter 2). They addressed different impacts: financial harm; physical harm; and damage to the moral climate, (that is, loss of trust in our institutions and leadership). They concluded that the indirect consequences of white-collar crime—that is, its impact on the social fabric of the community—are of considerably greater significance than dollar losses, no matter how high these latter may be. Based on this conclusion, Professors Meier and Short saw the need for a research program that

> studies directly the nature of this impact (on the social fabric), with attention to individual perceptions of the seriousness of white-collar crime and corporate criminality, one's relationship with major institutions, and the extent to which these institutions (and subunits within them) are able to generate trust and confidence in their performance.

The Role of Government in Containing White-Collar Crime

There are numerous government agencies engaged in containing white-collar crime. The term *containment* is used here to denote a mix of deterrence and prevention, investigation, prosecution, related civil litigation, and regulatory activity. Containment activities can be considered along lines of function, such as policing, prosecuting, or regulating. They can also be viewed along jurisdictional lines reflecting federal, state, and local efforts. There is much overlap among agencies that seek to deal with white-collar crime along functional lines, as well as among federal, state, and local agencies. It would have been impossible to examine the research possibilities of all feasible containment activities. We therefore asked Professor Ezra Stotland to consider "The Role of Law Enforcement in the Fight Against White-Collar Crime," (chapter 4) and Professor John M. Thomas to consider "The Regulatory Role in the Containment of White-Collar Crime" (chapter 5).

Professor Stotland chose to address the potential of one form of law-enforcement agency, the police, in white-collar-crime containment. Noting that police were much neglected and overlooked as a resource in this area, he suggested a number of research thrusts. Professor Stotland first stressed these points among others:

> The police are in the community and have sources of information not available to other agencies.

> Police involvement helps to maintain the salience of the criminal remedy for white-collar crime.

> Police engagement in white-collar-crime enforcement efforts will serve to make credible to the public the seriousness of government enforcement efforts against white-collar crime.

Among other research projects recommended by Professor Stotland were surveys of police to determine the extent to which they are the recipients of information or complaints about white-collar crime, and studies of their motivation to become more active in this field. He also suggests that there is evidence that police often are unaware that much white-collar criminal activity violates criminal laws, and that research testing this hypothesis might lead to a greater police focus on white-collar crime. The most interesting possibility he raises is that research that could lead to increased police activity in this area might also improve police performance in other, more-traditional realms of law enforcement.

Regulatory agencies play a vital role in white-collar containment. By acting as gatekeepers for much business activity, they are in a particularly good position to prevent white-collar abuses, to detect such abuses, and to act on them directly or by referring them to prosecutors for criminal prosecution. They are often in a position to act more quickly and effectively to protect the public than are traditional law-enforcement agencies, for example, through injunctive actions and denial of authority to operate in the business area they are regulating. Nevertheless, there may be negative elements in the regulatory role. Professor John M. Thomas addresses these issues in chapter 5. He describes regulatory objectives and considers them in relationship to the need to contain white-collar crime. He notes that regulatory objectives focus on achieving compliance rather than punishing violators, and that regulatory agencies are not inclined to seek sanctions where such action is not deemed likely to increase compliance. Thomas further notes that broad agency discretion to fashion remedies for violations and day-to-day working relationships with those regulated could work at cross purposes with criminal enforcement. Prominent among his recommendations for research are studies of how regulatory agencies exercise their very broad discretion to choose between remedies (including referral for criminal prosecution), and of the deterrent effect of cases they do refer for prosecution. Perhaps implicit in these recommendations is the need to develop data that can help regulatory agencies determine when and how criminal enforcement can contribute to regulatory objectives. Professor Thomas' stress on the need to understand different and often conflicting objectives among agencies operating in the same field comes up again later, in chapter 7, as one of the central issues raised by Edwin H. Stier on new and potential remedies for white-collar criminal behavior.

Characteristics of Offenders

Contemporary concern with white-collar offenders has, as noted previously, centered on the crimes of the powerful. Professor M. David Ermann and Richard J. Lundman were therefore asked to consider what it is about large organizations that leads to organizational deviance, or to individual deviance on behalf of organizations by those acting on their behalf. The authors elected to do this by examining corporate violations of the federal Corrupt Practices Act, an act that bans corporate political contributions. In chapter 3, "Corporate Violations of the Corrupt Practices Act: Descriptions and Analysis," they focus on one major case and conclude that there are identifiable "organizational and environmental pressures that impel individuals in the direction of corporate crime." They stress the need for research on these organizational forces, which they list as follows:

1. The availability of numerous, essentially accurate rationalizations for criminality.
2. The limited information characteristic of social forces in large organizations.
3. Selection and training of loyal employees.

Who Can Make Research Contributions?

It was noted previously that different disciplines have gone their separate ways to examine white-collar-crime issues through varying lenses, and with little or no awareness of other's work. A comprehensive research agenda to deal with any societal problem should consider all possible contributors, whatever their disciplines. Professor Simon Dinitz was therefore asked to consider "Multidisciplinary Approaches to White-Collar Crime" (chapter 6). In this chapter, he considers a content analysis of four years' worth of articles and editorials in *Fortune, Business Week, The Wall Street Journal,* and *Vital Speeches of the Day.* Dinitz discussed white-collar-crime issues with a selected group of persons from public administration, accounting, management, law, marketing and related disciplines, engineering, and nuclear physics. He considers the insights gained from this content analysis and from his interviews in the light of criminological perspectives and research. Dinitz concluded that, given the complexity of white-collar-crime issues, which involve many of the most-complex questions in our society, a multidisciplinary approach to research in this field is both necessary and desirable. In the course of this chapter he addresses broader issues concerning white-collar-crime research needs and makes a number of specific recommendations. These include research on "networking,"—that is, the establishment of multidisciplinary teams to analyze, investigate, and prosecute complex crimes; study of the "whistle blower" and the incentives and disincentives for his or her behavior; and the question of whether public attitudes toward white-collar crime determine enforcement action, or whether vigorous enforcement informs and shapes public attitudes toward such crime.

Remedies for White-Collar Crimes

Wrongful behavior comprehended by the term *white-collar crime* is subject to response by a multitude of enforcement, regulatory, and administrative agencies; invoking an almost infinite number of statutes and regulations; exercising extensive discretion; and calling for remedies of every imaginable kind. There is, nevertheless, great concern about the adequacy of remedies to achieve containment goals. For example, it is often asked whether financial impositions on convicted corporations constitute anything more than a cost of doing business, which, even when very high, is really only comparable to one bad business result among many compensating profitable results. Those engaged in combating white-collar crime, in criminal or regulatory agencies, continually question whether their arsenal of remedies is adequate to punish specific violators or to generally deter others. They are not necessarily concerned with the need to have more-severe remedies available, but they desire to have finely graded classes of remedies so that the "punishment can fit the crime." All too often, enforcement personnel are forced to choose between a remedy which is no more than the proverbial slap on the wrist and some draconian and therefore unusable infliction.

Edwin H. Stier is director of the New Jersey Division of Criminal Justice, an agency that is unusual in that it exercises strong, statewide, centralized control over criminal-justice enforcement. It has managed a high volume of significant white-collar investigations and prosecutions and has pioneered criminal-justice-enforcement approaches to new challenges, such as environment issues like illegal dumping of toxic waste. Mr. Stier's chapter, "The Interrelationships among Remedies for White-Collar Criminal Behavior," suggests that rather than formulate new remedies, we first must determine why existing remedies are not as effective as they should be. He concludes that the effective marshaling and application of existing remedies are prevented by the differing goals and objectives of agencies with concurrent jurisdiction to deal with the containment of specific white-collar crimes, and that these differing agency objectives present roadblocks to successful investigation and prosecution of offenses. Stier argues for a research program that will provide greater knowledge of the goals and objectives of related agencies and of the relationships among such agencies. To assist in this effort, he suggests a classification scheme for analysis of agency goals and activities as a framework for research.

Observations on Colloquium Issues

Following an oral presentation of each paper by the authors, another participant delivered a prescheduled response; the floor was then opened for comments by all colloquium participants. This section consists of brief observations on issues raised, under headings that pull together and add to comments made in the course of the sessions.

Definitions of White-Collar Crime

Definitional issues should not be permitted to become roadblocks that prevent initiation of otherwise worthwhile research projects. We cannot wait until everyone agrees on a definition. Nevertheless, the definitional issue is an important one, which should be directly addressed in any plan for research. The term *white-collar crime* may not be too general a description for a colloquium or for a National Institute of Justice program, but it is far too general to be invoked in a design for specific research. Greater differences exist between kinds of white-collar crime than between many specific white-collar crimes and other illegal acts that clearly would not carry this label. Are we addressing corporate crimes, consumer fraud, or con games? Those who would be comfortable in applying the label to all these crimes would still be troubled by the failure to specify which white-collar crime we are talking about.

Another definitional issue that should be clearly addressed is that of how even a specific white-collar crime is to be dealt with as a research question. For example, designs for environmental research should clearly specify the degree to which they will devote attention to criminal or civil aspects of the issues, or to the linkages between them.

Insistence that research designs be specific in their definitions will help us avoid much of the vagueness of approach that has characterized work in this field.

Impact of White-Collar Crime

The problems of assessing the consequences of white-collar crime have often been discussed. Two points made in the course of the colloquium warrant special attention. First, the harm we seek to measure should go beyond the financial, physical, and social categories advanced in the paper by Meier and Short to a consideration of other containment costs. Among the costs to be measured should be private expenditures for insurance, public and private expenses of pre- and postaudits, and systems designed to prevent and deter, to which might be added all those losses from transactions that never are consummated because of fear of white-collar crime and related abuses that are not remediable from the perspective of a potential victim.

Second, it was observed that the policy usefulness of impact data would be far greater to operating agencies if such data dealt with specific crimes. This kind of information, it was stressed, would be even more valuable for policy usefulness if organized along dimensions of the nature of the perpetrators and the nature of the victims, as well as the nature of the crime. Comparative studies between specific types of white-collar crime, or between groupings that could be shown to share common characteristics or consequences, should also be considered.

Interactions between Agencies

In one way or another, the issue of agency interaction was a major theme of this colloquium. In chapter 4, in which Stotland addresses the police role in white-collar-crime enforcement, such relationships are deemed vital. Police work may often be pointless unless it is appreciated by the prosecutor or by another agency that will consummate an investigation with a legal action. Thomas's presentation on the regulatory role (chapter 5) and Stier's discussion on remedies (chapter 7) focus in large part on the different goals and objectives of agencies that must work together, that have equally legitimate mandates to operate in the same cases, and that therefore strongly influence each other. Professor Dinitz (chapter 6) talks of "networking"—that is, operationalizing relationships between agencies whose resources, taken together, can succeed where individual agencies cannot. Stier adds an extra dimension here, suggesting that the challenge is not only to achieve agreement among agencies but also, even more, to develop a clear understanding of how the characteristics and missions of agencies determine their real goals. Implicit in Stier's view is the possibility that individual relationships between agency staffs may be important in particular instances, but that better understanding of agency goals and missions and their adjustment and reconciliations may foster structural changes and more-permanent improvements.

White-Collar Offenders

Much attention has been given to white-collar offenders indirectly, as in the case of disputes over the definition of white-collar crime and, more recently, in studies of those characteristics of large organizations that cause them or their employees to commit white-collar crimes. It has been suggested that researchers look at organizations that are considered less prone to delinquency, and attempt to determine characteristics that influence organizational behavior. These seem to be highly desirable approaches. In addition, however, we should draw finer distinctions in a number of related areas, asking about the roles and responsibilities of professional and occupational groups to help contain white-collar crime. How do controllers, auditors, and house counsel operate within large business organizations? Do they report to the highest levels of management, or do their findings have to go through hierarchical layers? Are outside counsel or auditors truly independent? How would these questions be answered in the case of delinquency-prone organizations, compared with those believed less prone? Research attention to such questions should be entertained.

Awareness of White-Collar Crime

Current plans for surveying public attitudes and perceptions undoubtedly will involve determination of the public's knowledge of whether particular behavior constitutes white-collar crime or some other abusive behavior that may be remediable by official action. Professor Stotland (chapter 4) raises an interesting point when he questions whether police are in a position to handle properly complaints of alleged white-collar criminal abuses, in light of some evidence that they themselves know little about white-collar crime. One should not limit such questions to the police. Prosecutors have expressed doubts as to whether public officials in local agencies know enough about white-collar crime to recognize the need to make reports of indications of fraud or other suspected violations to them or to the police. A study that could probe the knowledge of agency officials who do not customarily interact with criminal-enforcement agencies, to determine whether they would recognize a white-collar crime in their field if they saw one and to learn the standards that they would apply before referring a matter for prosecution, would be of major use to policymakers. It would help with agency interactions, provide a basis for remedial action within agencies that lack sophistication in this field, and add to our awareness of the gaps in our knowledge about the incidence of white-collar crime.

Crime-Producing Environments

Observers of white-collar crime have made frequent note of the fact that since laws often proscribe conduct, they may to that extent create criminal conduct where it did not exist before. One suggested route is decriminalization, or the substitution of stringent regulatory or civil-liability alternatives as a curb on conduct. This approach is acceptable when consciously applied to conduct of an equivocal nature; but it cannot be used in all situations in which the government, in some sense, produces crime. For example, research consideration should be given to the possibility that compliance violations may be a natural and predictable result of poorly structured government benefit or procurement programs, and that prescribed procedures for competitive bidding on government contracts may make it very difficult to submit a bid without skirting the line at which equivocal language becomes misrepresentation and fraud.

Summary

There appear to be three general themes that emerged from preparation for the colloquium, reinforced by the chapters that follow and also by the discussions they stimulated. The first is the necessity to distinguish between the different forms of behavior that fall under the rubric of "white-collar crime," since they may vary so widely in terms of motivation, characteristics or modus operandi, victims, impact, and amenability to responsive containment operations and legal remedies. The second is the all-too-apparent absence of reliable information about the incidence and impact of white-collar crime and related abuses, both overall and by specific categories. Third, and possibly most important to the design of research programs in this field, is the need to recognize, understand, and take into account the relationship among all the issues discussed previously and those directly addressed in the chapters that follow.

The importance of this third theme became even more evident during the colloquium. In the discussion of each paper, questions and comments reflected their interrelationships. For example, the implicit definitional decision on the part of many colloquium participants to focus on the behavior of high-status offenders could result in rather narrow boundaries for data to be collected on the impact of white-collar crime. Along the same lines, reservations expressed about the role of police in white-collar-crime containment clearly reflected doubts that police would be involved in white-collar-crime cases which involved such high-status offenders. It was also impossible to ignore the close linkage among criminal-justice, regulatory, and administrative approaches to the containment of white-collar crime; how each activity influences the other; and the inseparability of data generated by their operations. Finally, it was implicit in the colloquium papers that operational "networking" was of crucial importance in this field, compelling the conclusion that white-collar-crime research must contribute to greater understanding of the ways in which agencies (public and private) can better work together. The chapters that follow should be read against the backdrop of these common themes.

Notes

1. Edwin H. Sutherland, "White-Collar Criminality," *American Sociological Review* 5 (February 1940):1-12.

2. See Gilbert Geis, "On a Research and Action Agenda with Respect to White-Collar Crime," chapter 8 of this book.

3. See Robert K. Elliot and John J. Willingham, *Management Fraud: Detection and Deterrence* (New York: Petrocelli, 1980).

4. U.S. Attorney General, *National Priorities for the Investigation and Prosecution of White Collar Crime: Report of the Attorney General* (Washington, D.C.: U.S. Government Printing Office, 1980). See also Herbert Edelhertz and Charles Rogovin, eds., *A National Strategy for Containing White-Collar Crime* (Lexington, Mass.: Lexington Books, D.C. Heath and Company, 1980); see especially William Morrill, "Developing a Strategy to Contain White-Collar Crime," pp. 85-94; and Frederic A. Morris, "Meeting the Challenge of White-Collar Crime: Evolving a National Strategy," pp. 95-102.

5. Edwin H. Sutherland, *White-Collar Crime* (New York: Holt, Rinehart and Winston, 1949), p. 9; Walter C. Reckless, "White-Collar Crime," *The Crime Problem,* 5th ed., chap. 13 (New York: Appleton-Century-Crofts, 1973); Herbert Edelhertz, *The Nature, Impact and Prosecution of White-Collar Crime* (Washington, D.C.: U.S. Government Printing Office, 1970), p. 3; Susan Shapiro, "Thinking about White-Collar Crime: Matters of Conceptualization and Research" (Unpublished monograph, Yale University, 1979); Laura Shill Schrager and James F. Short, Jr., "Towards a Sociology of Organizational Crime," *Social Problems* 25 (April 1978):407-419; for further reviews of research in the field, see Peter Ostermann et all., *White-Collar Crime: A Selected Bibliography* (Washington, D.C.: NILECJ, LEAA, U.S. Department of Justice, July 1977); Herbert Edelhertz et al., "Bibliography of White-Collar Crime Reference Sources," *The Investigation of White-Collar Crime: A Manual for Law Enforcement Agencies* (Washington, D.C.: U.S. Government Printing Office, 1977), appendix C, pp. 314-324; "Institute Supports Wide-Ranging Inquiry into White-Collar Crime," *LEAA Newsletter* 8 (March 1979):12-14.

6. Gilbert Geis and Herbert Edelhertz, "Criminal Law and Consumer Fraud: A Sociolegal View," *American Criminal Law Review* 11 (Summer 1973):989-1010.

7. Miriam S. Saxon, *White Collar Crime: The Problem and the Federal Response,* Report No. 80-84 EPW (Congressional Research Service, Library of Congress, Washington, D.C., 14 April 1980), pp. 1-8; see also Reckless, "White-Collar Crime"; and Shapiro, "Thinking about White-Collar Crime."

8. See Saxon, *White Collar Crime,* pp. 8-19.

9. Joseph R. Gusfield, *Symbolic Crusade* (Urbana: University of Illinois Press, 1966).

10. *Report on the National District Attorneys Association Economic Crime Project: Fifth Grant Period* (Report to the National District Attorneys Association Economic Crime Project by Battelle Human Affairs Research Centers, Seattle, Wash., August 1980).

11. "Study on the Impact and Incidence of White-Collar Crime in American Society," Proposal JYFRP-80-R0031 to U.S. Department of Justice, 18 August 1980.

12. John Herling, *The Great Price Conspiracy: The Study of the Antitrust Violations in the Electrical Industry* (Washington, D.C.: Robert B. Luce, 1962), "Research Agreements Program on White-Collar Crime," Grant No. 78-NI-AX-0017, Marshall B. Clinard, *Illegal Corporate Behavior* (Washington, D.C.: U.S. Government Printing Office, 1979).

13. See, for example, the muckraking studies in *The Washington Post* and in Morton Mintz and Jerry S. Cohen, *America, Inc.* (New York: Dial Press, 1971); and Jonathan Kwitny, *The Fountain Pen Conspiracy* (New York: Knopf, 1973).

14. Edlehertz and Rogovin, *A National Strategy;* Bert H. Hoff, "Report of the National Strategy Conference of the National District Attorneys' Association Economic Crime Project," Washington, D.C., 19 July 1979; U.S. House of Representatives, Subcommittee on Crime, Committee on the Judiciary (95th Congress, 2nd Session), *Hearings on White-Collar Crime* (Washington, D.C.: U.S. Government Printing Office, 1979).

15. Guiseppe di Gennaro and Eduardo Vetere, "Economic Crime: Problems of Definition and Research Perspectives," (Paper presented at First European Symposium of Social Defense on Economic Crime, Rome, 28-29, October 1977.

16. Herbert Edelhertz, "Transnational White-Collar Crime: An Overview." Temple Law Quarterly 53 (1980):1114-1126.

17. See discussion of this issue by Saxon, *White-Collar Crime*, pp. 62-63; see also testimony of Donald R. Cressey, *Hearings on White-Collar Crime,* pp. 31-32.

18. See Edwin Stier, "The Interrelationships among Remedies for White-Collar Criminal Behavior," chapter 7 in this book.

19. See Geis and Edlehertz, "Criminal Law and Consumer Fraud."

20. Geis, "On a Research and Action Agenda."

21. See testimony by Cressey, *Hearings on White-Collar Crime,* pp. 31-32.

22. See Geis, "On a Research and Action Agenda."

23. Merek E. Lipson, "Compounding Crimes: Time for Enforcement?" *Hastings Law Journal* 27 (1975):175-211.

24. *S.E.C.* v. *Texas Gulf Sulphur,* 401 F. 2d 833 (2 Cir. 1968), modified on other grounds 446 F. 2d 1301 (2 Cir. 1971); Cert. den. 404 U.S. 1005 (1971).

25. An attempt has been made to answer some of these questions by gathering data from local prosecutors' offices. See *Report on the Economic Crime Project.*

2 The Consequences of White-Collar Crime

Robert F. Meier and
James F. Short, Jr.

White-collar and corporate criminality are commonly viewed by observers as among the most serious—for some, indeed, *the* most serious—forms of crime (for example, Ermann and Lundman 1978; Saxon 1978; Clinard 1979). These views appear to be related to the impact of this form of criminality on society, an impact so substantial that it equals or surpasses that of homicide, robbery, forcible rape, and mass murders. One might be tempted to challenge such opinions as conjectural and the result of personal idosyncrasies were they not so widely held and so ardently defended among criminologists. How are such judgments made? This is the central question addressed in this chapter in which a variety of issues of crime impact and its measurement are discussed. Because so little is known, however, special attention is given to kinds of data and substantive topics that future research concerned with this subject might consider.

Criteria of Criminal Harm

Although we wish to avoid the many conceptual problems associated with the definition of white-collar criminality (Geis and Meier 1977), it is necessary to provide a preliminary definition of the phenomenon under discussion. We have decided to follow, but not to defend here, the definition of white-collar crime adopted in a recent survey of data sources of white-collar lawbreaking. Reiss and Biderman (1980, pp. 51-52) define white-collar crime in terms of "1) the violator's use of a significant position of power for 2) illegal gain." These authors continue by noting that:

> The corollary condition that there be damage or harm to victims is an essential condition for all torts as well as crimes. . . . Although calculations of probable harm are implicit in the definition and classification of types of law violation and in the range of possible penalties attached to each violation, in practice the actual harm done to victims is more often than not the principal element in determining the offense alleged and, later, of sanctions.

This makes an evaluation of the impact of crime all the more important.

Three criteria are most often mentioned in determining the degree of harm from crime: financial loss, physical harm, and damage to the moral climate of the community. This abbreviated list does not exhaust the potential standards by which one can judge an act socially injurious, but it does seem to capture the dimensions on which observers rate white-collar and corporate criminality as harmful. Unfortunately, different definitions of white-collar crime make strict comparisons between white-collar and ordinary crime spurious. Moreover, the nature of these crimes makes complete detection and assessment impossible. This is compounded by the fact that each of the standards of criminal harm is difficult to evaluate unambiguously, making comparative statements between precise levels of harm among different categories of crime impossible.

Financial Harm

Although precise financial estimates of the economic impact of white-collar and corporate criminality do not exist, several estimates of such impact have been offered.

In 1974 the U.S. Chamber of Commerce estimated the short-run direct cost of white-collar crime to the U.S. economy at no less than $40 billion annually (Chamber of Commerce 1974, p. 5), an estimate that is consistent with that quoted by Congressman John Conyers in hearings before the Subcommittee on Crime of the Committee on the Judiciary in 1978 (Conyers 1978, p. 93). In 1976 the Joint Economic Committee of the U.S. Congress put the figure at $44 billion annually. Several observers since that time have pointed out that this estimate is very conservative and excludes a number of offenses (for example, Sparks 1978, p. 172; Rodino 1978, p. 146). Senator Philip Hart, as chair of the Judiciary Subcommittee on Antitrust and Monopoly, estimated that antitrust-law violations may illegally divert as much as $200 billion annually from the U.S. economy.

Congressman Peter Rodino, in hearings conducted in 1978, informed the Conyers committee that the Justice Department estimated in 1968 that the estimated loss due to violations of the Sherman Act alone was $35 billion, and a 1977 GAO study estimated that frauds against government programs in seven federal agencies alone cost the taxpayers roughly $25 billion (Rodino 1978, p. 138). Rodino placed the estimated loss from all forms of white-collar criminality as closer to $100 billion annually.

Estimates of total financial loss from white-collar crimes are in the billions of dollars each year, and estimates of financial loss from specific white-collar crimes are similarly high. The American Management Association has estimated that the loss due to employee pilferage—arguably a white-collar crime, but one that is not typically discussed as such—costs the business community $5 billion a year (cited by Clark 1978, p. 143).

The difficulty with estimates of specific white-collar crimes parallels that with estimates for white-collar criminality in general: The definition of white-collar crime varies from observer to observer, making such estimates impossible to reconcile. For example, the U.S. Chamber of Commerce estimate mentioned previously includes the estimated cost of shoplifting, but not that of price fixing. That report does not provide a strenuous defense of such a debatable choice of crimes.

Most observers are quick to point out that the estimates they provide are conservative, and that the actual loss is probably far greater. There is agreement, however, that the annual cost from white-collar and corporate crimes is far greater than that from ordinary crime. As we shall see, measurement of these costs is extremely complex. Data sources are inconsistent and plagued by problems of reliability and validity. A beginning has been made (see Reis and Biderman 1980), but many problems remain. It seems safe to say that statistics on white-collar crime are at a more-primitive stage than were statistics of street crime prior to the initiation of the Uniform Crime Reporting system.

Physical Harm

As high as financial estimates are, by most standards, they do not include the total losses that accrue from these offenses. For example:

> They do not cover the losses due to sickness and even death that result from the environmental pollution of the air and water, and the sale of unsafe food and drugs, defective autos, tires, and appliances, and of hazardous clothing and other products. They also do not cover the numerous disabilities that result from injuries to plant workers, including contamination by chemicals that could have been used with more adequate safeguards, and the potentially dangerous effects of work-related exposures that might result in malignancies, lung diseases, nutritional problems, and even addiction to legal drugs and alcohol. [Clinard 1979, p. 16]

Physical harm, like financial losses, can be directed toward at least three different groups: employees of offending firms, consumers, and the community at large (Schrager and Short 1978). Physical harm to employees includes unsafe working conditions, such as those found in many mining operations and in fiberglass plants. The effects of black-lung disease and asbestos poisoning, although relatively slow to develop, can result in death.

Harm experienced by consumers includes the sale of unsafe products (such as flammable clothing for children), food, and drugs. Perhaps the most dramatic and significant case of consumer harm in recent history arose over the manufacture and sale of an automobile, the Ford Pinto, which had been linked with a number of driver and passenger deaths due to an unsafe fuel tank. Although the criminal trial related to this case resulted in acquittal of the Ford Motor Company, commentators have been quick to point out that the principle of manufacturers' criminal liability for their products was more firmly established by the trial. Many other instances of severe physical harm might be cited, although they have not always resulted in criminal prosecution and conviction. For several years the Beechcraft Company allegedly used a fuel pump with a faulty design that caused a number of deaths of pilots and passengers in the Beechcraft "Bonanza" series of aircraft; the engine would often stall when the plane was banking lightly shortly after takeoff, causing a loss of power and control (Geis and Monahan 1976).

Harm to the community at large can take many forms, such as pollution—air, water, and noise. A recent report estimated that 14,000 persons in the United States who would have died in 1978 of lung cancer and other diseases related to air pollution were spared because of improvements in air quality since the enactment of the Clean Air Act of 1970 (*Lewiston (Idaho) Morning Tribune,* 22 April 1980, p. 4A). The estimate was derived from previous studies of the impact of air pollution.

Perhaps because physical injuries are not readily quantifiable in terms of dollars and cents, these consequences of white-collar and corporate criminality are viewed as more serious by citizens than are financial or property losses (Schrager and Short 1980). One problem is that it is often impossible to demonstrate that actions leading to physical injuries were intentional or were the result of faulty decision making or other "human-like" qualities. This, evidently, accounted for the recent court decision that found Ford Motor Company not guilty of the deaths of persons resulting from a Pinto fuel-tank explosion and fire. To cite the lack of complete documentation concerning corporate liability in such matters is not to deny that there are physical injuries; nor is it to argue against the notion that the public, regardless of strict legal criteria, may blame corporations and their officers for such acts. Nevertheless, it must be recognized that all the cautions concerning data sources regarding economic harm apply with even greater force in the case of physical harm.

Another difficulty in assessing this consequence is the absence of clear criteria or standards by which physical harm from criminal means can be evaluated. Life itself is physically risky in many respects; to claim that such risks are due to criminal conduct is quite another matter. The best-designed aircraft and the most intensively trained pilots still cannot eliminate completely the risk of flying. Until the idea of *minimum acceptable level of risk* is explicated and put into practice, discussions of physical harm from white-collar crimes are likely to be widely speculative. The idea of minimum acceptable levels of risk is not new, having been employed, for example, in determining unacceptable health risks for air and water pollution. Airborne particulates or water contaminates above specified medically determined levels are deemed unacceptable. If high levels of particulates or contaminants can be traced to a manufacturing concern, then state or federal sanctions can be imposed. Acceptable levels of risk for many types of pollution have not yet been determined, and they often shift as knowledge is expanded. This further complicates assessments of physical impacts of corporate behavior.

Damage to Moral Climate

Although few dispute that the financial loss and physical harm due to white-collar crime are enormous, perhaps the criterion of harm that has been stressed most strongly by sociologists is the set of broader social consequences of crimes committed by persons of high social status. Persons of wealth and high social standing are often held to very high standards of accountability for their conduct. As one observer put it: "It can be argued, convincingly I think, that social power and prestige carry heavier demands for social responsibility, and that the failure of corporation executives to obey the law represents an even more serious problem than equivalent failure by persons less well-situated in the social structure" (Geis 1972, pp. 380-381).

The notion that prestige carries with it greater responsibility toward the community is objectionable to some on the grounds that it may lead to standards of seriousness of crime that depend on characteristics of persons such as socioeconomic status, race, or gender. One of the charges against the traditional criminological focus on ordinary crime is that it does precisely this, since the most-serious crimes of this sort are heavily concentrated among those segments of the population of lower socioeconomic status. Still, it is unmistakable that some crimes *are* more serious than others, and more-serious crimes may indeed be those committed by persons in positions of power and prestige. In fact, one of the characteristics of white-collar crimes—that victimization patterns are spread over many more persons than with most conventional crimes—suggests that crimes by persons in power may have more impact precisely for this reason.

Because of the high social standing of white-collar offenders, some observers have maintained that these violations create cynicism and foster the attitude that "if others are doing it, I will too" (Saxon 1980, p. 12). Tax authorities have used this interpretation of the fact that after exposure of former President Nixon's tax deceits, false reporting of taxes increased substantially (Geis 1977). More fundamentally, it is held that white-collar crime threatens the trust that is basic to community life—for example, between citizens and government officials, professionals and their clients, businesses and their customers, employers and employees, and—even more broadly—among members and between members and nonmembers of the collectivity. Thus, Cohen (1966, pp. 4-5) argues that "the most destructive impact of deviance on social organization is probably through its impact on *trust,* or confidence that others *will,* by and large, play by the rules." Because both the offenders and the offenses are "high placed," this is a particularly troublesome feature of white-collar crime.

The relationship between white-collar crime and prevailing public attitudes about trust has neven been explored systematically. Yet it is precisely public trust—trust in social institutions, groups, and particular persons—that may provide the social glue that is social cohesion in the community. Once that cohesiveness is weakened or broken, the social fabric itself suffers. (We will return presently to these considerations, which deserve more than passing mention.)

These consequences, however, rest to a large extent on some unstated and untested assumptions, namely, (1) that high-status persons serve as moral role models for the rest of the population, who, in turn, pattern their behavior after those they emulate; and (2) that the public generally views such conduct as relatively serious, at least compared with street crime. The former assumption has never been tested empirically, and one could generate arguments both for and against it. The second assumption has received more empirical attention, both because public perceptions of crime seriousness may be important criteria of harm, and because these perceptions may be related to other criteria mentioned earlier. However, none of these studies can be considered definitive. Paradoxically, the accepted social-science view has been that the public does not view white-collar crime as serious in comparison with ordinary or street crime. This view may be related to the inconclusiveness of the research; if so, however, it is odd that the second assumption has been implied at all.

Public Reactions to White-Collar Crime

The conventional wisdom that members of the public do not view white-collar violations as terribly serious, compared with ordinary crimes, was succinctly summarized by the President's Commission on Law Enforcement and Administration of Justice (1967, p. 48): "The public tends to be indifferent to business crime or even to sympathize with the offenders when they have been caught."

This argument dates back at least to Ross (1907, p. 46), who claimed that

> the real weakness in the moral positions of Americans is not their attitude toward the plain criminal, but their attitude toward the quasi-criminal. The

shocking leniency of the public in judging conspicuous persons who have thriven by antisocial practices is not due, as many imagine, to sycophancy . . . but the fact that the prosperous evildoers that bask undisturbed in popular favor have been careful to shun—or seem to shun—the familiar types of wickedness.

Sutherland maintained this view in his major work on white-collar crime when he claimed that "the public . . . does not think of the businessman as a criminal; the businessman does not fit the stereotype of 'criminal' " (1949, p. 224). However, Sutherland, like Ross before him, did not support his claim with reference to data. Work subsequent to Sutherland has perpetuated this view. Clinard (1952, p. 355) and Aubert (1952) both subscribed to this view. According to Aubert, "The public has customarily a condoning, indifferent or ambivalent attitude," although he does admit that this conclusion is not based on systematic surveys.

Supporters of this conventional wisdom have often attributed this fact to the influence of white-collar violators in manipulating stereotypes and images of "the criminal" so as to exclude themselves. As Sutherland (1945, p. 270) observed: "Public opinion in regard to picking pockets would not be well organized if most of the information regarding this crime came to the public directly from the pickpockets themselves." Still other writers have quarreled with the reason for public indifference while at the same time maintaining its existence. Kadish (1963) takes as given the public's nonserious perception of white-collar crimes and uses it to support his argument that white-collar crimes must be processed differently (that is, administratively, not criminally).

The Evidence

What is the empirical evidence with respect to this conventional wisdom? Actually, there is very little. One small-scale study (one that was conducted as part of a larger survey on a topic quite removed from white-collar crime) is often cited in support of this view. Newman (1953) found that 78 percent of his 178 respondents did not rate violations of pure food and drug laws as comparable in seriousness to street crimes; but the respondents did favor stiffer penalties than the courts usually gave out for such violations. Aside from these findings, most of the research on perceived crime seriousness has suggested a far different conclusion: Members of the public do make discriminations among types of white-collar crime (as they do for street crime), rating some as more serious, some as less. Moreover, white-collar violations as a group are generally ranked as quite serious.

Reed and Reed (1975) found that 305 freshman at a southern university rated a number of white-collar crimes as being at least as serious as street crimes. Rettig and Passamanick (1959a,b) questioned respondents about the rightness and wrongness of fifty different acts, five of which involved business crime. Four of these business crimes were among the twenty-five eliciting the severest moral condemnation. (A follow-up showed, however, that most of these white-collar offenses elicited less condemnation with increasing age of the respondents.)

Gibbons (1969) questioned 320 San Francisco residents about their preferred punishments for a variety of offenses. Of the respondents, 70 percent preferred prison sentences for an antitrust violator, about the same percentage that preferred imprisonment for an auto thief. Forty-three percent preferred imprisonment for an advertiser who misrepresents his product, a figure similar to that for the imprisonment of one who assaults another person.

A 1969 Harris poll concluded that analysis of this list of white-collar and street crimes and rankings of seriousness leaves little doubt that immoral acts committed by "establishment" figures are viewed as much worse, by and large, than those of the antiestablishment figures who have caused all the recent flurry of public indignation (*Time,* 6 June 1969, p. 26).

Clinard (1952, pp. 89-114), in spite of his view that the public does not condemn white-collar crimes to the same extent as street crimes, indicated that polls conducted at the time of his study of Office of Price Administration (OPA) violations during World War II found that most persons (between two-thirds and 97 percent, depending on the specific poll of a national sample) favored OPA controls.

Hartung (1953) asked 40 meat company managers and 322 citizens to express their disapproval of ten different acts (five criminal, five civil and of the white-collar-crime variety). Citizens disapproved of the civil acts to the same extent—not more, but certainly not less—as the criminal acts; the meat managers, perhaps expectedly, disapproved more of the criminal acts.

A 1968 survey of U.S. citizen attitudes also found relatively high condemnation for one specific white-collar offender: the embezzler. Samples of 1,000 adults and 200 adolescents rated the embezzler as a less-serious criminal than the armed robber, murderer, or narcotics seller to minors, but as more serious than the burglar, prostitute, or rioter who engages in looting. There was no difference by sex of respondent in these ratings, but more highly educated and white respondents were more likely to favor lesser penalties for the embezzler (however, even here the degree of condemnation was high). In another part of the survey, respondents were asked how uneasy they would be working with a parolee who had been convicted of a crime. Only the armed robber provoked more anxiety than the embezzler who stole from a charity; much less anxiety was expressed over the prospect of working with a check forger, an auto thief, an income-tax defrauder, or a shoplifter. When asked about specific dispositions, 7 percent of the respondents were willing to place the embezzler on probation; but 43 percent favored a short period of confinement, and 42 percent a longer sentence. More-lenient handling was favored by the respondents for a 25-year-old burglar, with 20 percent favoring probation, 57 percent a short period of confinement, and 15 percent a longer sentence (Joint Commission on Correctional Manpower and Training 1968).

More-recent surveys show similar results. In a survey of Baltimore residents, Rossi et al. (1974) found that manufacturing drugs known to be harmful to users and knowingly selling contaminated food that causes a death were rated as more serious than armed robbery, child abuse, selling secret documents to a foreign government, arson, deserting the army in time of war, spying for a foreign government, or child molesting. Of the 140 offenses on this list, 20 could reasonably be considered white-collar crimes. Taken together, the white-collar offenses as a group were rated as more serious than spouse abuse, burglary of a factory, resisting arrest, bribing a public official, simple assault, or killing a suspected burglar in one's home.

Cullen, Link, and Polanzi (1980) replicated the rankings of Rossi et al. in a rural area in Illinois. On the basis of 105 responses, they conclude that citizens do view white-collar criminality as serious (more so, in fact, than did Rossi's respondents), although, as expected, they make distinctions in terms of relative seriousness on the basis of different kinds of white-collar crimes. Violent corporate offenses, in particular, were rated as highly serious. Knowingly selling contaminated food that causes death, for example, was rated as more serious than forcible rape, aggravated assault, or selling secret documents to a foreign government. Causing the death of an employee by neglecting to repair machinery was rated by the Illinois respondents as more serious than child abuse, making sexual advances to small children, and kidnapping for ransom.

Hawkins (1980) surveyed 662 undergraduates at the University of North Carolina. Students were asked to rank the seriousness of twenty-five different acts presented in scenarios that altered the nature of the acts and the actors. Six of the scenarios depicted white-collar offenses. One such act, that of a hotel owner who refuses to install a fire alarm, as a result of which one hundred persons die in a fire, was rated as more serious than the crimes of a 50-year-old man who rapes a babysitter, a young man who kills his parents, or a woman who shoots and injures her husband. The other white-collar crimes received differential ratings, although the lowest-rated white-collar crime—that of a man who fails to pay income tax—was rated sixteenth out of the list of twenty-five.

A preliminary analysis of data collected in a nationwide sample of 60,000 households by Marvin Wolfgang (1980) found that the public does indeed view white-collar crimes as serious. Wolfgang's data show that the crime of a legislator who takes a bribe of $10,000 was rated as more serious than a burglary of a bank that netted the burglar $100,000. The polluting of a city's water supply by a factory, resulting in the illness of only one person, was rated as more than twice as serious as the burglary of a private home in which the burglar steals $100. Consistently, certain white-collar violations—particularly those that result in injury or death—are rated as very serious, a view that is supported by a reanalysis of Rossi's data by Schrager and Short (1980), who found that white-collar crimes involving violence are rated as being as serious as street crimes of violence and more serious than nonviolent crimes of either variety.

The Confrontation of Empirical Evidence and Conventional Wisdom

One must wonder on what basis criminologists have maintained the view that the public is indifferent to white-collar crimes. Virtually all the research done so far suggests quite another conclusion: The public does condemn white-collar crimes, many of them as much as or more than forms of ordinary crime. Yet the conventional wisdom persists: "One must, of course, recognize that the public is far less fearful of dying a slow death as a result of air pollution, or of a disease caused by their occupation, than they fear being robbed or burglarized" (Clinard 1979, p. 16).

One could argue, we suppose, that the findings reviewed indicate increased awareness of such crimes on the part of the public, perhaps a shift in public knowledge; that is, the more one knows about these crimes—particularly about their harmful consequences—the more one condemns them. The problem with comparing the public with criminologists in this respect is that the latter have done very little research on white-collar crime compared with ordinary crime. At this point, it is questionable whether criminologists are better armed with scientific knowledge about white-collar crime than is the public. In this sense, the protestations of criminologists appear to be a case of "Do as I say, not as I do." Further, one could argue that increased public awareness and knowledge are products of the consumer movement, which has taken as its objective precisely this sort of public information dissemination. Yet even those studies done prior to the existence of the current consumer movement suggest that the public has hardly been indifferent to white-collar crimes. In any case, there are other plausible explanations for public awareness.

Heightened Social Consciousness. There seem to us to be at least three possible explanations for the discrepancy between the empirical evidence and criminologists' interpretation of that evidence. First, the moral condemnation displayed by criminologists is so intense, compared with that of the public, that anything less than total public outrage will be interpreted by criminologists as indifference. Such a hypothesis is clearly plausible and is, in fact, suggested by the work of many criminologists who have studied white-collar crime. Meier and Geis (1979), for example, have recently argued that criminologists have adopted a strict "correctionalist" stance with respect to white-collar crime. The works of Ross, Sutherland, Clinard, and many others seem to have been oriented more toward control and regulation than toward increasing social understanding of this form of criminality, an orientation that is often quite divergent from that which criminologists bring to the study of ordinary crime.

Whereas the ideological position of, say, Sutherland was masked by statements indicating that he viewed his contribution as "reforming criminological theory, and nothing else" (1949, p. 1), criminologists have recently been less subtle. Donald Cressey, a collaborator with Sutherland and himself a contributor to the literature on white-collar crime, has noted Sutherland's strong reformist inclinations with respect to the conditions he was studying (Cressey 1976, pp. 214-215). Recently, Cressey himself illustrated this tendency in testimony before the Subcommittee on Crime of the Committee of the Judiciary (Cressey 1978, pp. 113-114): "I am glad you invited me back because, among other things, my testimony in June didn't show enough *indignation*. I am quite indignant about white-collar crime, and my prepared statement this time expresses a little of that indignation. I am looking for solutions to our white-collar crime problem that involve something other than mere deterrence and defense."

Such indignation, of course, may simply reflect the greater consciousness among criminologists of the nature and extent of white-collar crime. It is true that many citizens do not realize that they are being victimized by some white-collar crimes (such as price-fixing or restraint of trade) and, under those circumstances, the public cannot be expected to react to such behavior. Yet the evidence reviewed suggests that the public does react negatively to white-collar offenses in its ratings of seriousness (for example, according to the consequences of the act and, perhaps, the characteristics of the actor). The public does not lump all white-collar crimes into the same cognitive category, as criminologists often do. Of course, there is nothing inherently improper about being indignant about white-collar crime as long as this attitude does not interfere with the scientific task.

What People Say and What They Do. Another possible explanation for the divergence of the empirical literature on public perceptions of seriousness and criminologists' interpretations of that literature is that criminologists are acutely aware that what people say is often different from what they do (Deutscher 1973). Finding that people regard some white-collar crimes as being as serious as some ordinary crimes may tell us nothing, for example, about the willingness of those same people to support legislation dealing more harshly with white-collar criminals; or to convict white-collar crimes from a safe distance, yet to accord white-collar criminals differential treatment at the hands of the law (or tolerate such treatment).

One reason for this apparent discrepancy between attitudes and actions may be that the kinds of contingencies that often mitigate criminal penalties are more prevalent among white-collar criminals (for example, no prior record or no record of violent acts, steady employment, ability to meet other social and financial obligations, few prospects for recidivism, and so forth). Moreover, one must consider that most white-collar criminals are not tried by juries (neither are most ordinary criminals, of course), but are dealt with by officials of regulatory agencies; the public seldom has an opportunity to influence directly either the nature of the penalties for these crimes or the application of those penalties that do exist with respect to specific violations.

Even if citizens were deeply sincere in condemning white-collar crimes, it could be that their outrage has no collective expression in the form of citizen groups and lobbyists. However, the tremendous increase in consumer advocacy suggests precisely the opposite—that citizens are not only concerned, but are finding political means to express their opinions (Geis 1974), even if some recent evidence has indicated that public opinion does not directly affect either the content or the administration of the criminal law (Berk, Brackman, and Lesser 1978).

Flaws in the Research. A third explanation for criminologists' interpretations of research concerning public reactions to white-collar crimes concerns various methodological defects of the research that render it implausible. One could ask whether respondents are willing to respond to an investigator's questions about the seriousness of white-collar crimes in a manner that is socially acceptable (at least to the investigator), and still regard white-collar crimes as less serious, on the whole, than ordinary crime. Moreover, it is true that some studies of public perceptions of crime seriousness have used nonrandom samples of citizens (for example, Newman 1953; Reed and Reed 1975; Hawkins 1980), making generalizations of results questionable.

Rossi et al. (1974) used a representative sample of Baltimore, Maryland, respondents (who may be atypical of citizens elsewhere); several other problems also limit complete confidence in their findings:

1. The method of rating crime seriousness is that suggested by Wolfgang and Sellin (1964), which presents respondents with a crime description and asks them to rate the crime from 1 to 9 (with 9 representing the most serious). This technique has proved troublesome in some respects (for example, Rose 1966); consequently, investigators increasingly have used a

technique known as *magnitude estimation*, whereby an arbitrary value (such as 100) is assigned to a criterion crime, and respondents are asked to rate other offenses as more or less serious (by assigning higher or lower values) than the criterion offense (see Erickson and Gibbs 1979, for a rationale for this procedure and an example of it; see also Wolfgang 1980). This method greatly increases the potential range of expressed seriousness, thus permitting more variability in seriousness ratings; moreover, one can most easily make comparative judgments about the relative positions of offenses, since this technique produces a ratio scale.

2. The number of persons who rated each of Rossi's crimes varied from crime to crime (each crime was rated by at least 100 persons). Thus, although the total sample may have been representative of Baltimore citizens, the representativeness of the sample for *each* crime varied. Rossi and his colleagues do not provide sufficient information about the sample for each crime to satisfy this nagging doubt.

3. Perhaps because of these difficulties, there appears to be a serious problem of response reliability in Rossi's findings. One crime, assault with a gun on a stranger, was inadvertently repeated in the survey. The first time it was asked, this crime was rated as eighteenth most serious out of the 140 total offenses. The second time it was asked, this crime fell to twenty-fourth position (Rossi et al. 1974, note, table 1, p. 229). Moreover, the standard deviation for this offense does not appear much larger than those for other offenses in the study, suggesting that reliability may be a problem for other offenses as well. In a subsequent publication, Berk and Rossi (1977, appendix A) address some of these issues, but not in a completely satisfying manner. Moreover, the subsequent discusssion raises yet another question, that of the possibility of low test-retest reliability.

This third problem of Rossi's study was evident in the replication of that study as well. Cullen, Link, and Polanzi (1980, p. 16) indicate that they inadvertently repeated three offenses, and that respondents rated the same crimes differently the second time. Armed robbery of a company payroll dropped from the twenty-ninth position to the thirty-sixth; burglary of a home with stealing of a color television set was ranked both seventy-seventh and eighty-second; and assault with a gun on a spouse was ranked twenty-seventh and thirty-seventh. Such differences in ranks for the same offenses cannot but raise questions about other crime rankings.

Alienation, Social Confidence, and the Moral Climate

If social scientists have misinterpreted (or do not accept) the evidence on perceived seriousness and public concern with white-collar crime, they have left virtually unexamined their own stress on damage to the moral climate and the social fabric. The complexity of these phenomena undoubtedly contributes to the lack of empirical work. Yet relevant theory and research exist, although the concepts and methods of inquiry of the body of this work have not been applied to the study of white-collar crime. In this section we discuss two areas of inquiry that seem especially relevant to our concerns, and the implications of these for the study of white-collar crime. Following this, we discuss research strategies suggested by these implications, as well as strategies designed to permit greater precision concerning seriousness ratings.

Alienation

The "alienation syndrome" (Seeman 1975, p. 91) is based on "root ideas concerning personal control and comprehensible social structures." Some of the varieties of alienation that scholars in this tradition delineate relate directly to the lack of trust that is hypothesized to result from white-collar crime. The most obviously relevant variety of alienation in this respect is normlessness, which is prominent in both structural and social-psychological theories. Here, the focus is on standards of behavior, not on the behavior of individuals. The relationship between the two may be regarded as problematic. Structurally, the concept of normlessness refers to "the condition in which norms have lost their regulatory powers"; at the individual level, the concept "refers to expectations or commitments concerning the observance of established norms of behavior" (Seeman 1975, p. 102). Operationally, attempts to measure normlessness suggest the concept's affinity to trust; for example, in "Dean's (1961) usage (his item: 'Everything is relative and there just aren't any definite rules to live by'), or McClosky and Schaar's (1965) measure of 'anomy' (item: 'People were better off in the old days when everyone knew just how he was expected to act')" (Seeman 1975, p. 103). Trust has also been a major focus of recent work on political issues (for example, Finifter 1970; Converse 1972) and on interpersonal trust (Rotter 1980).

    Studies of normlessness suggest, as Seeman (1975, p. 104) notes, that trust is not a "unitary personality feature, a thread which binds attitudes toward oneself, toward others, and toward the polity into a generally positive (or negative) orientation." A clear implication for study of the impact of white-collar crime is that interpersonal referents of trust must be differentiated from institutional ones. Institutions, broadly conceived, have been differentiated in the next body of research to be considered. Before turning to this research, however, mention should be made of other possibly relevant varieties of alienation.

Powerlessness is the dimension of alienation most extensively studied by social scientists. Defined as "a low expectancy that one's own behavior can control the occurrence of personal and social rewards" (Seeman 1972, p. 473), powerlessness might be expected to result from white-collar crime to the extent that trust in large corporations, government, or other seemingly responsible organizations is eroded by its occurrence. A less-studied dimension, "cultural estrangement"—"the perceived gap between the going values in a society . . . or subunit thereof . . . and the individual's own standards," again following Seeman (1972, p. 473)—might be expected to rise in response to the crimes of apparently responsible officials in business, government, and other offending institutions.

Another dimension of alienation delineated by Seeman and others is *meaninglessness.* "Things have become so complicated in the world today, that I really don't understand just what is going on" is an item on Middleton's (1963) alienation scale. Yet another is *self-estrangement,* perhaps the alienation theme with the most-venerable history, from Marx to the present. Finally, there is *social isolation,* which, in Wilson's (1968) usage, has a strong trust component, being based on "a desire for the observance of standards of right and seemly conduct" (p. 27). These are also important to consider as we study the impact of white-collar crime on moral climate and the social fabric.

Although alienation relates in a general way to the moral-climate and social-fabric impacts of white-collar crime, Seeman's cautions suggest the desirability of differentiating trust and other types of impact into more-specific institutional areas than has been customary in the alienation literature. Alienation scales have tended to concentrate on *interpersonal* and *political* trust, and on disaffection in these areas and in one's *work* situation (see, for example, Robinson and Shaver 1973, chaps. 4 and 5), areas that may or may not be affected by one's experience with and/or perceptions of white-collar crime. Both general and more specifically directed effects require investigation, as the next body of research to be examined suggests.

Confidence in Institutions

Since 1972, the General Social Survey (GSS), a project of the National Opinion Research Center (NORC), and the Louis Harris polling organization have been questioning samples of the U.S. population about their confidence in major institutions. The form of the questions occasionally varies, but the following GSS version is representative and has remained constant throughout the history of GSS (1973-1980):

> I am going to name some institutions in this country. As far as the *people running* these institutions are concerned, would you say you have a great

deal of confidence, only some confidence, or hardly any confidence at all in them?

Similarly, precise descriptors have varied between GSS and Harris, with GSS being more consistent. GSS descriptors, since 1973, were the following: major companies, organized religion, education, executive branch of the federal government, organized labor, press, medicine, television, U.S. Supreme Court, scientific community, Congress, and the military. In 1975, banks and financial institutions were added. Harris descriptors have been identical in many instances, and very similar in most others. Smith (1979) has examined at length the impact of these and other differences between GSS and Harris. His conclusion is that, with proper caution, the confidence items used by GSS and Harris can be used "as measures of the fluctuating state of trust in major institutions" (Smith 1979, p. 93). Trust was the single most frequently given definition of confidence by a randomly chosen subsample of the 1978 GSS sample. "In general . . . confidence means to the vast majority of people trusting or having faith in the leadership, while a secondary group emphasizes competence, and a much smaller group stresses the concepts of serving either the common good or personal interests" (Smith 1979, p. 76). These differences in definition of confidence were not found to be related to the *level* of confidence expressed by respondents.

Smith (1979, p. 87) suggests that a major problem that lends instability to confidence measures relates to the abstract nature of the items. "This can make it harder for items to become crystalized and, as a result, make changes in responses easier and more common." Again,

> Attitudes about confidence are not usually consciously preformulated in a summary and coherent fashion and cannot be simply or automatically plugged into *any* scale of responses. In essence, the nature of the topic of confidence in institutions probably helps to keep many attitudes uncrystalized and thus makes them more susceptible than average to changes. [Smith 1979, p. 88]

It thus appears that confidence is a viable concept, in the sense of being widely and correctly understood, but that the particular institutional items studied are ambiguous enough to introduce an element of instability. It is possible—and, we think, probable—that more-specific institutional referents, related to more-specific events, might elicit more sharply focused, reliable, and valid responses. Such a strategy would require detailed questioning about knowledge, awareness, and concern before respondents were questioned about confidence and the meaning of the concept. Such a procedure is well worth the effort, given the potentially important relationship between the concept of confidence and white-collar criminality.

The Impact of White-Collar
Crime: A Proposal

The impact of white-collar crime may now be restated in terms of the issues discussed earlier. Impact is of three types: (1) economic harm, (2) physical harm, and (3) damage to the social fabric (including moral climate or climates). The first two of these may be identified with objective—although difficult to measure—criteria, such as monetary costs and health hazards associated with white-collar crime. Economic and physical harm depend to some extent on each other, most typically in the form of economic costs associated with physical damage (to health, as a result of disease or injury, and, in the extreme case, death). Similarly, damage to moral climate or social fabric is presumably partly a function of perceived and experienced economic and physical harm. By its very nature, however, the social fabric represents more than individual experiences or perceptions of harm, or their accumulation. Although debate about precise meanings is unlikely to be stilled by any definition—nor should it be—based on the "alienation" and "confidence" literature, the notion of *trust* appears to be crucial.

Trust is an element of both normlessness and social isolation, as they have been measured. Its relationship with other types of alienation, and the relationship of white-collar crime to each type of alienation, are problems worthy of attention. Trust has been defined as a "generalized expectancy held by another individual that the word, promise, oral or written statement of another individual or group can be relied on" (Rotter 1980, p. 1). This suggests that an institutional or collective counterpart to interpersonal trust could be defined as the expectancy that institutions can be relied on to meet the expectations constituents have for them. To the extent that expectations are not met, constituents may become alienated from these institutions, and may reduce or eliminate participation in them. Thus the inability of political institutions to produce effective and meaningful majorities through elective procedures, such that persons can readily identify the most-effective means by which they can attempt to satisfy their political self-interest, may reduce the percentage of persons who vote in elections (see also Janowitz 1978). Similarly, the inability of economic institutions to produce high-quality goods at "fair" prices without resorting to deceptive and illegal means, may lead to economic boycotts, consumer advocacy, and suspicion of the business community.

The rest of this chapter examines problems associated with the measurement of each of the types of impact. Since our own research is focused on public assessments of white-collar crime, and on damage to the social fabric, we will concentrate on these areas and will devote less attention to the assessment of economic and physical harm. We will, however, begin our discussion with the latter.

Data Sources on White-Collar Lawbreaking

Until recently, no attention has been given to the problem of data sources on white-collar and corporate criminality, aside from the plaintive suggestions of criminologists that current sources are inadequate. Toward that end, Reiss and Biderman (1980) and their associates have surveyed public and private data sources on white-collar lawbreaking. Their state-of-the-art survey reveals a multitude of data sources, as well as problems in their interpretation. Their concluding observations, although focused on social indicators and substantive theories of white-collar crime, are no less applicable to the problem of assessing many of the consequences of such crime. They indicate that

> the current state of federal agencies' information systems makes it difficult to develop a system of social indicators on white-collar law-breaking without substantial alteration in their data collection, processing, and reporting subsystems. . . . Quite often the current data cannot provide satisfactory tests of substantive theory, yet they are nonetheless put to it. The result is a body of empirical investigations that are inappropriate and inaccurate tests of theory.

This is true also with respect to assessment of the consequences of white-collar crime. Reliable and valid social indicators of white-collar crime are crucial to any such assessment. Yet, just as the Uniform Crime Reports provide little information about the consequences of even Class I crimes, social indicators of white-collar crimes are unlikely to provide complete information about its consequences. Reiss and Biderman (1980, p. 697) acknowledge that seriousness often enters into measurement considerations in a variety of ways, but conclude that "it seems premature . . . to attempt any classification of illegal gains or harms" and that such problems are "worthy of systematic investigation."

At present, there are substantial problems with virtually every known data source on the consequences of white-collar crimes. Records and statistics maintained by offending organizations, for example, are unlikely to have this sort of information; and, if such information is maintained, it is unlikely to be available to outsiders. Records of enforcement and sanctioning agencies are more likely to have information about the nature of the offense than about its impact (except, perhaps, in very general terms). Moreover, those who would attempt victimization surveys that concentrate on white-collar crimes would somehow have to compensate for the fact that victims are often unaware of their victimization, a situation that is very different from that for street crime. Yet until such work is attempted, discussions of the physical and economic impact of white-collar crime are doomed to be shrouded in controversy and speculation.

Public Assessment

Public assessment of the impact of crime has most often been studied by means of seriousness ratings. Contingencies of perceived seriousness have seldom been studied directly. Rather, they have been inferred from variations in ratings of crimes associated with, for example, age, sex, and other characteristics of the victim and the offender, and the relationship between the victim and the offender. We propose to study these relationships directly by inquiring about the influence on perceived seriousness of dimensions of harm, such as those suggested by Reiss and Biderman (1980). We propose, further, to study the effect on perceived seriousness of the *degree of harm* associated with crimes, that is, the economic, physical, and "community" (social fabric and moral climate) criteria, as noted earlier.

Earlier research suggests strongly that physical harm is perceived as more serious than is economic harm, for both white-collar and ordinary crime. However, the range of such variation, and the influence of victim-offender relationships, has hardly been studied at all. This is particularly true with respect to white-collar crime in which such relationships may be critical, as between employers and employees; between producers of products and consumers of those products; or between the general public or segments thereof and those who offend against them, such as polluters of the environment or corrupters of common trust (see, for example, Schrager and Short 1978, 1980).

Little systematic research of this sort has been undertaken—none, to the best of our knowledge, concerning white-collar crime. Sykes and West (1978) report exploratory research concerning "how people perceive various crimes and how the elements composing these images influence their evaluations" (p. 3). Fifty respondents from randomly selected households in Charlottesville, Virginia, were interviewed concerning their images of ten crimes (none, unfortunately, white-collar crimes) selected from the Rossi et al. (1974) study. Asked "what factors would, in their judgment, make each crime more or less serious," respondents volunteered "at least eight major factors at work":

> First, as might be expected, the degree of bodily hurt and the degree of economic damage or loss a crime caused were both cited. In addition, however, many respondents also pointed to the degree of psychological or emotional damage caused by a crime; the degree to which a crime posed a threat to persons other than the victim or its *potential* for harm; the presence or absence of intent—that is, the extent to which the crime was "voluntary"; what the offender expected to achieve by the crime, which can be called *purpose*; why the offender had that purpose, which can be called *motive*; and finally the presence or absence of something that can be called *fair play*. Judgments concerning the seriousness of crimes are apparently based not simply on some concept of financial or physical injury, but represent instead a complex set of evaluations in which the character or

nature of the criminal is no less important than the consequences for the victim. [Emphasis in original.]

These findings are suggestive, but hardly (as Sykes and West readily acknowledge) definitive, again particularly with respect to white-collar crimes in which both perpetrators and victims often are organizational, or at least are far more numerous than is the case for the common crimes studied. Such findings, in any case, call even more strongly for the inclusion of possibly relevant contingencies in determining public perceptions of white-collar crimes.

Measuring Social Impact: Seriousness and Harm

No social impact of white-collar crime involves all the complexities of the phenomena so labeled, as these are understood and reacted to by citizens, both individually and in a variety of collectivities. Experienced and perceived economic and physical harm, however measured, are both related to social impact, but in largely unknown ways. As we have seen, studies of perceived-seriousness yield impressive empirical regularities with respect to the relative seriousness of particular crimes and combinations of victim and offender characteristics. Yet little is known of the precise bases for perceived seriousness, that is, the characteristics of crimes that are associated with as signed seriousness ratings. We know that, *in general,* crimes resulting in physical harm are rated as more serious than are crimes resulting in economic harm, and that the degree of each type of harm is associated with perceived seriousness. Yet this knowledge is quite limiting and is unlikely to generate any new insights about public perceptions of crime seriousness or, more grandly, public perceptions of trust and confidence in social institutions.

This insight, however, does not take us very far unless we take other sources of complexity into account. Two such factors that are worthy of attention include personal experience with crime, and the relationship between white-collar crime and values. Instances of white-collar crimes may result in trivial individual harm (for example, persons victimized by a price-fixing conspiracy may be charged only one cent more for a product as a result of that crime); yet those small individual harms can be aggregated into losses that are indeed substantial (Reiss and Biderman 1980). Given the literature reviewed earlier, individual perceptions of crime seriousness may rely less on *personal experience* with crime—such as being victimized directly and substantially—than on other bases. Moreover, values such as those placed on private ownership of property and enterprise (and its uses), as well as other fundamental values (Rokeach 1979), seem likely to be related in more-complex ways to white-collar than to ordinary crime.

A second aspect of measuring social impact concerns various dimensions of trust, drawing on the literature of alienation and on confidence in major social institutions. Here, the focus is on the social fabric. The rich literature on alienation and institutional confidence unfortunately has little reference to white-collar crime. Substantive findings in both literature and research on political efficacy are of considerable interest and relevance, however. It is known, for example, that better-educated persons and those of high socioeconomic status generally have lower scores on powerlessness and normlessness scales, and higher scores on scales of political efficacy. These same persons seem more likely to be knowledgeable about white-collar crime both in general and with respect to particular instances that have achieved notoriety, such as the Thalidomide and Love Canal disasters, and price-fixing by major electrical companies. Nisbet (1979), among others, has pointed to the great difference between public understanding and reaction to widely publicized events such as the accident at Three Mile Island, and reaction to less-publicized but perhaps even more-serious conditions, such as contamination of waterways by chemical dumps. It will be important, therefore, to study carefully a variety of segments of the population, and *general* perceptions of economic and physical harm caused by white-collar violations, as well as knowledge of and reactions to particular events.

In general, powerlessness and normlessness are positively related to one another, and both are negatively related to political efficacy. But the relationship of these to the phenomena of white-collar crime is not known. The politically and economically powerful are *less* likely to suffer personally devastating consequences of white-collar crime—and, by definition, are more likely to be engaged in such crime than are the less powerful. Awareness of the seriousness of violations that threaten the environment—air, water, and esthetic quality, for example—may make them *more* concerned than others who are less aware and less knowledgeable. However, beliefs in political efficacy—confidence in their ability to control events—may lead them to be less alienated from the system. Because white-collar violations so often involve corporate enterprise and its relationship with government, political philosophies become involved in attitudes toward such phenomena. This is evident in lobbying efforts related to legislation that affects corporate behavior as well as enforcement. A prime example is Occupational Safety and Health legislation (OSHA), about which labor and business groups hold strongly opposing views. At issue are activities to be defined as in violation of law, as well as policies and practices of law enforcement and how these are to be reported and, therefore, understood by interested groups.

Political and economic issues involved in the assessment of the impact of white-collar crime are illustrated by recent polls concerning confidence in business and government regulation. Defenders of private enterprise have been quick to point out that declining confidence in corporate business has not been paralleled by beliefs that government regulation of business should be increased. If the polls are to be believed, in fact, quite the opposite has occurred. Majorities of those questioned express the opinion that government regulation of business should be decreased. The polls also show, however, that confidence in government has eroded in recent years. Lack of support for government regulation may, therefore, reflect a lack of trust in government rather than, as some have suggested, a lack of faith in the efficacy of government regulation or in the system in general.

These interpretations also are clouded by finding that confidence in business varies a good deal by broad product categories. Confidence in the drug industry, for example, has been found to be relatively low compared with that in most other industries (Lipset and Schneider 1979, p. 8). Although it is possible that the drug industry is tainted by association in the minds of some with illegal drugs, such as heroin, it is also true that the industry has been involved in some of the more-notorious cases of widespread physical harm, such as the use of thalidomide and diethyl stilbestrol (DES), for which large court penalties have been assessed. Clearly, there is a need for careful assessment of public knowledge and opinions about the behavior of specific industries, and perhaps of specific companies.

In addition to targeting specific categories of white-collar offenders, it is necessary to target segments of the population according to their status, or potential status, as victims. This can be done both by identifying "known groups" of victims and by specifying groups in the general population with differing probabilities of victimization. In each case, there is reason to believe that *classes* of victims should be distinguished. It has been suggested that individuals may be victimized by virtue of their status as employees, consumers, or members of the general public; that is, white-collar violators may victimize persons in the workplace, as consumers of products, or as members of the general public by virtue of common dependence on air, water, and soil. To this list can be added the possibility of victimization as coowners, as in the case of stockholders of companies who are defrauded or are victims of embezzlement.

In spite of all this, however, the precise relation of victimization to perceptions of crime seriousness and/or trust and confidence in institutions is troublesome. Thus, although personal experience may be less important than previously thought, one's relation to a *class* of potential or real victims may be very important in determining such attitudes.

These considerations all point to a research design that is sensitive to different populations; that employs multiple indicators of concepts such as social trust, perceived seriousness of different crimes, and value positions; and that attempts to examine the consequences of white-collar and corporate criminality within the larger context of "community." For some time, sociologists have maintained that the most-devastating impact of white-collar crime lies in the nature of social relationships that may be altered as a result of declining trust and confidence in institutions, which provide the setting for most interaction. Up to now, there has been little empirical work to generate a more-refined statement of this impact. This is precisely what we call for here. At this point there is ample reason to believe that white-collar and corporate criminality may have consequences that are far more harmful to the nature of communities than those of ordinary crime. Hence, the sociological agenda seems self-evident.

Summary and Conclusions

The impact of white-collar crime in economic and physical terms has occupied most of the attention of criminologists, although the estimates of such harms are imprecise. Increased precision might be achieved with more attention to the notion of "minimally acceptable level of risk," devising standards of such risks, and applying these standards across a broad number of behavioral areas. It seems likely that until such criteria can be developed, estimates of the extent to which white-collar crime constitutes socially injurious conduct will continue to be speculative.

The impact of white-collar crime on the social fabric of the community is perhaps the most-serious harm discussed by sociologists; but no one has yet devised a method by which such an impact can be determined empirically beyond very general statements of "social harm." We propose that (1) the impact of white-collar crime on the social fabric is perhaps the most important, long-term harm caused by such offenses; (2) sociologists need to devote a good deal more conceptual and theoretical attention to the nature of the social fabric, as well as to begin to explore such concepts empirically; and (3) a reasonable starting point for such work would lie in the notions of alienation, confidence in major institutions, and collective trust. The research that has been devoted to these areas so far has not recognized their possible relationship with white-collar crime, although the implications of these relationships pose intriguing and seemingly fruitful areas of inquiry.

The research program envisaged here is one that studies directly the nature of this impact, with attention to individual perceptions of the seriousness of white-collar and corporate criminality, one's relationship with major institutions, and the extent to which those institutions (and subunits within them) are able to generate trust and confidence in their performance. Until such questions are posed directly, discussions of the consequences of white-collar crime will suffer from the narrow focus that presently characterizes them.

References

Aubert, Vilhelm. 1952. "White-Collar and Social Structure." *American Journal of Sociology* 58:263-271.

Berk, Richard E.; Brackman, H.; and Lesser, S. 1977. *A Measure of Justice.* New York: Academic Press.

Berk, Richard E., and Rossi, Peter H. 1977. *Prison Reform and State Elites.* Cambridge, Mass.: Ballinger.

Chamber of Commerce. 1974. *A Handbook on White Collar Crime: Everyone's Problem, Everyone's Loss.* Washington, D.C.: Chamber of Commerce of the United States.

Clark, Ramsey. 1978. *Testimony.* See Subcommittee on Crime (1978).

Clinard, Marshall B. 1952. *The Black Market.* New York: Holt, Rinehart and Winston.

––––––. 1979. *Illegal Corporate Behavior,* National Institute of Law Enforcement and Criminal Justice. Washington, D.C.: U.S. Government Printing Office.

Cohen, Albert K. 1966. *Deviance and Control.* Englewood Cliffs, N.J.: Prentice-Hall.

Converse, Phillip E. 1972. "Changes in the American Electorate." In Angus Campbell and Phillip E. Converse, eds., *The Human Meaning of Social Change,* pp. 263-337. New York: Russell Sage.

Conyers, Congressman John. 1978. *Testimony.* See Subcommittee on Crime (1978).

Cressey, Donald R. 1976. "Restraint of Trade, Recidivism, and Delinquent Neighborhoods." In James F. Short, Jr., ed., *Delinquency, Crime and Society,* Chicago: University of Chicago Press.

––––––. 1978. *Testimony.* See Subcommittee on Crime (1978).

Cullen, Francis T.; Link, Bruce G.; and Polanzi, Craig W. 1980. "The Seriousness of Crime Revisited: Have Attitudes toward White-Collar Crime Changed?" Unpublished paper, Department of Sociology, Western Illinois University, Macomb.

Dean, D. 1961. "Alienation: Its Meaning and Measurement." *American Sociological Review* 26:753-768.

Deutsches, Irwin. 1973. *What We Say/What We Do: Sentiments and Acts.* Glenview, Ill.: Scott Foresman.

Edelhertz, Herbert. 1978. *Testimony.* See Subcommittee on Crime (1978).

Erickson, Maynard L., and Gibbs, Jack P. 1979. "On the Perceived Severity of Legal Penalties." *Journal of Criminal Law and Criminology* 70:102-116.

Ermann, David, and Lundman, Richard, eds. 1978. *Corporate and Government Deviance.* New York: Oxford University Press.

Finifter, A.W. 1970. "Dimensions of Political Alienation." *American Political Science Review* 64:389-410.

Geis, Gilbert. 1972. "Criminal Penalties for Corporate Criminals." *Criminal Law Bulletin* 8:377-392.

———. 1974. "Avocational Crime." In Daniel Glaser, ed., *Handbook of Criminology*, pp. 273-298. Chicago: Rand McNally.

———. 1977. "White-Collar Crime: It Pays." *Washington Post*, 16 September, p. 11.

Geis, Gilbert, and Meier, Robert F., eds. 1977. *White-Collar Crime: Offenses in Business, Politics and the Professions*. New York: Free Press.

Geis, Gilbert, and Monahan, John. 1976. "The Social Ecology of Violence." In Thomas Lickona, ed., *Moral Development and Behavior*, pp. 342-356. New York: Holt, Rinehart and Winston.

Gibbons, Don C. 1969. "Crime and Punishment: A Study in Social Attitudes." *Social Forces* 47:391-397.

Hartung, Frank E. 1953. "Common and Discrete Values." *Journal of Social Psychology* 38:3-22.

Hawkins, Darnell. 1980. "Perceptions of Punishment for Crime." *Deviant Behavior* 1:193-215.

Janowitz, Morris. 1978. *The Last Half-Century*. Chicago: University of Chicago Press.

Joint Commission on Correctional Manpower and Training. 1968. *The Public Looks at Crime and Corrections*. Washington, D.C.: U.S. Government Printing Office.

Kadish, Sanford H. 1963. "Some Observations on the Use of Criminal Sanctions in Enforcing Economic Regulations." *University of Chicago Law Review* 30:423-449.

Lipset, Seymour Martin, and Schneider, William. 1979. "The Public View of Regulation. *Public Opinion*, January-February, pp. 6-13.

McClosky, H., and Schaar, J.H. 1965. "Psychological Dimensions of Anomy." *American Sociological Review* 30:14-40.

Meier, Robert F., and Geis, Gilbert. 1979. "The White-Collar Offender." In Hans Toch, ed., *Psychology of Crime and Criminal Justice*, pp. 427-443. New York: Holt, Rinehart and Winston.

Middleton, Russell. 1963. "Alienation, Race and Education." *American Sociological Review* 22:670-677.

Newman, Donald J. 1953. "Public Attitudes toward a Form of White-Collar Crime." *Social Problems* 4:228-232.

Nisbet, Robert. 1979. "The Rape of Progress." *Public Opinion*, June-July, pp. 2-6.

President's Commission on Law Enforcement and Administration of Justice. 1967. *The Challenge of Crime in a Free Society*. Washington, D.C.: U.S. Government Printing Office.

Reed, John P., and Reed, Robin S. 1975. "Doctor, Lawyer, Indian Chief: Old Rhymes and New on White-Collar Crime." *International Journal of Criminology and Penology* 3:279-293.

Reiss, Albert J., Jr., and Biderman, Albert D. 1980. *Data Sources on White-Collar Law-Breaking.* Washington, D.C.: Bureau of Social Science Research.

Rettig, Solomon, and Passamanick, Benjamin. 1959a. "Changes in Moral Values over Three Decades." *Social Problems* 6:320-328.

———. 1959b. "Changes in Moral Values as a Function of Adult Socialization." *Social Problems* 7:117-125.

Robinson, J.P., and Shaver, P.R. 1973. *Measures of Social Psychological Attitudes.* Ann Arbor, Mich.: Institute for Social Research.

Rodino, Congressman Peter W., Jr. 1978. *Testimony.* See Subcommittee on Crime (1978).

Rokeach, Milton, ed. 1979. *Understanding Human Values.* New York: Free Press.

Rose, G.N.G. 1966. "Concerning the Measurement of Delinquency." *British Journal of Criminology* 14:256-263.

Ross, Edward A. 1907. *Sin and Society.* New York: Harper and Row.

Rossi, Peter H.; Waite, Emily; Bose, Christine E.; and Berk, Richard E. 1974. "The Seriousness of Crimes: Normative Structure and Individual Differences." *American Sociological Review* 39:224-237.

Rotter, Julian B. 1980. "Interpersonal Trust, Trustworthiness, and Gullibility." *American Psychologist* 35:1-7.

Saxon, Miriam. 1980. *White-Collar Crime: The Problem and the Federal Response.* Washington, D.C.: Congressional Research Service, Library of Congress. Report No. 80-84 EPW.

Schrager, Laura Shill, and Short, James F., Jr. 1978. "Toward a Sociology of Organizational Crime." *Social Problems* 25:407-419.

———. 1980. "How Serious a Crime? Perceptions of Organizational and Common Crimes." In Gilbert Geis and Ezra Stotland, eds., *White-Collar Crime: Theory and Research,* pp. 14-31. Beverly Hills, Calif.: Sage Publications.

Seeman, Melvin. 1972. "Alienation and Engagement." In Angus Campbell and Phillip E. Converse, eds., *The Human Meaning of Social Change,* pp. 467-527. New York: Russell Sage.

———. 1975. "Alienation Studies." *Annual Review of Sociology* 1:91-123.

Smith, Tom. 1979. "Can We Have Confidence in Confidence? Revisited." In Denis F. Johnston, ed., *The Measurement of Subjective Phenomenon.* Washington, D.C.: Government Printing Office, in press.

Sparks, Richard. 1978. *Testimony.* See Subcommittee on Crime (1978).

Subcommittee on Crime. 1978. *White-Collar Crime.* Hearings, 21 June, 12 July, 19 July, and 1 December 1978. House of Representatives, Committee on the Judiciary. Committee print, Washington, D.C.

Sutherland, Edwin H. 1945. "Is 'White-Collar Crime' Crime?" *American Sociological Review* 10:132-139.

Sykes, Gresham, and West, Stephen R. 1978. "The Seriousness of Crime: A Study of Popular Morality." Paper presented at the annual meeting of the Eastern Sociological Society.

Wilson, James Q. 1968. "The Urban Unease." *The Public Interest* 12:25-39.

Wolfgang, Marvin E. 1980. "Crime and Punishment." *The New York Times,* 2 March, p. 4E.

Wolfgang, Marvin E., and Sellin, Thorsten. 1964. *The Measurement of Delinquency.* New York: Wiley.

3

Corporate Violations of the Corrupt Practices Act

M. David Ermann, and
Richard J. Lundman

Introduction

Discussion of whether corporations have responsibilities to the general public would have seemed peculiar to Americans of a few centuries ago. They assumed that public service was the major goal of every bank or manufacturer seeking to be incorporated. Their assumption also was law.[1] Historically, an American organization could be created only if its incorporators showed British monarchs and, later, state legislators that issuance of a charter to incorporate would enhance the public good. The issue was not just whether the new corporation would be law abiding and inoffensive. Corporations had a positive responsibility for public service.[2] In order to ensure that a new corporation would serve the public good, state legislatures reviewed requests for incorporation one at a time and required that the potential incorporator demonstrate how issuance of a charter to incorporate would serve the interests of the public at large.

However, states soon realized that they could attract business and thereby increase tax revenues and employment opportunities by relaxing incorporation standards and procedures. New York became the first state to undertake such relaxation, in 1827,[3] and other states quickly followed in an effort to compete. In the decades that followed, positive public service as a condition for incorporation faded rapidly. Present-day requirements for incorporation are the will to do so, the ability to pay a relatively modest fee, and enough creativity to discover an original name for the corporation.[4] Currently, corporations have no positive obligation to serve the public at large.

Instead, corporations are held to minimum standards of not violating the law. Corporations have many of the same legal obligations as individuals. Laws prohibiting false advertising, for instance, are essentially similar to laws prohibiting fraudulent acts by individuals.[5] Corporations also confront special laws intended to protect the public at large from certain corporate actions. The Corrupt Practices Act is one such law. In the early part of the twentieth century, Congress added Section 610 to Title 18 of the United States Code.[6] This act made it illegal for business corporations to make direct or indirect financial contributions to candidates for federal office. Many states quickly passed similar laws making it illegal for corporations to make financial contributions to candidates for state office.

Purpose of the Chapter

The purpose of this chapter is to describe and analyze corporate violations of Section 610 of Title 18 of the United States Code, the Corrupt Practices Act. It begins by sketching the origins of this act and its enforcement immediately following the Watergate break-in. Then, descriptive and analytical attention is directed at one corporate violator, the Gulf Oil Corporation.

In describing and analyzing corporate violations of the Corrupt Practices Act, we will suggest some of the elements of a research agenda on white-collar crime. First, we believe it necessary to begin to examine the processes surrounding the criminal labeling of corporate actions. Therefore, we will illustrate the nature of this analysis by briefly sketching the origins of the Corrupt Practices Act.

Second, we believe it is crucial to begin to probe the origins of corporate criminality. In undertaking such analysis, we seek to discover the ways in which organizational forces, not just individual proclivities, relate to corporate criminality. Therefore, we will provide an organizationally sensitive analysis of some of the forces that helped propel Gulf Oil employees in the direction of corporate violation of the Corrupt Practices Act.

The Corrupt Practices Act

Prior to 1907, corporate campaign contributions were both legal and frequent. The privately owned United States Bank, for instance, spent $80,000 just for pamphleteering in the 1832 presidential campaign. Sugar refiners spent large sums in an effort to dictate sugar tariffs in 1892. And the Standard Oil Company, one of the first truly national corporations, spent $500,000 in the 1896 and 1900 elections.[7]

The corporations that made campaign contributions were generally those most directly dependent on government regulations and decisions. For instance, between 1888 and 1900, politicians were attempting to decide where to locate a canal linking the Atlantic and Pacific Oceans. Corporations interested in building the canal variously lobbied that it be located through Nicaragua or across the Isthmus of Panama. As Overbacker relates:

> The elder Senator La Follette tells us that preceding the presidential election of 1888, Republican leaders urged him to support the Nicaraguan

Canal Bill because parties interested in its passage had offered to contribute $100,000 to the Republican campaign fund if the bill was acted upon favorably. A similar amount had been offered to the Democrats.[8]

Corporate campaign contributions first became a public issue in the United States in the late 1800s, in part because of the passage in 1883 of a British law forbidding corporate contributions and in part because "some . . . deplored the part which banks and other corporations played in financing the Republican campaign of 1896."[9] But the issue reached the general public's attention only in the 1904 presidential election. In the final weeks of that campaign, the Democratic candidate for president, Judge Alton B. Parker, charged that his Republican opponent, Theodore Roosevelt, had accepted large contributions from corporate interests wanting favors from the government.

Judge Parker and other Democratic campaigners refused to take any corporate contributions, although these were legal at the time. They also tried to link Republican support for high tariffs to corporate contributions, considering this an issue with which many voters would sympathize. On 24 October 1904, for instance, Judge Parker asked:

> Shall the creations of government, many of which pursue illegal methods, control our elections, control them by moneys belonging to their stockholders, moneys not given in the open and charged upon the books as moneys paid for political purposes, but hidden by false bookkeeping?[10]

Republicans did not address Judge Parker's charges directly, since the issue had been raised very late in the campaign. Instead, they noted that both parties had habitually received corporate contributions, denied that they had made any promises in return for contributions, and claimed that Democrats also were receiving corporate money.

In the words of one observer at the time, public opinion "had not been sufficiently aroused to declare itself . . . " in the election.[11] There was more concern about the amounts of these funds than about the fact that they existed. However, the issue was strong enough to outlive the election and help foster subsequent changes in the sources and public disclosure of political contributions.

In his message to Congress in December 1905, President Roosevelt recommended a law abolishing corporate political contributions. In January 1907, Congress passed such a bill. In some quarters, there was a clear understanding of the need for this kind of protection for the public at large, as the court showed in one decision upholding the law's constitutionality in 1916: "Its purpose is to guard elections from corruption, and the electorate from corrupting influences in arriving at their choice."[12]

Simlar laws were passed at the state level. By 1905, five states already had statutes prohibiting corporate political contributions. Sixteen more states added such laws by 1910, and fourteen more between 1911 and 1920.[13] These laws, along with their federal counterpart, came to be known as "corrupt-practices acts" and dealt with many aspects of electoral money. They reflected a public concern with the general problem of political corruption, with corporate contributions representing only one aspect of the overall problem. As a result, many people were ambivalent about these recently criminalized corporate actions.

Ambivalence about corporate contributions is well illustrated in a 1929 case involving a local utility company in Iowa. The company violated state law by spending several thousand dollars to defeat a mayoral candidate who had attacked company rates and had promised to try to establish a municipal electric plant. The judge, probably sharing some of the mixed feelings of his fellow citizens, saw no distinction between political expenditures by citizens and those by corporations. He said in his decision: "I infer that the power company was attacked, and it is asking too much of human nature to expect the corporation not to defend itself. On the other hand, if the corporation set out to corrupt the electorate, it must certainly be punished. . . ."[14] Despite his ambivalence, the judge ruled that the company had made an illegal campaign contribution.

Federal and state bans on corporate political contributions have remained in effect since 1907; only the ways in which they are enforced and the specification of how they are to be interpreted have changed. Their impact, however, is still unclear. It is probably safe to agree with some earlier observers that prohibitive legislation did not dry up corporate political contributions, but did reduce them from what they had been or would have been. It also seems probable that there was clear but not fervent public support for banning corporate cash contributions.

Perhaps because of a general lack of public concern, enforcement of the Corrupt Practices Act has been essentially nonexistent. Illegal corporate contributions have been described as a "part of life,"[15] but contributors and recipients of these illegal funds have not been quick to reveal their illegal transactions. Additionally, enforcement officials have not devoted resources to the discovery and prosecution of corporate offenders. Consequently, until Watergate, these laws rarely were enforced.

Enforcement Following the Watergate Break-In

On 17 June 1972, a private security guard encountered evidence of a break-in at the Watergate complex in Washington, D.C. Police were called, and five men were arrested inside the Democratic National Committee Headquarters.[16]

By June 19, 1972, links had been established between the Watergate break-in, the Committee to Reelect the President (CREEP), and the White House.[17] The break-in was linked with CREEP when it was learned that one of the burglars, James J. McCord, Jr., was security coordinator for CREEP. The break-in was linked with the White House when it was learned, further, that two of the burglars carried address books with the name of Howard Hunt and the notation "W. House." Calls to the White House revealed Howard Hunt's employment as an aide to Charles Colson, special counsel to President Nixon.

Parts of the ensuing investigation focused on identifying the sources of funding for the Watergate break-in and related actions. In July 1973, Watergate Special Prosecutor Archibald Cox announced that his office had evidence that American Airlines had made an illegal $55,000 corporate contribution to CREEP.[18] Mr. Cox requested that other corporations voluntarily disclose their illegal contributions to CREEP.

Also during the summer of 1973, Common Cause brought suit against CREEP, asking that all corporate contributions be revealed.[19] Common Cause won its suit, and that action, coupled with Mr. Cox's request for voluntary disclosures, was the first step in a process that culminated in the conviction of eighteen corporations for violations of the Corrupt Practices Act. The corporations, most of which pleaded guilty, were: American Airlines; American Shipbuilding; Ashland Oil; Associated Milk Producers; Braniff Airways; Carnation Company; Diamond International; Goodyear Tire; HMS Electric; Gulf Oil; LBC&W, Incorporated; Lehigh Valley Co-op; Minnesota Mining; National By-Products; Northrup Aviation; Phillips Petroleum; Time Oil; and Ratrie, Robbins and Schweitzer.[20] Fines were levied in amounts ranging from $1,000 (National By-Products) to $25,000 (Ashland Oil).[21] Gulf received the modal fine of $5,000. The aftermath of Watergate saw the first federal prosecutions of corporations for violation of the Corrupt Practices Act.

The Gulf Oil Corporation

Among the reasons for focusing on Gulf's actions are two of prime importance. First, Gulf's criminal actions were investigated extensively by government agencies and Congressional committees, thus permitting detailed description and analysis.[22] Second, Gulf's actions are representative of a frequent type of corporate criminality. In addition to the eighteen corporations actually convicted of violating the Corrupt Practices Act, another three hundred also were reported to have made illegal contributions.[23]

Analysis of Gulf's actions should help illuminate this frequent type of corporate crime. For these important reasons, the Gulf Oil Corporation is the focus of our descriptive and analytical attention.

Description of Gulf's Actions

Gulf's violations of the Corrupt Practices Act began over twenty years ago.[24] Around 1959, four of Gulf's top executives—William K. Whiteford, Gulf's chairman of the board and chief executive officer; Joseph Bounds, executive vice-president; Archie Gray, general counsel; and William T. Grummer, comptroller—became alarmed over what they perceived as "creeping encroachment" by government toward the oil industry.[25] They complained publicly about arbitrary oil-import quotas, attacks against depletion allowances, the unwillingness of government agencies to grant Gulf a fair hearing, and conflicting government regulations. A pamphlet sent to stockholders and employees argued:

> We have seen the development of a situation in which Gulf—and the industry—had been subjected to increasing attacks while in the political climate of our times, it has increasingly been denied a fair hearing.[26]

The pamphlet also called on employees and stockholders to "get involved" in politics,[27] and announced the opening of a Government Relations Office in Washington, D.C.

The immediate problem confronting the Gulf executives committed to a more-active political involvement was gathering the money needed for such an undertaking. Apparently aware of the Corrupt Practices Act, they initially attempted to gather voluntary contributions from Gulf executives. This "flower fund" scheme failed, and those involved in the origins of Gulf's illegal actions were faced with what was presumably a difficult decision: whether corporate funds would be diverted to permit contributions to candidates for public office.

For reasons we later will make clear, Gulf's top executives decided to violate the Corrupt Practices Act by giving "laundered" corporate funds to candidates for public office.

Laundering: The Bahamas Connection. For laundering chains originating in the United States, the initial step occurs when money is secured from a source that does not want to be identified.[28] The money then is sent to another location, usually a person and bank in a foreign country. There, the original money is exchanged for foreign currency, and that currency is used to buy back U.S. dollars. "Clean" dollars then are returned to the United States for distribution. Laundering is a chain of cash transactions intended to make identification of the original source difficult.

Bahamas Explorations was a nearly inactive Gulf subsidiary located in Nassau. Each year it applied for and received a small number of exploration licenses, and it occasionally undertook exploratory surveys. Prior to 1959, Bahamas Exploration appears to have been a holding operation, reserving Gulf a place should significant deposits of petroleum or natural gas be found in the Bahamas.

Bahamas Exploration was Gulf's money-laundering center. At Gulf's home office in Pittsburgh, money was listed fraudulently as deferred charges to be paid to suppliers by Bahamas Exploration. A deferred charge is a future debt with money reserved for payment. If a deferred charge is fraudulent, then no voucher for its payment is ever received, and the money is freed for use. Therefore, money was sent from Pittsburgh to Bahamas Exploration in Nassau to pay fraudulent deferred charges.

William C. Viglia, an assistant comptroller for Gulf stationed in Nassau, was responsible for accounting at several Bahamian subsidiaries, including Bahamas Exploration. In 1961 he was called to Gulf's corporate headquarters in Pittsburgh by Executive Vice-President Joseph Bounds. Bounds told him that "there would be certain funds, monies, coming down to the Bahamas, that he was to deliver this money to . . . [the head of Gulf's Government Relations Office in Washington, D.C.] and to Bounds, and that's it."[29] Viglia did as he was told, returned to Nassau, and established the first of several bank accounts.

Viglia then awaited instruction regarding return of the clean money. The money moved as follows:

> After receipt from Viglia of an envelope containing cash, Bounds locked it in the safe which [Chairman of the Board and Chief Executive Officer William] Whiteford had asked him to maintain in his office in the 31st floor of the Gulf Building. After a delivery, Bounds informed Whiteford . . . [who] . . . thereafter entered Bound's office during the latter's absence, opened the safe, removed the envelope, and left the safe open. The safe remained open and empty until another Viglia delivery, when the same procedures were followed.[30]

In a three-year period starting in about 1961, $669,000 was returned to the United States in this way. Mr. Bounds retired in 1965, and the more than $5 million earmarked for politicians was delivered to another Gulf employee, Claude Wild.

In 1959, Claude Wild was a legislative analyst for the Mid-Continent Oil and Gas Association. He was known to have extensive contacts with members of Congress and their aides when Gulf officials hired him to head their newly created Government Relations Office in Washington, D.C. The executives who hired Wild told him that Gulf had been "kicked around, knocked around by government,"[31] and that Gulf intended to change that. They also told him that illegal corporate campaign contributions were "a part of life,"[32] that Gulf would join other corporations in making such contributions, and that he would get a minimum of $200,000 per year to distribute to candidates.

Until at least 1962, Wild's funds came via the route just described. After 1965 all deliveries were made directly to Wild by Viglia. Both men took special precautions to shield their actions from outsiders:

> Viglia . . . never . . . [came] . . . to Wild's offices . . . no records were maintained. . . . [W]hen Wild needed funds he telephoned Viglia and Viglia delivered the cash. . . . Wild and Viglia met at various points throughout the United States, but never in a Gulf office.[33]

Distributing: the Washington Connection. Claude Wild was responsible for distributing the laundered funds. However, $5 million is an enormous amount of money for one person to distribute, especially in small amounts, as was Gulf's custom. According to Wild, it was "physically impossible for one man to handle that kind of money."[34] Consequently, he used three people in his own office, seven of his office's regional vice-presidents, and seven others, including Gulf employees and personal friends, to help distribute the money.

In distributing these funds, Wild indicated that the sole criterion was that "the money be spent in the general interest of Gulf and the oil industry."[35] Following this general guideline, he handled nearly all the payments to candidates for national office, whereas his assistants generally handled the payments to candidates for state and local offices.

Of the $5 million given to candidates for public office, it is possible to identify the recipients of only $870,000. On advice of counsel, Wild declined to identify recipients. He also declined on grounds that he could not ever recall informing any recipients that they were receiving laundered corporate funds.

Despite Wild's concern with maintaining the image of the public officials who accepted laundered Gulf funds, it is possible to construct a partial listing of recipients. The single largest known contribution was to CREEP. The amount was $100,000, and a member of the Senate Watergate Committee described how it was solicited:

> Mr. Lee Nunn . . . came to Wild's office and told him that the Committee to Re-Elect the President would handle the 1972 Nixon campaign outside the normal Republican channels. . . . Nunn suggested that if Wild wanted verification of Nunn's role in the effort, he should get in touch with Attorney General John Mitchell. Wild met with Mitchell in his office at the Department of Justice and Mitchell indicated that . . . [CREEP] . . . was a legitimate operation and that Mitchell had full confidence in Nunn.[36]

Wild called Viglia, obtained $50,000 in cash, and delivered it to Nunn. Some time later, Secretary of Commerce Maurice Stans called Wild and told him that a "kind of quota for large corporations of $100,000" had been established.[37] Wild again called Viglia and then delivered the additional money to Stans, thus meeting CREEP's quota.

However, Gulf contributions were not limited to presidential candidates. Gulf funds also were distributed to congressional campaign committees, to candidates for the U.S Senate and House, to their aides and friends, and to candidates for state and local offices.[38] Apparently Gulf felt that it had been "kicked around, knocked around" not only by federal government but also by state and local governments.

Disclosure: the Watergate Break-In. Gulf's illicit activities were a well-kept secret, despite the involvement of numerous Gulf employees and hundreds of recipients. Members of the general public did not know that Gulf was subverting the electoral system. Were it not for the Watergate break-in, there is little reason to believe that the actions of Gulf and hundreds of other corporations ever would have been disclosed.

Analysis of Gulf's Actions

In the remainder of this chapter we probe for some of the origins of corporate violations of the Corrupt Practices Act. In pursuing this analysis, we assume that organizational forces rather than individual pathologies best explain corporate criminality. We thus agree with Schrager and Short's recent observation:

> While organizations cannot act independently of the people that constitute them, it does not follow that determination of the culpability of individuals should be the primary focus. . . . Preoccupation with individuals can lead us to underestimate the pressures within society and organizational structures which impel those individuals to commit illegal acts. . . . Recognizing that structural forces influence commission of these offenses . . . serves to emphasize *organizational* as opposed to *individual* etiological factors, and calls for a macrosociological rather than individual level of explanation.[39]

Given our shared animating assumption, we now seek preliminary answers to the following question: "What is it about life in and around large organizations that impels individuals to commit illegl acts?

Rationalizing Criminality. *Rationalizations* are explanations for actions taken or planned.[40] People use rationalizations to explain past actions to themselves and, if questioned, to others. People also use rationalizations in advance of certain actions, literally permitting their release. These prebehavior rationalizations are especially important in permitting release of actions known to be improper or illegal. They are the reasons a person provides in advance in criminality, explanations as to why it is necessary and acceptable to engage in actions that otherwise would make one uncomfortable.

Corporate structures and environment provide top-level executives with large numbers of essentially accurate rationalizations for criminality. In the case of Gulf, the available rationalizations were so numerous and so accurate that most individuals finding themselves in the same positions as Gulf's executives also would have decided to violate the Corrupt Practices Act.

Gulf's elites could tell themselves that other corporations were doing what they were considering. Illegal contributions were believed to be a routine part of corporate and political life, with Gulf at a disadvantage compared with less-inhibited corporations. Additionally, the Corrupt Practices Act had been in existence for over half a century. Yet despite its long history, the act had never been enforced. Further, Gulf's elites could take special precautions to minimize the possibility of detection. Corporate funds coult be twice laundered, being listed as deferred charges and then passed through a sleepy Bahamian subsidiary. Finally, if the unlikely did occur and Gulf's criminal actions somehow did come to the attention of law-enforcement agencies, the consequences certainly would not be serious. Stockholders were unlikely to react negatively since Gulf's actions clearly were intended to increase corporate profits. The government could fine Gulf, but the amount would not be large. Government was not in the business of crippling important corporations with large fines.

Not only were the opportunities for rationalization numerous, but they also were essentially accurate. Gulf *was* at a disadvantage compared with the more than 300 other corporations known to have made illegal contributions. Disclosure literally *was* an accident. Stockholders were not upset, as stock prices actually increased in the months following disclosure.[41] And Gulf was fined only $5,000.

Social Roles in Large Organizations. Social roles are the smallest subunits of organizations.[42] Associated with each role are a limited set of work-related expectations. Social roles are integrated with one another to facilitate attainment of organizational goals. Typically, role interpretation is hierarchical, with role occupants of one level responsive to the direction of their organizational superiors. Generally, individuals are neither encouraged to look beyond their particular role requirements nor rewarded for doing so.[43]

Once corporate crime is set in motion by top-level executives, the nature of social roles in large organizations limits the information and responsibilities of other participants. Most of the individuals who participated in Gulf's criminal actions did not have, or need, or probably want complete information. Additionally, none had complete responsibility. They simply had to do what was decided for them as part of their jobs. This was true for individuals occupying roles at all levels at Gulf.

Consider the limited information and responsibility of Gulf's comptrollers. [44] As can be seen in table 3-1, three individuals followed the comptroller who helped launch Gulf's criminal actions. None of the three had to make any difficult decisions, much less involve themselves in criminal actions. All they were told was that they would receive requests for money from certain employees. All they did was write notes to treasurers asking that these employees be provided with the requested money.

Gulf's treasurers also knew and did little. All they were told was that the Bahamas Exploration account was "highly sensitive and confidential."[45] All they did was send checks to that account upon receipt of a note from a comptroller.

Dozens of other Gulf employees engaged in similar actions. John Brooks describes one of Gulf's money-toting bagmen:

> Most often the delivery would be at an airport or at the recipient's office, but occasionally it would be at a place suggestive of a desire for secrecy. . . . In 1970 he handed an envelope to Representative Richard L. Roudebush, of Indiania . . . in the men's washroom of a motel in Indianapolis. . . . Time and again, asked . . . whether he knew what was in the envelope he had delivered, he replied, "I do not," or "I have no knowledge." A minor figure . . . apparently content to spin constantly above the cities, plains, and mountains of America, not knowing why, not wanting to know why. . . .[46]

Corporate criminality is made easy for individuals by the nature of social roles in large organizations. Most participants have only limited

Table 3-1
Persons Occupying Four Top-Level Positions within Gulf Oil, 1958-1973

Chief Executive Officer and Chairman of the Board	Comptroller	Treasurer	General Counsel
W. Whiteford,[a] 1958-1965	W. Grummer,[a] 1958-1964	H. Moorhead, 1958-1972	A. Gray,[a] 1959-1960
E.D. Brockett, 1965-1971	W. Henry, 1964-1966	P. Weyrauch, 1972-1973	D. Searls, 1960-1961
R. Dorsey, 1971-1973	F. Anderson, 1966-1968		R. Savage, 1961-1969
	F. Deering, 1968-1973		M. Minks, 1969-1973

Source: *Securities and Exchange Commission* v. *Gulf Oil Corporation*, Civil Action No. 75-0324, United States District Court, District of Columbia, Report of the Special Review Committee of the Board of Directors of Gulf Oil Corporation, 30 December 1975, pp. 64-85.
[a]Initiator of laundering and illegal compaign-contributions operations.

information. Most have responsibilities that in themselves are not illegal. Although the sum of these work-related actions is corporate criminality, it generally does not seem that way to individual employees.

Selecting and Training Loyal Employees. All organizations have sensitive and important secrets and thus are dependent on the loyalty of employees.[47] Additionally, all organizations engage in actions that could prove embarrassing were they to be stripped of their organizational context and displayed in a public arena.

Organizations therefore select and train loyal employees. Selection involves searching applicants for signs of loyalty. The major sign of loyalty is similarity—being like the people who previously have proved loyal to the corporation:

> Forces stemming from organizational situations help . . . promote social conformity as a standard for conduct . . . managers choose others who can be "trusted." And thus they reproduce themselves in kind. . . . Forces insisting that trust means total dedication and non-diffuse loyalty . . . serve to exclude those . . . who are seen as incapable of such single-minded attachment.[48]

Training of new organization members involves verification of the loyalty of those selected. The technique is a gradual and piecemeal introduction of the corporation's sensitive and important secrets.[49] No one individual, especially initially, need know all or even most of what the corporation is doing. All that is required is a willingness to do one's job and to keep the bits and pieces of secrets safe. With time, with sufficient verification of loyalty, and as the need arises, particularly loyal employees are rewarded with promotion and thus with exposure to more-complete and more-important secrets.

Gulf's employees were the loyal products of these routine selection and training procedures. Not one went public with rumor or evidence of criminality. Not one took advantage of numerous opportunities for personal enrichment.

Rumor and evidence of criminality were widespread within Gulf as an organization. Comptrollers received cautious instructions to write notes when told to do so by corporate subordinates. Treasurers sent money to the off-the-books account of a subsidiary that never did much of anything. Typists and clerks told jokes and stories of men with "the little black bags" of Gulf money.[50] But no Gulf employees went public with information of their corporation's criminal actions.

Large numbers of Gulf employees had easy access to over $5 million of essentially untraceable corporate funds. For obvious reasons, formal records were not kept; thus there was no reliable method of verifying that laundered corporate funds actually had been delivered. Despite numerous opportunities, those involved were "corporate Boy Scouts," totally "trustworthy, loyal . . . thrifty, brave . . ." in their roles as Gulf employees:

> No evidence has been uncovered or disclosed which established that any officer, director, or employee of Gulf personally profited or benefitted by or through any use of corporate funds for contributions, gifts, entertainment or other expenses related to political activity. Further . . . [there is] . . . no reason to believe or suspect that the motive of the employee or officer involved in such use of corporate funds was anything other than a desire to act solely in . . . the best interests of Gulf and its shareholders.[51]

We now have established some of the origins of Gulf's criminal actions. Until and unless contradictory data become available, we submit that elite access to numerous essentially accurate rationalizations for criminality, the limited information and responsibilities characteristic of social roles in large organizations, and the selection and training of loyal employees are among the elements of life in corporations that impel individuals to commit illegal acts.

Symbiotic Big-Business–Big-Government Relations. However, Gulf's criminal actions would not have been possible were it not for the willing involvement of literally hundreds of recipients. Politicians obviously were selling something that Gulf was willing to buy. In order to understand Gulf's actions more fully, it is necessary to examine big-business–big-government relations.

People in top-level positions in government and business have much in common with one another.[52] They generally share common life-styles and values. They frequently exchange positions, moving between positions of power and responsibility in business and those in government. If there is a difference between persons in government and business, it is that politicians lack direct access to corporate resources.

Persons in government and business also need each other. A presidential attempt at voluntary price controls needs the cooperation of large corporations. Corporations need government assistance in protecting certain markets from foreign competition.

This regular contact and cooperation signals symbiotic rather than adversarial relations, as the economist Daniel R. Fusfeld has noted:

> The United States has moved well down the path toward a corporate state. Economic power is concentrated in the hands of a relatively few super-corporations. . . . Political power has shifted heavily into the hands of the executive branch of the federal government. . . . These two centers of economic and political power have developed a growing symbiosis.[53]

Looked at in this way, Gulf Oil and the Watergate burglary it helped fund emerge as part of the symbiotic fabric of the corporate state. Gulf's actions were part of an exchange relationship in which each party fully expected to benefit—and most likely did.

For the politicians who run government, Gulf and other contributing corporations were solving a problem by providing politicians with access to corporate resources. Being a politician is costly, and access to money is fundamental to political success. The higher the office, the grander the ambition, the more costly it is to be a politician. To Spiro Agnew, for instance, the corporate and other contributions and kickbacks that ultimately forced his resignation were

> essential to survival, a basic platform from which he could continue to pursue higher office. Having entered big time politics without benefit of wealth . . . [h]e accepted groceries from a supermarket executive. His restaurant tabs were picked up. . . . He used funds given . . . him when he was Governor to stock a winecellar. . . .[54]

In exchange, politicians did not have to sell their votes or themselves. All Gulf was paying politicians for was the predictability all corporations need in order to survive and prosper.[55] Gulf's chief complaint was that inconsistent government regulations were making rational calculations difficult. The corporation was asking and paying for a more-consistent set of regulations, ones that would permit the "calculable adjudication and administration" fundamental to the existence and growth of corporate capitalism.[56] The precise content of the regulations was less important than the calculability of their consequences.[57]

Gulf's criminal actions thus were indicative of the shared interests of big business and big government. They were a routine and accidentally discovered part of the symbiotic fabric of the contemporary corporate state.

Summary and Conclusions

This chapter has examined corporate violations of the Corrupt Practices Act. It has sketched the origins of the act and its enforcement following the Watergate break-in. It has described and analyzed the actions of one corporate violator, the Gulf Oil Corporation.

We draw three conclusions from our efforts. First, as compared with the origins laws applicable to vagrancy, marijuana use, sexual psychopathology, and other criminal acts primarily performed by individuals, considerably less is known about laws primarily applicable to corporations.[58] Our brief sketch of the Corrupt Practices Act suggests that it is possible to examine the "criminalization of corporate behavior."[59]

Second, compared with the generally detailed description of the actions of particular delinquents, professional thieves, fences, and addicts, much less is known about the actions of criminal corporations.[60] Our description of Gulf's actions suggests that it is possible to begin to provide material descriptive of the actions of criminal corporations.

Third, our analysis of Gulf's actions suggest that it is possible to devote primary attention to the organizational and environmental pressures that impel individuals in the direction of corporate crime. We believe we have helped demonstrate that it is useful to emphasize "organizational as opposed to individual etiological factors" in probing the origins of corporate crime.[61]

Notes

1. For a history of corporate chartering, see David Finn, *The Corporate Oligarch* (New York: Simon and Schuster, 1969); and Ronald E. Seavoy, "The Public Service Origins of the American Business Corporation," *The Business History Review* 52 (Spring 1978):30-60.

2. See Paul J. McNulty, "The Public Side of Private Enterprise: A Historical Perspective on American Business and Government," *Columbia Journal of World Business* 13 (Winter 1978):122-130.

3. See Seavoy, "Public Service Origins."

4. For a particularly clear example, see Ted Nicholas, *How to Form Your Own Corporation without a Lawyer for Under $50.00* (Wilmington, Del.: Enterprise Publishing Company, 1972). Mr. Nicholas advocates incorporating in Delaware since the state is dependent on corporate-charter-fee revenue and thus places very few restrictions on corporations.

5. Edwin H. Sutherland, *White Collar Crime* (New York: Holt, Rinehart and Winston, 1949), p. 32.

6. *Securities and Exchange Commission, Plaintiff* v. *Gulf Oil Corporation, Claude C. Wild, Jr., Defendants,* Civil Action No. 75-0324, United States District Court, District of Columbia, Report of the Special Review Committee of the Board of Directors of Gulf Oil Corporation. 30 December 1975, p. 3. Hereinafter identified as SEC, *Report.*

7. *Materials for this section are derived from Herbert Alexander, ed., Political Financing* (Beverly Hills, Calif.: Sage Publications, 1979); Perry Belmont, *Return to Secret Party Funds* (New York: G.P. Putnam's, 1927; reprinted, New York: Arno Press, 1974); Louise Overbacker, *Money in Elections* (New York: Macmillan, 1932; reprinted, New York: Arno Press, 1974); Lester A. Sobel, ed., *Money and Politics: Contributions, Campaign Abuses and the Law* (New York: Facts on File, 1974).

8. Overbacker, *Money in Elections,* p. 175.

9. Ibid., p. 234.

10. Quoted in Belmont, *Return,* p. 175.

11. Ibid., p. 47.

12. Overbacker, *Money in Elections,* p. 240.

13. Ibid., p. 294.

14. Ibid., p. 337.

15. SEC, *Report,* p. 7.

16. Carl Bernstein and Robert Woodward, *All the President's Men* (New York: Warner Paperback Library, 1975), p. 16.

17. Ibid., pp. 20-23.

18. Leon Jaworski, *The Right and the Power: The Prosecution of Watergate* (New York: Simon and Schuster, Pocket Books, 1977), p. 21.

19. SEC, *Report,* p. 7.

20. Jaworski, *The Right and the Power,* pp. 344-345.

21. Ibid., pp. 344-345.

22. SEC, *Report.* Also see John Brooks, "The Bagman," in Rosabeth Moss Kanter and Barry A. Stein, eds., *Life in Organizations: Workplaces as People Experience Them* (New York: Basic Books, 1979), pp. 363-372.

23. Marshall B. Clinard, *Illegal Corporate Behavior* (Washington, D.C.: U.S. Government Printing Office, 1979, Stock No. 027-000-00843-7), p. 200.

24. The source for this section is SEC, *Report,* pp. 31-92, pp. 199-298, and appendixes A-D. The page locations of specific quotations will be identified. Also see Brooks, "The Bagman."

25. SEC, *Report,* p. 62.

26. Ibid., p. 62.

27. Ibid., p. 62.

28. For a discussion of laundering in the context of Watergate, see Bernstein and Woodward, *All the President's Men,* pp. 38 ff.

29. SEC, *Report,* p. 43.

30. Ibid., p. 43.

31. Ibid., p. 63.

32. Ibid., p. 63.

33. Ibid., p. 65.

34. Ibid., p. 66.

35. Ibid., p. 66.

36. Ibid., p. 70.

37. Ibid., p. 71.

38. Ibid., pp. 64-85.

39. Laura Shill Schrager and James F. Short, Jr., "Toward a Sociology of Organizational Crime," *Social Problems* 25 (April 1978):410.

40. The imagery and vocabulary advanced in our discussion of rationalizations are from Gresham Sykes and David Matza, "Techniques of Neutralization: A Theory of Delinquency," *American Sociological Review* 22 (1957):664-670.

41. Brooks, "The Bagman," p. 372.

42. For a general discussion of this point, see Marvin E. Olsen, *The Process of Social Organization* (New York: Holt, Rinehart and Winston, 1968), pp. 103 ff.

43. See Diane Rothbard Margolis, *The Managers: Corporate Life in America* (New York: William Morrow, 1979), pp. 54-66; Clinard, *Illegal Corporate Behavior,* pp. 3-10.

44. Based on SEC, *Report,* pp. 242-266.

45. Ibid., p. 223.

46. Brooks, "The Bagman," p. 369.

47. For an early discussion of this point, see Max Weber, *On Law in Economy and Society,* ed. and annotated by Max Rheinstein, trans. Edward Shils and Max Rheinstein (New York: Simon and Schuster, 1967), pp. 334-335.

48. Rosabeth Moss Kanter, *Men and Women of the Corporation* (New York: Basic Books, 1977), p. 68.

49. All the persons with access to Gulf's sensitive and important criminal secrets had served long corporate apprenticeships. See SEC, *Report,* pp. 242-266.

50. Ibid., p. 223.

51. Ibid., pp. 216-217.

52. See C. Wright Mills, *The Power Elite* (New York: Oxford University Press, 1956); Michael Useem, "Studying the Corporation and the Corporation Elite," *American Sociologist* 14 (May 1979):97-107; Gwen Moore, "The Structure of a National Elite Network," *American Sociological Review* 44 (October 1979):673-692.

53. Daniel R. Fusfeld, "The Rise of the Corporate State in America," *Journal of Economic Issues* 6 (March 1972):1. See also Arthur S. Miller, *The Modern Corporate State: Private Governments and the American Constitution* (Westport, Conn.: Greenwood Press, 1976).

54. James M. Naughton, John Crewdson, Ben Franklin, Christopher Lydon, and Agie Solpukas, "How Agnew Bartered His Office to Keep from Going to Prison," in Gilbert Geis and Robert Meier, eds., *White-Collar Crime: Offenses in Business, Politics, and the Professions* (New York: Free Press, 1977), p. 226.

55. For a discussion, see Neal Shover, "The Criminalization of Corporate Behavior: Federal Surface Coal Mining," in Gilbert Geis and Ezra Stotland, eds., *White-Collar Crime* (Beverly Hills, Calif.: Sage Publications, 1980), pp. 98-125.

56. Max Weber, *General Economic History,* trans. F.N. Knight (New York: Collier, 1961), p. 208; cited in Shover, "Criminalization of Corporate Behavior," p. 123.

57. See Shover, "Criminalization of Corporate Behavior."

58. See, for example, William Chambliss, "A Sociological Analysis of the Law of Vagrancy," *Social Problems* 12 (1964):66-77; Howard S. Becker, *Outsiders: Studies in the Sociology of Deviance* (New York: Free Press, 1963), pp. 121-162; Edwin H. Sutherland, "The Diffusion of Sexual Psychopath Laws," *American Journal of Sociology* 56 (September 1950):142-148; Anthony M. Platt, *The Child Savers* (Chicago: University of Chicago Press, 1969).

59. Shover, "Criminalization of Corporate Behavior."

60. See, for example, Clifford R. Shaw, *The Jack-Roller: A Delinquent Boy's Own Story* (Chicago: University of Chicago Press, 1930); Edwin H. Sutherland, *The Professional Thief* (Chicago: University of Chicago Press, 1937); Carl B. Klockars, *The Professional Fence* (New York: Free Press, 1974); Richard P. Rettig, Manual J. Torres, and Gerald R. Garrett, *Manny: A Criminal-Addict's Story* (Boston: Houghton Mifflin, 1977).

61. Schrager and Short, "Toward a Sociology," p. 410.

4 The Role of Law Enforcement in tl Fight against Whi Collar Crime

Ezra Stotland

Introduction

White-collar crime is a nationwide problem. It occurs in government, in business, and in not-for-profit enterprises; on the streets, in people's homes, and in hotel rooms. It is perpetuated by con men, business people, housewives, and almost all professionals. It ranges in size and scope from the smallest bank-examiner fraud to multinational theft. In fact, we export our "surplus" crime to other countries.

Such a pervasive national problem obviously requires a pervasive national effort to control and even eradicate it. Focusing efforts to control it on just one locus of its occurence, except for pragmatic reasons of limited resources, can have only a temporary and limited effect. If the establishment implicitly condones unethical, illegal standards of behavior in one part of the marketplace by simply ignoring them, then sooner or later these standards will begin to generalize to other parts. Some potential criminals would perceive it as "inequitable" not to have the same chance as others to make a fast buck or to make a lot of money slowly but illegally. Some law-enforcement officials and regulatory-agency personnel may implicitly, albeit covertly, share the same outlook. Thus, no segment of our national life should be overlooked as a potential locus of illicit white-collar actions.

Yet the effort to control and eradicate white-collar crime has tended to be piecemeal and sporadic. Some federal agencies have dealt with the problem much more vigorously and consistently than have others. In some states, law-enforcement and regulatory agencies have likewise been diligent; in others, they have not. The same is true at the local level. This uneven crime-control effort has contributed to the movement rather than the control of crime; to the perpetrators' waiting out enforcement efforts, rather than giving up crime; and to uncertainty and ambiguity about our ethical and legal standards on the part of many people.

Obviously, what is needed is a consistent, long-term effort to control and eradicate white-collar crime on many fronts, involving all the appropriate regulatory and law-enforcement agencies. Such an effort requires not only that many agencies be involved, but also that a whole range of tools be available, from the gentlest administrative reprimand, through civil-court actions, to criminal sanctions. Different types of loci of crime require different remedies, but all should be available for use when appropriate.

One of the greatest untapped reservoirs of manpower and organization that must be mobilized in the effort is the police. As will be articulated later, the police can make unique and significant contributions to the total effort, as well as providing sheer volume of energy and personnel nationwide. The purpose of this chapter is both to articulate what some of these contributions might be and to support some very specific lines of research that can enhance these efforts.

The role of police officers and departments in the fight against white-collar crime has only recently begun to the recognized and appreciated. Each year, more large urban departments have established units that deal with white-collar crime, going well beyond the traditional limits of police work (street bunco, simple embezzlements, forgeries, rubber checks, and so forth). Special investigative units dealing with more-complex and larger-scale white-collar crime have been established in Los Angeles, Chicago, San Francisco, Portland, Atlanta, New York, and elsewhere, with all but the first having been inaugurated fairly recently. State police or similar agencies have had such units in Michigan, New Jersey, Washington, and California. The Federal Bureau of Investigation has recently made white-collar crime one of its top-priority crimes, with spectacular results as it has shifted from bank robbery to robbery of banks. The International Association of Chiefs of Police has recently produced a series of training keys focusing on white-collar crime. The association's organ, *Police Chief,* has published a number of articles on white-collar crime in the past two or three years. Police officers have applied in increasing numbers for training at the Battelle National Center on White-Collar Crime. No doubt the FBI's efforts will inspire local and state departments to enhance their efforts to fight white-collar crime.

These developments have not been part of a concerted, directed effort. No clarion call has been heard at a convention of police chiefs or police detectives. No chief has emerged as a leader in this effort, although Patrick Murphy, president of the Police Foundation, has strongly endorsed such efforts. No standards or goals have been articulated, beyond the obvious ones of investigating certain types of fraud, forgery, embezzlement, and so forth. Issues related to the unique contribution that police can make, to the most-effective way of organizing and conducting the police effort, to the effects that police participation will have on the police themselves, to the most-effective way of meshing police efforts with other branches of the criminal and civil justice systems—none of these issues have been addressed to any significant degree. Obviously, systematic research on these issues can be beneficial both to the police and to other related parts of the justice system.

In this chapter, we will first address the question of the special, if not unique, values of involving the police in the fight against white-collar crime. Some of the values of a total national effort, including the police, were set forth previously. But the specific contributions of the police need to be articulated, in addition to some values more or less unique to the police.

In the next section of the chapter, we will examine the traditional police role of gathering information, and will consider the possibility that this role can be extended into the area of white-collar crime. As we will show, information on white-collar crime either can come to the police in the normal course of their activities, or can be sought out more proactively by the police. Programs to enhance police effectiveness in this respect, as well as research to evaluate them, will be proposed.

Following this discussion of the theoretical possibility of such police activities, we will address the problem of their practical feasibility and of the motivation of police officers to engage in them. Possible pilot studies on these issues are described.

These considerations lead into the next section, which deals with the ways in which police agencies can be organized to function most effectively in the area of white-collar crime. There are many organizational problems that plague both police and other law-enforcement agencies and that need to be addressed and researched, including methods of evaluating performance and effectiveness.

Finally, we will face the whole issue of the difficulty of knowing how to deploy resources for the most-effective long-range efforts—that is, the issue of the use of strategic intelligence to provide a basis for the mobilization of police and other agencies.

The Value of Involving the Police in Fighting
White-Collar Crime

One main value of involving the police in the fight against white-collar crime is simply that police can provide a greater deal of information for investigative or intelligence purposes. It is obvious that the enormity of the problem means that the federal government can deal with only a part of it. Police—functioning out in the community, on the streets, in stores, in homes—can provide eyes and ears to observe possible crimes that office-bound personnel may never encounter. The police may be able to alert the criminal-justice system to white-collar crimes early in their development, before they reach the stage at which many more people have been hurt.

There are additional reasons for involving the police in the effort against white-collar crime. First, the activities of the criminal-justice system against white-collar crime have multiple functions, one of them being to educate the population at large that society is demanding closer adherence to legal and ethical standards in the marketplace. Unless the public at large appreciates and supports these efforts, the fight against white-collar crime will be lost in the long run. Police participation greatly enhances the effort to educate the populace, especially since the very involvement of the police communicates clearly that this type of crime is considered just as wrong as "blue-collar" crime. The sense that the "big cats" get away with it, while the little ones do not, would be reduced somewhat if the same agency went after both big and small cats. The notion that the public really does not care if the big, white-collared cats get away, and is willing to overlook such animals, may not now be true, or may not have ever been true. However, recent research by Wolfgang (1980) and by Short and Schrager (1980) has shown that the public does, in fact, take white-collar crime seriously, and thus would be impressed that society, including the police, is moving against it.

Second, the involvement of the police tends to ensure that the criminal remedy is not neglected, both because of their very presence and because of their articulateness. This is not to argue that the criminal remedy is the only significant one to be used against white-collar crime, but rather that all remedies need to be kept available so that the most-appropriate one can be used in specific cases. Brintnall (1978) reports that more of the investigations in which the police assisted the prosecutor lead to criminal prosecution than of those in which the prosecutor had help from other agencies or no help from outside entities.

Third, the public nature of the police involvement would tend in many areas, such as ghettos, to aid in the fight against common crime. If the police established greater rapport with the community by helping, say, residents of a ghetto or a barrio against a consumer defrauder, this could lead to more cooperation with the police in fighting common crime. This cooperation can take the form of reporting more crimes sooner, willingness to be a witness, and—as has been found in some storefront police substations—even turning in fugitives.

Fourth, the recent movement of organized criminals into legitimate businesses indicates that not only do organized criminals commit white-collar crimes in conducting their traditional activities, but also that they can reasonably be expected, in the long run, to commit more common white-collar crimes in their newly acquired legitimate businesses. Thus the involvement of the police as the natural enemies of organized crime brings to bear significant additional resources against white-collar crime. Fights against both types of crime will benefit, and there is less likelihood that certain types of crime will escape detection by falling between the two types of targeting agencies.

The police are chronically placed in situations in which they are subjected to corrupting influences. Subcultures have frequently developed in police departments that tolerate at least some corruption, and police scandals unfortunately are not rare events. Since such scandals often are themselves a form of white-collar crime, a police officer's active participation in the fight against white-collar crime outside of his department may very well lead him to become less tolerant of it in his own department. Social-psychological research has indicated that when an individual chooses to take actions that violate his private attitudes, he is likely to change his attitudes to be more consistent with his actions. Thus, an officer with a relaxed approach to extortion conducted by his colleagues might become indignant toward them after he has worked on white-collar-crime cases, and has made many choices among courses of actions while doing so. Since both measures of the degree of corruption in police departments (Sherman 1978) and measures of police officers' views of corruption have been developed, before-and-after studies of the effect on police corruption of involvement in fighting white-collar crime are clearly feasible.

Police as Potential Sources of Information about White-Collar Crime

We have now seen some of the values of involving the police in the fight against white-collar crime. The next section concerns the types of white-collar crime that police are likely to detect.

It is obvious that some forms of white-collar crime would be very unlikely to come to the attention of even the most-diligent and observant police officer, such as false billing, advance-fee schemes, churning, stock fraud, and so forth. Nevertheless, many forms can, in principle, come to the attention of an observant or a even nonobservant police officer. Brintnall (1978) reports that in the thirty-five jurisdictions in the Economic Crime Project, police referrals were the source of only 3 percent of the prosecutors' cases, but that the losses to the victims in these cases were about equal to those in all the other cases; that is, the police were involved in cases that went far beyond the typical ones of bunco or petty embezzlement. Some examples of this will be presented later, along with research strategies for determining, first, the amount of relevant information that could in fact be gathered by police officers under optimal conditions, and, second, the amount of such information that is in fact at least noticed by the police.

The first set of crimes are those whose manifestations an officer can notice in the ordinary course of his work, without any victims or witnesses informing him.

Automobile-Insurance Fraud ("Accidental" Damage to Vehicles). Insurance companies estimate that around 10 percent of claims against them are fraudulent. Information on the signs of insurance fraud have already been developed by the Insurance Crime Protection Institute (ICPI). The signs of a contrived automobile accident have been spelled out in detail in Training Key 241, a publication of the International Association of Chiefs of Police (IACP) (1976). Among the indicators of a contrived accident are crash scenes at places where the volume and type of traffic will of necessity distract an officer's attention; crash locales in dark areas on rainy nights; victims in different cars who appear to be acquainted or who appear to know a lot about insurance and can point up the amount of damage; at-fault drivers who "confess" too readily; "painful" injuries with little outward sign, such as whiplash; declinations of treatment at the scene; cars that have obviously been damaged before, presumably in previous "accidents"; absence of appropriate skid marks; and so forth.

Signs of a "paper" accident are also cited in the aforementioned training key: The victim reports the accident with an "over-the-counter" police report; the victim reports soft-tissue injuries, such as back strain; one person reports for two drivers; there are inconsistencies in the vehicle identification number; both vehicles reportedly are sent to the same repair shop; there is a lack of witnesses; one driver has too complete knowledge of the other's personal and insurance situation; and so forth.

Staged Residential Burglaries. Many police officers are cynical about the validity of a large percentage of the burglaries reported to them, since a police report is usually required in order to collect burglary insurance. The same IACP training key points out that amateurish burglaries may be fraudulent; that fraud may be indicated by an unlikely place of entry or damage at the point of entry inconsistent with a real burglary. Other signs of staged burglaries are reports of losses inconsistent with the person's lifestyle, a series of reported break-ins, and so forth.

Staged Commercial Burglaries. These can be perpetuated by both employees and employers. Signs might include remarks by employees that the missing stock was recently moved elsewhere, burglaries that appear to be inside jobs, and so forth.

For each of the aforementioned types of insurance fraud, it would be very helpful to patrol officers, detectives, and managers of investigations to know which of the signs of fraud is most indicative both of a fraud and of a prosecutable fraud. The earlier in the process of investigation the officer or supervisor can determine whether enough of these cues are present, the sooner decisions about pursuing an investigation can be made, thereby permitting the most-efficient use of resources. Thus, one major research project should parallel the one done by Stanford Research Institute (SRI) on predicting the value of continuing an investigation of a common crime on the basis of information available at the time of the preliminary investigation. (This direction of research is discussed later.)

The suggested research program on insurance fraud will follow a format that we shall call a *cyclical research program*. This format will be applied later to other types of crime, but it will be illustrated by its application to insurance fraud. This research would be performed in the following steps:

1. Determination of how many of the aforementioned cues of fraud are actually reported in current accident and burglary reports. This could be done by an examination of both patrol officers' reports and detective reports.
2. Determination of which cases were investigated by the police and which by insurance investigators—and, in both instances, of which cases actually lead to prosecutable cases.
3. Determination of the relationship between the amount and types of information included in current patrol and detective reports, on the one hand, and the successful completion of the investigation on the other. The results would give a first approximation of the potential for the use of that information to predict which investigations should be pursued. It would also give a picture of which types and amounts of information from patrol officers lead detectives to follow through on cases.
4. Determination of the possibility of gathering further information by surveying police officers and detectives to determine which of the possible cues of fraud they had noticed in, say, the last accident report they made, but had not reported in writing. It may well be that officers do not fully report the information because they may not appreciate the significance of what they observe, or may not believe that anyone will bother to investigate the cases in which they do suspect fraud. The influence of these reasons for nonreporting could also be determined in the survey.
5. On the basis of the results of the first four steps, performance of a field experiment to enhance officer observation and reporting of potential insurance fraud—partly through training, partly through improved procedures, and partly through enhanced reward systems. The effects of each of these types of upgrading efforts on the reporting of cases, on the initiation and completion of investigation, and on the filing of charges could be examined.

This model of research can be applied to many types of white-collar crime, as will be suggested later. In fact, lists of indicators that white-collar crimes are probably occurring have been developed in spheres in which the police generally do not function. For instance, a list of indicators of probable crimes has been developed for auditors (Sorensen, Grove, and Sorensen 1980); for observers of local government (Lyman, Fletcher, and Gardiner 1978); for stock fraud by the SEC; and so forth.

Home-Repair Fraud. Although in the area of home repair there is no institute such as the ICPI that can establish a formal list of signs of home-repair fraud, much is already known by the police, although not formalized. Much can be observed by patrol officers because of the highly organized quality of one group of perpetrators, the Williamson gang. This secretive, cohesive, extremely well organized gang has accumulated much wealth by systematically "working" areas in which prime potential victims reside. Some external earmarks of the presence of these gangs that have been noticed are:

1. Out-of-state licenses on home-repair trucks, especially roofing trucks.
2. Perpetrators who live close together in a trailer court regularly used by them.
3. Ownership of very late model, luxury cars; they may keep them only a year before selling them.
4. Prowling in areas in which elderly people reside.
5. Young, very polished men making approaches to potential victims.
6. Equipment, especially in roofing trucks, that would not pass any safety test.
7. If confronted, failure to produce a business license. (This also could lead to citation and even to arrest.)
8. A rash of blacktoppings of driveways, reinforcements of chimneys, and so forth, in a neighborhood.

In addition, many police-department detectives and intelligence units have pictures of some of the perpetrators and organizers, so that patrol officers might recognize them on the street.

Obviously, a cyclical research format paralleling the one for insurance fraud could be done in the area of home-repair fraud, although it is unlikely that the first step in the research program (dealing with current observation and reporting of crime) will bear much fruit. On the other hand, some police departments, such as in Los Angeles, have already alerted patrol officers from time to time about the Williamsons.

Door-to-Door Salesmen and Other Street Operators. The signs of fraud committed by door-to-door salesmen have not yet been highly articulated, but the presence of young people soliciting from door to door, especially if they are selling magazine subscriptions, may indicate not only a fraud but also an abduction of groups of young people who are transported by adults from place to place to perpetrate frauds. The police might observe this type of fraud commited by people who work the streets or go door to door: salespersons of phony burglar alarms; collectors for phony charities; itinerant auto mechanics who promise to "repair that dent right." Obviously, a research program using the cylical format could be performed here as well.

Consumer Fraud. An officer could very well become aware of consumer frauds just through his own observations, without necessarily any input from citizens. These observations are probably more likely to occur if an officer gets to know a district very well by repeatedly patrolling it. For example, he may notice a close-out sale that never ends, a fire sale that occurs without a fire, or a car that is advertised in the newspaper by a used-car dealer but is not actually obvious on the lot. Again the cyclical research format can be used here.

Welfare Fraud. As Hutton writes in *The Police Chief*, (1979):

> Indications of welfare fraud are often evident to the peace officer aware of . . . eligibility factors. Simple cohabitation frauds can be seen during calls for service in the home, during disturbing the peace or family fight calls, during checks of driving and vehicle registration records, and during service of arrest warrants (such as for unpaid traffic tickets) at the residence. [Hutton, G.U., "Welfare Fraud and the Police," *The Police Chief*, November, 1979, pp. 46-47. Reprinted with permission.]

However, as indicated later, reports by police of such probable welfare frauds may lessen the number of calls for service they receive from some neighborhoods, even in the case of serious felonies.

Environmental Safety. This is a relatively new area for possible enforcement by police officers; however, the mobility of patrol and their constant observation may prove invaluable (Greenberg 1979). For example, state police officers in New Jersey were highly instrumental in detecting and investigating the wanton piling up of barrels of toxic wastes in obscure areas under a skyway. Officers may detect other forms of pollution, such as excessive emission from smokestacks, dumping in streams, pile-up of garbage, and so forth. Again, cyclical research can be conducted on how much opportunity there might be for officers to detect this and to generate prosecutable cases.

Other Suspicious Information Encountered through Ordinary Patrol. No doubt there are areas other than insurance fraud, home-repair fraud, and so on in which the cyclical format can be applied. For example, local police in New Jersey observed the diversion of diesel fuel during a period of shortage. Increasingly, police have uncovered large-scale white-collar schemes simply in the course of normal police work. A major bank embezzler was detected because an officer's investigation of the smashing of the rear end of the perpetrator's car led to the literal uncovering of a large number of bookie slips. A major instance of official corruption was found because an officer examining a car overdue from a rental agency found a cache of government checks. A series of automobile-repair frauds were uncovered because one officer noticed that there were regular verbal and fist fights around a given garage between the owner and some customers—who usually called the former a crook. Fraudulently obtained bank cards have been picked up in the course of routine arrests for common crimes.

Sometimes, in an area they know well, police officers may simply notice unusual events that are suggestive of white-collar crime. A patrol officer became suspicious about the rapid turnover of used cars in a residential driveway and uncovered an odometer roll-back operation. The movement in and out of a business of goods not appropriate to that business may indicate a bankruptcy fraud (or a fencing operation). The sudden "unexplainable" wealth of a given citizen may be suspicious as may be the sale of land that is apparently useless or the use of land in obviously inappropriate ways.

Research to determine how often these instances occur would be difficult to conduct because the nature of the events attracting the officers' attention varies so much. However, questionnaires to officers about incidents in which their suspicions were aroused but not reported might prove fruitful. So might recording increases in the number of reports by officers who are sensitized to the problem of white-collar crime in general. This sensitization may occur among officers who participated in one of the cyclical research programs described previously.

Communications from Citizen-Victims

So far the focus has been on possibilities of detection of crime through observation by officers, not through reports to them by victims or witnesses. It is not uncommon for officers to be approached by citizens with complaints about having been cheated. The traditional police response has been to refer the citizen to his or her lawyer, or to some noncriminally oriented lawyer. However, in many cases criminals may go undetected because the citizen was too discouraged to seek other help. The police officer encounters the person at the most-crucial point, when he is most involved and most motivated to act. The officer can be the symbol of the total governmental establishment; a referral to another agency or to the citizen's lawyer may aggravate a problem because of the disappointment involved. The citizen may also be frustrated by the delay, the lack of certainty of an effective response from the referee, and so on. In any case, we have no clear knowledge of how much valuable information for investigative or intelligence purposes is lost to the criminal-justice system because of an ineffective response from the police.

Thus a survey could be done of police officers to determine the frequency, nature, and setting of the phenomenon of citizens telling an officer that they had been cheated. Detailed examination of the officers' recollection of such citizen complaints could suggest whether the complaint indicated that a criminal act had occurred. This act could be any one of a number of types: consumer fraud, automobile-repair fraud, pyramid schemes, land (in some locales), or even traditional street bunco. When police officers are socially integrated into their patrol area (as in team policing or basic car plans), or in small communities, the officers might be the first to learn of more-sophisticated crimes, such as stock frauds, land frauds, complex embezzlements, complex frauds against the government, graft, and so forth, simply because the police officer is a friend to whom people talk, even when they might not believe that the officer can help them in any way. A properly designed research project could determine whether in fact such intelligence is available to police officers, and of what kind. More than one officer has remarked bitterly about the white-collar crime he hears about but does not feel he can act on. Such research would also shed some light on such issues as the sociological-demographic characteristics of complaining victims, especially if some additional research can be developed to deal with noncomplaining victims, or victims who complain to other agencies. The amount of social organization among complaining victims, their status and role in the community, and so forth are also valuable types of information for the police to develop.

Attempts have been made to make the police more available for receiving complaints from citizens; one of these is the storefront that the Los Angeles Police Department established in a Chicano neighborhood, called (in Spanish) Operation Swindler (Edelhertz et al. 1977). Local residents can bring their consumer complaints to this office, which is manned by Hispanic officers and workers. The officers taking the complaints can either conduct initial investigations to determine whether crimes have possibly occurred, or can refer the cases to their civil-law or administration colleagues and officemates from other branches of the municipal government. This storefront has been so successful that others have been established in other, more-Caucasian neighborhoods. Similar but probably less-effective storefronts have been established in Denver and other cities. The effectiveness of such storefronts in generating useful leads to crimes could easily be researched by examining the files of such units and by studying their histories of operations.

Communications from Citizen-Whistleblowers

If police officers—patrol and detectives—are well integrated into their community, they are highly likely to become known to some of the peripheral, or even central, participants in a scheme. Should any of them ever decide to blow the whistle, either sub rosa or publicly, the police officer would be available to them. These whistleblowers might be peripheral participants who have been cheated by the principals; peripheral or principal participants who have finally had pangs of conscience; principals who fear that the scheme is about to be detected and wish to bargain from a position of strength; and so forth. Patrolmen and detectives may hear about such people, but, often lacking the orientation to deal with white-collar crime, may not capitalize on these opportunities to uncover schemes as well as to secure excellent witnesses. This sort of communication obviously would be likely only in certain locales, such as jumping-off points for offshore banks or office areas in which boiler-room operations might be easily established. In any case, cyclical research programs such as the one for insurance fraud could gather information about the frequency with which police receive such information. This research could also generate valuable information about the whistleblowers themselves: their personal characteristics, their particular position and role in the schemes, their motivation for blowing the whistle, and so forth. This information could help guide investigators who are attempting to penetrate a conspiracy, as will be elaborated later.

Feasibility of Police Officers Becoming Sources
of Information about White-Collar Crime

Given that there is a theoretical possibility that the police can gather information regarding white-collar crimes, the next question concerns the practicality of having them do so. A common complaint heard about giving the police additional responsibilities is that the police are overburdened as it is—how can they do more? The retort is that much of the time patrol officers have little to do except patrol preventatively, an activity whose value has seriously been questioned. In fact, boredom on certain shifts in certain areas is a major problem. Much of the free time occurs during the daylight hours Monday through Thursday, time when it is probably most likely that white-collar crimes occur. It is likely that little can be learned about white-collar crime from Saturday-night barroom brawls. In any case, the research projects described earlier could incorporate questions about the times and places in which information was obtained, either by observation or by communication.

Motivation of Officers to Fight White-Collar Crime

If, as we have argued, it is both theoretically and practically possible for police to detect white-collar crimes, then how motivated would they be to use these opportunities to detect such crimes and criminals? The point made earlier concerning police officers' beliefs about white-collar crime raises the general question of the motivation of police officers to fight against white-collar crime. The question is important because police on the street have so much freedom to choose which types of offense to investigate that their motivation and preferences become crucial.

Part of this motivation to work on white-collar crime may be intrinsic to the work itself. Unlike some other additional responsibilities that the police have been asked to assume in recent years, the fight against white-collar crime is a genuine traditional law-enforcement function. Many officers appear to delight in the challenge of the work—the opportunity to do some "real" detective work, rather than writing reports about suspects named by witnesses. Since only 15 percent of police time is actually spent dealing with serious felonies, an addition to that time can only legitimately and properly enhance the police officer's view of himself as a crime fighter.

Furthermore, police may simply value honesty in the marketplace as much as, if not more than, other citizens. Although research has often found police conservative politically, these studies have not directly raised the possibility of police being populists, pitting the "man on the street" against any organization of great size, be it governmental or private. As Goldstein (1975) writes:

> The average officer—especially in large cities—sees the worst side of humanity. He is exposed to a steady diet of wrongdoing. He becomes intimately familiar with the ways people prey on one another. In the course of this intensive exposure he discovers that dishonesty and corruption are not restricted to those the community sees as criminal. He sees many individuals of good reputation engaging in practices equally dishonest and corrupt. An officer usually can cite specific instances of reputable citizens defrauding insurance agencies by false claims, hiding earnings to avoid taxes, or obtaining services or merchandise without payment. It is not unusual for him to develop a cynical attitude in which he views corruption as a game in which every person is out to get his share. [p. 25].

The police themselves have no doubt been victimized both personally and as a group. With their twenty-year career patterns, many police plan for their postretirement careers by investing, often in land. Many officers moonlight and may encounter white-collar crime in their second jobs (some have taken it on themselves to investigate in these cases). Obviously, they can be victimized. Recently, charitable fundraising by police has been subject to a good deal of milking by con men, to the detriment of law enforcement's status and prestige (Ely 1980).

Furthermore, law-enforcement officers may sympathize with certain types of victims, especially those who are relatively defenseless: widows who can be taken by con men; older people unable to repair their homes; people with little comprehension of the English language, families of the terminally ill, and so forth. For some officers, observation of street bunco and its victims can lead by stages into an interest in large-scale white-collar crime. Police who fill out accident or burglary reports that they suspect are fraudulent may become very angry at being forced to participate in a crime. For a number of reasons, police might well have a great latent—and perhaps realized—motivation to fight against white-collar crime. It is possible that some may prefer to make a more-active, involved response to citizen-victims than saying, "Tell it to your lawyer."

I have already done some pilot research to determine the strength of the motivation of police officers to fight the types of white-collar crime they probably are most likely to encounter. As part of this research project, officers were asked to indicate how interested they would be in dealing with particular instances of white-collar crime. The instances and the associated questions were presented in the format illustrated in the following example:

> There was a door-to-door encyclopedia business which encouraged customers to buy a set of expensive encyclopedias ($275.00) in order to receive savings on a number of other books and atlases over a ten-year period. The purported "special" or "reduced" price was in fact neither one, and purchasers did not obtain the savings that were promised. The encyclopedia business declared that contracts could not be cancelled, when in fact state laws gave customers a right to cancel. The business had no intention of ever honoring the promise of savings they had stated. This is a theft in the 2nd degree and constitutes a class C felony.

A) How interested do you think patrolmen would be in enforcing the law in this predicament?

Extremely _____ Not at all
interested 1   2   3   4   5   6   7 interested

B) How interested in this particular case do you feel a detective would be?

Extremely _____ Not at all
interested 1   2   3   4   5   6   7 interested

C) Can you suggest any ways in which patrolmen can help in this situation?

_____

_____

_____

D) Can you suggest any ways in which detectives can help in this situation?

_____

_____

_____

E) If you were freed of your other duties, how interested would you as a law officer be in fighting this crime?

Extremely _____ Not at all
interested 1   2   3   4   5   6   7 interested

Other instances that were used in the questionnaire concerned: Medicaid fraud by a doctor, odometer roll-backs, home-improvement fraud committed against a retirement home, automobile-repair fraud, a short-weighting food-processing company, business-opportunity fraud, bait and switch, dangerous children's toys, and roof-repair fraud. Pilot and exploratory studies were done with seventy-five police attending a college class and with recruits in a police academy (with the help of Carol Crosby, Cindy McCann, Becky Larned, and Harvey Chamberlin).

The questionnaires showed a high degree of internal consistency, with all the scores on the three questions that were used for each crime for all the situations being significantly correlated across crimes. On a 7-point scale with 1 as the "most interested," the mean score was 4.42 for the question of how interested they thought patrolmen would be in enforcing the law. But when police were asked how interested they would be if relieved of other duties, the mean rating dropped to 3.55, showing more interest. The standard deviations were 1.8 and 1.9, showing quite a wide spread of close to 4 points in a 7-point scale. In short, the exploratory study showed that there may well be an attitude toward white-collar-crime enforcement that is general across types of crime; that officers as a group would show at least a moderate interest; and that the officers vary greatly as a group in their attitudes toward fighting white-collar crime. In response to the questions about what patrolmen and detectives can do in the situations, very few of the officers answered that they would simply say it was a civil matter for the victim's lawyer. Many of them said that they would make a report for another agency. In further research, it would be valuable to determine how many officers and even investigators feel that the victims, individuals, or organizations are seriously to blame for their losses—even to the point of being unworthy of society's help—because they are essentially victims of their own greed, carelessness, or stupidity. If this view is commonly held, then educational programs would be warranted showing the vast range of motives of victims, including the most laudatory, as in charity frauds, and the most human, as in seeking phony therapies. The officers might also learn of the extreme difficulty of preventing victimization because of the cleverness of the perpetrators or the difficulty of getting accurate information.

The research described earlier is designed to measure the "natural" degree of interest of police officers and others in fighting white-collar crime. However, this can be enhanced in a variety of ways. The results of the type of study suggested here can help point to the best way to approach officers, what sorts of crimes interest them the most, what sorts of officers are more likely to be interested, and so forth. Sheer knowledge that these offenses are crimes increases interest. In pilot preliminary tests of the foregoing questionnaire, there were no descriptions of the events as "crimes"; we found that many, if not most, of the officers did not know that they were crimes. When the offenses were identified as crimes in the items themselves, the officers responded quite differently to the questionnaire. Once police officers begin to act on these offenses, they may discover some extraneous motives for fighting white-collar crime. As indicated earlier, they may find that their rapport with local communities may increase, especially in ghetto communities, if they indicate that they are on the side of justice no matter who the unjust are. This rapport may lead to better law enforcement against both common and organized crime—a bonus for the officers—as well as to more confidence in the "establishment" as exemplified by the police officer.

Patrick Murphy has suspected that confidence in the police can be enhanced because anti-white-collar-crime activity can put suspicions that the police have been corrupted by white-collar criminals, since otherwise, "How can the crooks survive?" Murphy stated before Congressman Conyers's committee:

> Some of the credibility of the street police officer in today's urban setting is weakened by the existence of white-collar crime about which the officers can do nothing but for which the officer may be blamed by less sophisticated members of the community. Consumer fraud is an example. Even police departments which may be among the most honest and enjoy reputations for integrity are not spared questions of poor people who often assume that the police are somehow part of the consumer fraud problems, that graft, payoff, some kind of cover up may exist. [House Judiciary Committee 1977]

The viability and longevity of any police effort to fight white-collar crime depends in part on the strength of the motivation of the officers involved after such anti-white-collar-crime activities get under way. Thus, some more-sophisticated versions of the aforementioned questionnaire could be administered to police departments that have ongoing anti-white-collar-crime efforts, so that the degree of intrinsic and extrinsic rewards experienced by the officers can be measured—for example, the perceived efficiency of their own work. Furthermore, the perception of the police in the communities could be studied, although measures other than survey questionnaires may be necessary in some situations. The results of both the police study and the community study could be compared to the results of parallel studies in the same department and communities prior to the inception of the increased effort against white-collar crime, or in other departments and communities in which no such efforts have been mounted.

If these studies are done properly, they can uncover obstacles that officers might have experienced: subtle or direct pressure not to pursue powerful targets; complaints about those who use law enforcement as a "bill collector," ceasing their cooperation after the complainee has paid them back or paid them off; difficulties caused by having to investigate a person or group in the community on whom law enforcement is dependent for other, legitimate reasons, such as assistance in tracing stolen and fenced property; and so forth. Such research might also ask investigators about how such problems are dealt with.

So far, we have treated the question of motivation at the level of the individual officer, and have not addressed factors that could lead organizations *as such* to enhance their efforts against white-collar crime. But without organizational commitment, the individual's own interest reaches a dead end. As mentioned at the beginning of the chapter, a number of local and state police departments have recently made a shift in priorities toward the area of white-collar crime. A very useful historical-reasearch project could be done to determine what political, sociological, or other factors lead to the decision to establish anti-white-collar-crime units in police departments. Obviously some of these units have the potential to harm powerful entities in the community, so that the political forces strong enough to overcome the apparent resistance can be identified.

The Organization and Techniques of Investigation

Up to now, we have examined the significance and potentiality of police forces to detect white-collar crimes and the degree and type of motivation they have and might develop for action against white-collar crime. We now turn to investigations and more-proactive operations by police departments. These investigations and other activities can be conducted in investigative units within police departments, in patrol, or in collaborative efforts between them. We will examine each in turn.

For the most part, patrol-officer roles in the anti-white-collar-crime effort are most effective in the area of detection and preliminary investigation. Officers can receive training and information about white-collar crime in the police academies, but also in roll calls and during in-service training. The Los Angeles Police Department has produced a series of flyers, to be given to police officers at roll call, which vividly describe current ongoing schemes, giving officers information not only on how to detect the outward signs of white-collar crimes but also on how to conduct preliminary investigations. For example, if a home-repair fraud is suspected, one or two officers in a car might approach the probable victim out of earshot of the suspect, while his partner engages the suspect in distracting conversation. The first officer can simply ask the probable victim if the suspect made him or her a business offer—and, if he did, ask him for his business license. Or the officers might secure information about the elements of a consumer fraud so that they can interview witnesses with better results. The IACP Training Keys mentioned earlier also point in these directions, and supply much information on the legal elements of a consumer fraud. Other materials could also be developed, such as an equivalent of the 49-page, pocket-sized *Police Guide on Organized Crime* (LEAA 1972). In any case, the effectiveness of this type of training can be evaluated, partly by questionnaires testing knowledge of controls, but mostly by asking officers about the practical value of the type of information. How has it helped them in preliminary investigations? Although attractiveness, interest, and informativeness of such handouts are important, the key evaluation variable is their usefulness.

Perhaps more important than an evaluation of these training techniques is a study of the system of information flow, decision making, and rewards and punishments in the relationship among street officers, their immediate supervisors, and detective units that are assigned to work on white-collar crime. Since a patrol officer has the technical ability and resources to do complete investigations on only a few of the incidents he uncovers, it is important to find out such things as what happens to his initial report (and whether the patrol officer even learns the fate of his report); what immediate, personal help he gets from detectives when he needs further help in investigation; who gets the credit for any arrests—patrolmen or detectives; how much personal contact there is between detectives and patrolmen; how often the detectives go to roll call to describe the latest scheme or current prime suspects or fugitives; and how information is collected so as to detect patterns readily. The Rand study of the investigative function in police departments uncovered many anomalies, and emphasized the need for collaboration between the two types of police officers. If their departments are properly organized, patrolmen should receive credit for cases that they may only have opened, with the detectives following through on the referred cases. A systems analysis of the relationship between white-collar-crime detective units and patrol could prove very valuable for police managers.

The possibilities of positive relations between state investigative agencies and local and state police are articulated by Steir, the director of the New Jersey State Department of Justice:

> And I know now that with the development of a sense of pride, a sense of accomplishment in law enforcement in this state, the quality of law enforcement at all levels has been upgraded . . . we devote a great deal of these resources to strengthening, bolstering, training the county and local level law enforcement. [House Judiciary Committee 1977, p. 208]

He reports that local officers make more referrals, and more arrests.

An important part of this system is deciding which leads to follow up, which cases to investigate. Two related but separable types of issues are involved in such decisions: the possibility of successfully completing an investigation, and the significance of the case. This latter issue, which also bears on the problem of evaluating white-collar-crime investigative units, will be discussed later. The issue of judging the probable success of cases is very important because investigators frequently take a long time and are very demanding of resources. As mentioned earlier, a clue to how to grapple with this problem may be derived from the recent development of methods for predicting the fruitfulness of investigations of a crime of a particular type, such as burglary. These methods involve a checklist of items such as availability of eyewitnesses, or knowledge of serial numbers of stolen goods. Given the great range and growing variety of white-collar crimes, it would be all but impossible to develop a system as specific and concrete as those being developed for common crime. Nevertheless, some broad categories of checklist items might be developed for broader categories of crime. Bowley (1974) suggests the number of victims and their location in the jurisdiction. The articulateness and the judged reliability of witnesses might be included. Edelhertz's (1977) analysis of the elements of fraud could constitute a framework for developing such a checklist for white-collar crimes that appear to be frauds (and not, say, embezzlements or computer crimes). The value of such a checklist might first be tested by going through archival data and recording whether or not information in each of the categories of the elements of the crime was available at the end of the preliminary investigation, and then determining whether the number of elements about which there was information correlated with successful completion of the investigation, or whether the presence of information with respect to a subject of elements was sufficiently predictive. As Richards (1977) points out, it may be necessary to continue the preliminary investigation in order to provide information with respect to parts of the checklist about which little is known one way or the other. He also points out that unless the investigations begin to show some direction, some movement, the detectives will soon lose their motivation, and waste their time. The proper selection of cases for long-term investigation is crucial. This procedure might be especially helpful in the area of consumer fraud, since many nonpolice as well as police agencies receive a very high volume of complaints, only a small percentage of which actually involve crime. Consumer fraud may be a sufficiently delimited area to make a rather specific and concrete checklist possible.

The results of this analysis could then provide the basis for testing the model in a predictive fashion on current investigations. The value of formalizing the process of decision making could be tested by determining whether the rate of successful completion of investigations was higher than when some comparable procedure was used.

When investigations go beyond the initial, preliminary stage, the requisite skills become more complex and sophisticated. These skills may be more available in police departments than might be assumed, since many officers moonlight, make investments for their early retirement, study law, and so forth. However, the possibility of hiring accountants or former businessmen, for example, as civilian members of fraud investigative units should not be overlooked, although the benefits of restricting such units to sworn officers were set forth earlier.

One major area of difficulty in the investigation of white-collar crime by police, as well as by any other agency, is the time involved. The enormous amount of detailed researching of records and tracing of paper along the trail often makes the task so formidable that some important cases may have to be overlooked because of considerations of resources and time. Although computers may help in many instances, this is not always the case. Some way of speeding up the scanning of paper to detect certain information would be of enormous assistance. For instance, computers that read may perhaps be devised to search through bank checks for numbers and/or names that are specifiable in advance. The world of business machines may have devices now in use that could be easily adapted for investigative purposes.

In the section on detection of white-collar crime, it was pointed out that research on whistleblowers would be quite valuable. Most white-collar crime is detected initially by personal communication—by reports, tips, complaints—rather than through close observation by government or private monitors. Although we argued earlier that much more can be done to facilitate detection by such monitors, personal reports will always be of great significance, so that it is important to maximize the input from these sources. Studies of such people would also be of great value for the investigative process in which the investigators are no longer in the position of simply being available if some victim/witness or participant decides to communicate with the police. In most investigations, the process is more proactive; the investigator seeks out possible informants and/or witnesses. Thus, studies could be done on the demographic, organizational, experimental, and personal characteristics of persons who are whistleblowers of various types: for example, witnesses, victims, or participants who cooperate with law enforcement on request, or those who do so only on a basis of bargaining or under pressure. Such research could use data from the various hotlines, investigators, investigative reporters, prosecutors, and so forth, and, where possible, from the whistleblowers themselves. This information could be coded into various categories that could be defined broadly enough to be applicable to all sorts of informants. Such information would provide systematic information about the demographics of whistleblowers and whistleblowing, as compared with other people; the "moral careers" of their involvement; the whistleblowers' positions in the conspiracy, peripheral or central; the role of persons in logistical support roles, such as advertising agents or printers; the role of competitiors as whistleblowers;

the immediate cause and basic motivation for blowing the whistle; the obstacles—organizations, personal and so forth—to doing so. Bogen (1978) honestly discusses ways in which management might "handle" potential whistleblowers in industry so as to minimize their "disruption" of the organization. Peters and Branch (1972) document the ways in which whistleblowers have been punished by their organizations. Some journalistic work has already been done on whistleblowers (Nader, Petkas, and Blackwell 1972), which suggests such hypotheses as whistleblowers being people who have group affiliations outside a conspiracy, or people who have been mistreated by the other conspirators. This information may be of great value to investigators. As Condon (n.d.) points out, choosing a "safe" but informed person to approach is often difficult, and a mistake in choosing an informant can expose an otherwise secret investigation.

A problem in recent complex (or even simple) investigation is that prime attention is given to the collection of data, and even to the organization of such data in flow charts, organizational charts, and so forth, by crime analysts. However, the availablity and organization of such information does not guarantee that the investigators or their supervisors will be able to think through some of the problems and possibilities. Psychology has shown repeatedly that it is only too natural to fit incoming, new information into a pre-existing set of ideas, concepts, and mental organizations of data. These mental sets may sometimes—we cannot tell how often— blind the investigator about what actually occurred, causing him to miss cases or misconstrue them. Psychology has also developed techniques for overcoming these effects by freeing the mind to look at information in different ways. No doubt some applied psychological research could examine how such techniques would be applied to investigations and case development so as to enhance investigators' decision making.

Evaluation and Reward

Even if the personnel of an organization are knowledgeable and motivated to deal with white-collar crime, the evaluation and reward systems within an organization and of the organization as a totality need to support and enhance efforts against white-collar crime. Evaluation has been very difficult in this area, with respect to both individuals and agencies, partly because the usual technique of counting the number of investigations and cases closed is highly inappropriate. Such counting tends to ignore the extreme complexity of some investigations, the length of time and resources needed, the great significance that one case might have on deterring other crimes by the perpetrators or by others; the value one case might have in educating the community of potential victims; the amount of money and other valuables that have been lost or that might be retrieved by victims directly through restitution or indirectly through civil suits; the harm inflicted on people of moderate means, as compared with the loss to the wealthy; the significance of the case in upholding (or restoring) public faith in the integrity of the establishment.

Some professionals have thrown up their hands at the complexity of this problem, but the need to evaluate both individuals and units have forced them to use whatever means possible to justify themselves to their sources of funds, promotions, and so forth. These sources are characteristically oriented toward simple statistical measures such as number of cases cleared. In order to deal with this orientation, not only are the number of ongoing and closed investigations and cases now reported, but also the dollar losses that have been suffered, the probable loss that was prevented, the number of victims, and so on. In addition, narrative reports of significant cases are made. An example from the Atlanta Georgia Police Department is shown in table 4-1.

However, no valid overall model has been developed that is widely used. Research on how to develop summary indexes of the productivity of a person and/or a unit would therefore be beneficial. Such an index might be developed in collaboration with economists and sociologists who could provide ways of measuring or estimating such factors as the number of

Table 4-1
Types of Investigations Conducted by the Atlanta (Georgia) Police Department, 1979

Case Type	Loss in Dollars	Comment
Embezzlements	68,585	Actual loss
Credit-card fraud	2,300,000/yearly	Five major Atlanta banks
Employee thefts	49,869	Probable loss
Fraudulent employee agencies	8,300	Probable loss
Illegal practice/abortion	NA	Investigative leads used to draft new legislation
Stock forgery	4,600,000	Investment prevented
Insurance-fraud ring	1,000,000	Estimated loss
Mail-order schemes	Undeterminable	—
Extortion attempt	1,200	One case; no loss
Arson	145,000	One case; no loss
Airline-ticket fraud	24,000/month	One case; projected loss
Bankruptcy fraud	753,560	Monitored case

Note: NA = Not available.

probable victims, the loss to each, and the proportion of a person's total assets that the loss represents.

Maltz (1975) proposed that in evaluating the Financial Crimes Bureau of the Illinois Attorney General's Office, an index be developed based on the components of property loss, physical injury, and psychological injury. In measuring property loss, he suggests using the number of days' pay lost by the victims; or, when the state is the victim, using the amount lost to the state divided by the average income of people in the state. One possible route that such research might take is the development of a procedure whereby the weights given to the aforementioned considerations or criteria can be changed as a matter of agency or individual policy. Making such a weighting procedure systematic and known would force agencies to articulate their policies and procedures, thus facilitating open discussion of policy issues. A generally accepted index that recognized some of the issues mentioned earlier might also facilitate the decision-making process inside agencies with respect to whether or not to open a full investigation on the basis of the results of the preliminary one. Obviously, some estimates will have to be made about some of the variables going into the index; but if the estimates are made within the framework of the index, they would be used more validly. The results of such an evaluation of a case after preliminary investigation could be reviewed along with the index of the probability of successfully completing an investigation, mentioned in an earlier section. With both of these indexes in mind, the manager can make a better-informed decision.

One major source of input for such indexes is the deterrent value of prosecutions. It has been an article of faith that the "rational" or calculating approach of the criminals makes white-collar crime more susceptible to the deterrence because of the probability and cost of being caught. However, very little research has been conducted to demonstrate the effect empirically. Hoover Institute economists have recently concluded a study showing that antitrust enforcement does lead to lower prices in an industry (Block, Nold, and Sidak 1978). Barlow and Laymen (1976) found that twenty people convicted of white-collar crime at various times in one county in Washington did not repeat their crimes, to the knowledge of public agencies, for a period of two years after the filings of the charges. Stotland et al (1980) found that increased prosecution of home-repair contractors for failure to have a license (bond) slowed the rate of increase in home-repair fraud, as indexed by complaints to consumer-protection agencies. Not only might such studies encourage investigators and prosecutors, but they also can give them the means to evaluate their productivity in terms of deterrent effects. These studies suggest possible sources of data on the occurrence of crime, and a statistical format for evaluating the deterrent value of their activities. The basic format of such studies is the development of some index of a given type of crime in a community, and recording of the level of this index before, during, and after the initiation of a program of investigation and/or prosecution. By means of a regression analysis applied to time series, it is possible not only to detect significant changes in the level of the index, but also to account for the effects that other factors, such as changes in local economy, might have on the level of crime. Measures of such other factors are often available. Studies of this sort, however, need to be supplemented by examination of the channels of information in a community regarding convictions; the resultant changes, if any, in potential offenders' or ongoing offenders' perception of the probability of being sanctioned; and their perception of the severity of sanctions. Obviously, more such studies should be performed, in order to provide a much broader base of information, both to justify the anti-white-collar-crime effort in general (if deterrence continues to be demonstrable) and to provide a format for establishing indexes of deterrence for a given case, or set of cases. Such research could provoke economists into providing more indexes of the amount of white-collar crime, such as the total amount of money (after considering inflation) a community spends on automobile repairs, compared with some standard of how much they would be expected to spend (M. Brintnall, personal communication, 1979). This research also might help to determine the types of perpetrators or illicit activities most susceptible to special or general deterrence.

Strategic Intelligence

In law enforcement, the term *intelligence* usually refers to the collection and analysis of data regarding particular persons or organizations that have been known to commit crimes. Intelligence units seek information that is not developed to the level required for formal investigation directed immediately toward prosecution. Since such intelligence is, at least in principle, one or two steps away from formal investigation, it should more accurately be called *tactical intelligence*. On the other hand, the term *strategic intelligence* should be used to refer to information and analysis that deals with the "big picture"—trends in society or in a community that point to the probability that crimes of a certain type will increase or decrease in a given area. Thus, changes in the rate of business activity could lead to changes in the ratio of certain crimes—for example, a downturn in a local economy might lead to more arson for profit.

   The expectation that strategic intelligence can lead to predictions about where crimes of certain types will occur in the future bears on a major problem in fighting whtie-collar crime: the known advantages to the criminals of the very long lag time between the perpetration of a crime and effective governmental response. Ordinarily, the police function primarily in a reactive mode—investigating complaints and leads made by or supplied by other entities, individual citizens, government agencies, the attorney general, newspapers, and so forth. Such a reactive mode makes the allocation of resources subject to influence by the degree of knowledge that people in these other entities have of white-collar-crime activities, their ability to recognize it as criminal behavior, and their willingness to report it to the authorities. Since white-collar crimes, unlike other crimes, are often hidden and/or not recognized as such, the dependency of the police on the other entities places the police at a distinct disadvantage. It is therefore possible for white-collar crime to exist undetected for considerable periods of time and thereby to inflict considerable damage on people and institutions. Thus, more proactive strategies and tactics by government, including law enforcement, are vital.

In order to promote such proactive strategies, the possibility should be considered of establishing research teams of economic historians, systems analysts, sociologists, and lawyers, to develop strategic intelligence for white-collar crimes. The organizational and procedural difficulties of establishing such multidisciplinary teams in these areas of concern should be examined through research (see chapter 6 by Dinitz). On the basis of guidelines stemming from this research, some pilot multidisciplinary teams could work on developing models for strategic intelligence to predict where and when there will be increases in white-collar crime and the occurence of new types. These predictive models could be developed on the basis of examination of historical data, which would be used to predict the historical increases and changes in white-collar crime, although the ultimate model would be based on more-current possible sources of data. The measures of past white-collar crime could be indexes based on newspaper reports, indictments, and so forth. The models could then be tested on more-current data, and, it is hoped, would be so devised that they could be used by agencies at all levels of jurisdiction, from local to national.

On the assumption that the predictive models prove themselves, the possibility should be explored of establishing local, regional, and even national entities that could develop and propose the most-appropriate strategy and tactics with respect to specific predicted upsurges in white-collar crime. Possible approaches could include "sunshine laws," criminal prosecutions, civil or administrative sanctions, system changes, monitoring procedures, or public education or warnings. Research could be done using available data on the effectiveness of each of these approaches for each type of white-collar crime. The technology developed by Sherman (1978) for indexing the degree of corruption in police departments could be translated into a schema for estimates of the actual amounts of white-collar crime in an area, so that some systematic way of estimating the efficacy of various tactics could be developed. These overall strategic considerations could imply which tactical approach might be most effective in gaining information about the probable locus of the crime, if any. Some types of crime might demand more emphasis on victim reports, whereas other types might be more susceptible to proactively confronting participants who are more likely to turn.

An example of what might be called strategic intelligence comes from Hagen (1979), although he does not use the concept of strategic intelligence. He shows how one can start from general knowledge about the economy and wind up with a very specific, completely proactive investigation—a practice that probably saved his community many thousands of dollars.

A.Case Example: The White-Collar Intelligence Process Operationalized

Scenario Introduction

You have been reading in the newspaper over the past three months how the national rate of inflation is continuing to rise abnormally. The prime interest rate offered by major east-coast banks rose again for the third consecutive time in a three-month period. The current rate constituted a five-year high. This morning's paper indicated that the major west-coast lending institutions were following the lead of their east-coast counterparts.

Ideally, this scenario should prompt the following type of questions of those involved in the white-collar-crime intelligence process:

1. What impact will the economic factors described in the newspapers have on the business community in my jurisdiction?
2. What has been the impact on the east-coast business climate since the first increases in the prime interest rate started to occur?
3. In what ways could a white-collar criminal gain monetarily from the economic climate described?
4. What would be indicators of such criminal activities being designed or perpetuated in my jurisdiction?
5. What would be logical information sources to review for such indicators?

Based on your prior experience, you know that numerous increases in the prime interest rate for corporate loans over a short period of time may be indicative of a tight money market. Such raises may have little impact on your community if the business climate has been stable with minimal growth or new business start-up. However, if the growth pattern has been escalating with the upswing of inflation and many new businesses are being started, then the ingredients of an "advance-fee scam" are present.

Specific to an advance-fee scam, the following questions must be addressed:

1. Has there been an increase in new business starts?
2. Has there been an increase in new-construction or land-development activity?
3. Has there been an increase in new industrial start-up or expansion activities?
4. Has there been an increase in loan denials or reduction in existing lines of credit?
5. Has there been a decrease in solicitation of loans by private individual or lending institutions?

If the answers to these questions are generally "yes," then the advance-fee target should be considered viable with future information collection of the intelligence process being focused on the determination of the existence of concrete indicators of the crime. The mere existence of the ingredients does not justify the conclusion that the scam exists, even from an intelligence perspective. Key indicators might include:

1. Financial-source activity soliciting loan business in spite of economic climate.
2. Financial source requiring a finder's or processing fee in advance to cover acquisition of the loan monies and the completion of the required paperwork.
3. Financial source not headquartered in the United States.
4. Financial source's financial statement suggests tremendous assets, often of the type that are subjectively valuated or capable of excessive inflation (foreign or domestic landholdings, mining claims, other loans, horse stables, and so forth).

Hagen then shows how the use of these fear indicators led him to focus on one brokerage house, where an intense investigation revealed a criminal operation.

In the area of organized crime, commissions have been set up to engage in such strategic intelligence, such as the New Mexico Governor's Organized Crime Prevention Commission (Hartz 1977). Such commissions may not only indicate the areas toward which resources should be directed, but may also warn the public, stimulate discussion of preventive measures, and so forth.

Even local neighborhood groups of citizens can devise strategic intelligence processes before Congress. Scondia (1977) showed how an analysis of the deterioration of housing in an area and the increase in ,absentee ownership could be used to predict an increase in arson for profit.

Conclusion

This chapter focused first on the process of gaining information about the occurrence of white-collar crime, either reactively or proactively; second, on the motivation of the police for gaining such information and using it most effectively; third, on the techniques for investigation; fourth, on evaluation of anti-white-collar-crime efforts; and, finally, on strategic considerations. In each instance research was suggested that could enhance the contribution of police to the overall effort to control and eradicate white-collar crime. The research projects suggested are not exhaustive, but they appear to be the most relevant to the purpose of the police role as a stable information-processing agency. These projects could also be usefully conducted in nonpolice investigative agencies such as prosecutors' offices, regulatory agencies, inspectors-general offices, and so forth, since they need to be part of the total, pervasive effort that was called for at the beginning of the chapter.

References

Barlow, S.R., and Loman, M.F. 1976. *White Collar Crime Project Evaluation.* Olympia, Wash.: Law and Justice Planning Division.

Block, M.K.; Nold, F.C.; and Sidak, J.G. 1978. *The Deterrent Effect of Anti-trust Enforcement.* Stanford, Calif.: Center for Econometric Studies of the Justice System, September.

Bogen, K.T. 1978. "Managing Technical Dissent in Private Industry." Unpublished paper.

Bowley, G. 1974. "Law Enforcement's Role in Consumer Protection." *Santa Clara Law Review* 14 (Spring):555.

Brintnall, M. 1978. "Police and White Collar Crime." Department of Political Science, Brown University. Unpublished paper.

Condon, R. *Managing Investigation into Public Corruption.* Seattle, Wash.: Battelle Law and Justice Study Center.

Edlehertz, H. 1970. *Nature, Impact and Prosecution of White-Collar Crime.* Washington, D.C.: Law Enforcement Assistance Administration.

Edelhertz, H.; Stotland, E.; Walsh, M.; and Weinberg, 1977. *Investigation of White-Collar Crime.* Seattle, Wash.: Battelle Institute and Law Enforcement Assistance Administration.

Ely, E.S. 1980. "Raising Money in the Name of the Law." *Police,* January.

Goldstein, Herman. 1977. *Policing a Free Society.* Cambridge, MA: Ballinger Publishers.

Greenberg, M.A. 1979. "Introductory Guidelines: The Police Role in Environmental Safety." *Police Chief* 47 (11):48-49.

Hagen, R.E. 1979. *Intelligence Process in White Collar Crime Investigation.* Seattle, Wash.: Battelle Institute.

Hartz, H.L. 1977. "Combating Organized Crime." *Police Chief,* September.

House of Representatives. Committee on the Judiciary. Subcomittee on Crime. (Conyers committee). 1977. *New Directions for Federal Involvement in Crime Control,* 95th Congress, 1st Session. Washington, D.C.: U.S. Government Printing Office.

Hutton, G.U. 1979. "Welfare Fraud and the Police." *Police Chief,* November.

International Association of Chiefs of Police. 1976. *Training Key: Insurance Fraud, No. 241.* Gaithersburg, Md.: IACP.

Law Enforcement Assistance Administration. (LEAA). 1972. *Police Guide on Organized Crime.* Washington, D.C.: U.S. Superintendent of Documents.

Lyman, T.; Fletcher, T.; and Gardiner, J.A. 1978. *Prevention, Detection and Correction of Corruption in Local Government.* Washington, D.C.: LEAA.

Maltz, M. 1975. *A Plan for Evaluation of the Financial Crimes Bureau of the Illinois Attorney General's Office.* Chicago Circle: University of Illinois.

Nader, R.; Petkas, P.S.; and Blackwell, K. 1972 *Whistleblowing: Report of the Conference on Professional Responsibility.* New York: Grossman.

Peters, C. and Branch, T. 1972. *Blow the Whistle.* New York: Praeger.

Richards, P.R. 1977. "Feasibility Study: A Rational Method of Choice in Selecting Crime Investigations." *Police Chief,* September.

Sherman, L. 1978. *Scandal and Reform.* Berkely: University of California Press.

Short, James F., and Schrager, L. 1980. "How Serious a Crime? Perceptions of Organizational and Common Crimes." In Gilbert Geis and Ezra Stotland, eds., *White-Collar Crime: Theory and Reserach.* Beverly Hills, Calif.: Sage Publications.

Sorensen, J.E.; Grove H.D.; and Sorensen, T.L. 1980. "Detecting Management Fraud: The Role of the Independent Auditor." In Gilber Geis and Ezra Stotland, eds. *White Collar Crime: Theory and Research.* Beverly Hills, Calif.: Sage Publications.

Stotland, E.; Brintnall, M.; L'Heureux, A.; and Ashmore, E. 1980. "Do Convictions Deter Home Repair Fraud?" In Gilbert Geis and Ezra Stotland, eds., *White Collar Crime: Theory and Research.* Beverly Hills, Calif.: Sage Publications.

Wolfgang, M. 1980. *National Survey of Crime Severity.* Philadelphia: Center for Studies in Criminology and Criminal Law, University of Pennsylvania.

5 The Regulatory Role in the Containment of Corporate Illegality

John M. Thomas

Introduction

Regulatory agencies define and enforce legal rules in areas in which government has decreed that the unhindered play of market forces can create serious liabilities for society. These rules are derived from statutes governing such diverse problems as antitrust violations, securities fraud, tax evasion, environmental pollution, worker health and safety, consumer fraud, and discrimination.[1] To the extent that an essential aspect of the regulatory process is the interpretation of vague legislative mandates, regulatory officials are able to define what constitutes illegal behavior on the parts of individuals and business organizations.[2] In addition, the exercise of discretion by regulatory officials influences the agenda of other law-enforcement agencies required to prosecute offenders.

The early, seminal writings on the nature of white-collar crime recognized the importance of the regulatory process. The problem of a regulatory approach was a prominent theme in Sutherland's conception of white-collar crime. According to Edelhertz:

> He [Sutherland] forcefully pointed out that our legislation had established a unique legal structure with a complex of administrative proceedings, injunctions, and cease and desist orders to meet common law fraud if committed in a business context, thus largely preempting the field of enforcement and making criminal proceedings unlikely or seemingly inappropriate. [Edelhertz 1970, p. 4]

Later Newman (1958) noted that "the vast bulk of white collar legislation is regulatory rather than penal in philosophy, is administrative in procedure, and by its qualifications is directed chiefly toward the business and professional classes of our society." And Kadish's (1963) analysis of the use of criminal sanctions in economic regulation distinguished this area of law enforcement by the fact that "the responsibility for investigation, detection, and initial prosecution is often vested in a specialized agency or other body rather than left with the usual institutions for policing and prosecuting criminal violations" (Kadish 1963; see also Caldwell 1958).

The concept of economic crime committed by business organizations has become increasingly complex and bewildering as regulatory statutes and agencies continue to proliferate.[3] As a consequence, it is difficult to propose a comprehensive typology of these offenses and to generalize about the role of the regulatory function in the containment of white-collar crime. There are, however, several important dimensions of regulatory offenses that should be noted. First, these offenses encompass a wide variety of victims: the general "public" in the case of environmental laws; individuals who are members of the violator organization in the case of worker health and safety and discrimination; and specific members of the public, such as shareholders and consumers, in the case of consumer fraud, antitrust violations, and drug statutes.[4] Second, it is not always clear that these offenses include the use of deception or the explicit disguise of purpose (see Edelhertz 1970, p. 14). Some regulatory violation may be committed in the absence of fraud, such as in the environmental and health and safety areas. This is not to say that these types of offenses could not be accompanied by other fraudulent transactions. A hypothetical example provided by Shapiro is the case of Plant X, which fails to abide by EPA emissions standards, versus Plant Y, which fails to abide, claims compliance, and "files for tax breaks for the installation of non-existent antipollution devices" (Shapiro 1979, p. 38). Third, regulatory problems lend themselves to what has been termed *compliance*, rather than *sanction-oriented* enforcement methods (Mileski 1971; Hawkins 1980a). The goals of enforcement in these situations include change in an undesirable illegal condition or state of affairs. Sanctions may not be imposed immediately because it is felt that negotiation between the regulator and regulated will bring about the necessary corrective action. Sanctions are used as a threat to secure compliance and deter future violations. In this sense, regulatory offenses can be said to require *conciliatory*, in contrast to *penal*, systems of legal control. A conciliatory system of law refers to "remedial styles . . . assistance for people in trouble . . . what is necessary to remedy a bad situation" (Black 1976, p. 4). Finally, although all regulatory agencies possess broad powers to investigate criminal activity and determine violations, this does not extend to criminal-prosecutorial authority. At the federal level, agencies refer cases to the Department of Justice for criminal prosecution. In addition, agencies have the option to pursue a variety of other remedies—for example, civil prosecution, which can result in fines, injunctions, or consent decrees.[5]

Although there have been many empirical studies of the private corporation, comparatively little research has been focused on the behavior of regulatory bureaucracies. Recently, a British scholar has noted:

> It is commonplace in the sociology of the law to observe that a characteristic of industrialized societies is the use of the criminal laws to regulate economic life. Yet it is remarkable that so few analyses of the nature of the regulatory process are to be found in the literature, especially

given the fact that post-war Anglo-American sociology of law is largely a sociology of criminal justice. [Hawkins, Keith, "The Use of Discretion by Regulatory Officials: A Case Study of Environmental Pollution in the United Kingdom," presented at a conference at SUNY at Buffalo, June 2-3, 1980]

In general, the regulatory process is concerned with how officials define and apply regulations, and the impact on compliance and deterrence of various enforcement remedies available to regulatory agencies—decisions to refer for criminal prosecution, to proceed with civil prosecution, or to undertake formal administrative procedures (see Clinard 1979; *Harvard Law Review* 1979). Central to the problem of administrative discretion (see Davis 1969) are decisions concerning the selective enforcement of violations, strategies for obtaining compliance, the use of sanctions, and the way agencies acquire information about regulatory problems (see Gifford 1972).[6]

The purpose of this chapter is to analyze the relationship between the exercise of discretion by regulatory officials and the control of corporate illegality through regulatory sanctions. The issue of discretion is important because of the problem of compliance and the traditional ambivalence about assigning blame attached to many of these offenses (see Kadish 1963).[7] The second section of the chapter discusses recent general trends in the regulatory control of corporate illegality, involving a growing emphasis on laws designed to protect the consumer and provide for public health and safety. The next section presents a general conceptual framework for considering future research on the regulatory process. This framework focuses on two problems in the exercise of discretion: the negotiation of compliance and the choice of legal sanctions. In summary and conclusion, the final section suggests several projects that might be included in an agenda of future research. A basic assumption of the following discussion is that systematic, empirical efforts to evaluate the impact of various regulatory sanctions, or to test new alternatives, should be informed by a greater understanding of the behavior of regulatory bureaucracies. As Jerry Mashaw has recently observed, a useful evaluation study "is research that is embedded in the policy process, i.e., research responsive to the world as the administrative decision maker sees it and constrained by the policy guidelines that the bureau recognizes" (Mashaw 1980, p. 75).

Trends in Government Regulation

Over roughly the past fifteen years, there have been a number of significant developments in the effort to control corporate illegality through the regulatory process. First, there has been an increased willingness on the part of the federal government to advocate criminal sanctions for regulatory offenses. Traditionally, criminal penalties have been ancillary to other sanctions, used as a last resort when other types of sanctions proved unworkable (see *Harvard Law Review* 1979).

An example of the recent prominence given to criminal penalties is the 1975 case of *United States* v. *Park*. In this case, both ACME Markets, Inc., *and* its chief executive officer, J.R. Park, were found guilty of the 1938 law against storing food shipped in interstate commerce in a rodent-contaminated, unsanitary building. In interpreting the Food and Drug Administration (FDA) legislation, the Supreme Court upheld the Park conviction and argued that a corporate officer with the authority and responsibility to prevent or correct a violation of the FDA act, and who does not do so, may be held criminally liable for the violation. Recent legislation in environmental regulation also supports this trend. The 1972 amendments to the Federal Water Pollution Control Act provide for the criminal prosecution of corporate officers for the abuse by these organizations of the environment. First offenders face imprisonment of up to one year and fines of $2,500 to $25,000 per day; additional offenses can be punishable by up to $50,000 per day and a prison term of up to two years. The increased penalties for price fixing under the Sherman Act also reflect a desire by Congress to impose greater personal criminal liability on corporate officers.

On the other hand, many regulatory agencies have limited the use of available criminal penalties. Although the teeth in such remedies have been sharpened by the courts and Congress, agencies have not utilized these weapons. Edelhertz has summarized the nature of this general phenomenon as follows:

> Except in rare instances [IRS and SEC] agency enforcement officials are prone to avoid considering cases for criminal prosecution. Agents or auditors alert to criminal issues lose their goal in a climate of discouragement and delay, or in the course of administrative and civil settlement negotiation. [U.S. House of Representatives 1978, p. 8]

It can also be hypothesized that the goals of compliance and deterrence in regulatory enforcement create uncertainty about the function of criminal sanctions. Arguably, the principal objective of statutes governing "corporate crime" is "not to punish morally culpable violators but to deter undesirable conduct regardless of culpability" (*Harvard Law Review* 1979, p. 236).

In contrast, the use of civil money penalties by administrative agencies has increased; federal agencies now rely on these fines to a much greater extent than on criminal referrals. There is some evidence that the adoption of civil penalties is associated with agency preferences for maintaining control over the process of negotiating settlements, a goal that has been reinforced by the congressional grant of authority to federal agencies to settle money claims. Thus, it has been argued, "The differing degrees of prosecutorial control exercised by regulators is bound to influence their selection of enforcement sanctions" (Diver 1980, p. 288).

Knowledge of the major influences on the exercise of discretion in the use of civil money penalties is important because such fines have been advocated as a more-effective deterrent to regulatory offenses than are criminal sanctions.[8] The impact of the civil alternative, however, can be blunted by implicit criteria employed by the regulatory bureaucracy in these decisions. Research on the assessment and collection of civil fines has revealed that proportionately less-severe penalties were levied, the larger the enterprise or the more serious the risk of harm (Diver 1980, p. 291).

Another significant trend in government regulation is the growth of what has been termed the "new social regulation" (Lilley and Miller 1977; Bardach 1979). In contrast to the traditional commercial regulation represented by such organizations as the Interstate Commerce Commission, the Securities and Exchange Commission, Federal Communications Commission, and the Civil Aeronautics Board, a vast number of new agencies have been created in functional areas that cut across industry lines (Weidenbaum 1978). A partial listing of this new legislation includes the National Environmental Policy Act, 1969; the Consumer Product Safety Act, 1972; the Equal Employment Opportunity Act, 1972; and the Occupational Safety and Health Act (OSHA), 1970. A prominent impetus for these laws is the desirability of doing something about a specific problem, often defined as a moral imperative (see Kagan 1978, p. 9). In part, this is a function of a political dynamic that tends to create new regulation, what Mashaw has recently termed "the ideology of governmental efficiency—the view that government is, and must be, an effective agent for getting things done" (1979, pp. 44-51). The end result was a set of new definitions of illegality that symbolized the legitimacy of continued government regulation of matters previously left to the private sector (see Wilson 1972, p. 166).

The problem of administrative discretion and compliance is complicated, however, because many statutes of the new social regulation reflect an objective that conflicts with the moral imperative to eliminate damage to the environment, remove unsafe products from the market, or guarantee a safe and healthful workplace. This goal embodies what Kagan has termed the utilitarian value in the U.S. legal tradition, specifically the need for maintaining economic efficiency: "regulators are expected to moderate police-mission enforcement whenever it comes too strongly into conflict with other important social interests and values, such as economic stability and efficiency" (Kagan 1978, p. 10). For example, the Consumer Product Safety Act states that the promulgation of standards shall include consideration of the public's need for the product involved, the probable impact of a regulation on the cost and availability of the product, and efforts to achieve objectives that minimize adverse effects on competition and commerce (Consumer Product Safety Act of 1972, 15 U.S.C., S 2058 c(1), 1976). Similarly, the Toxic Substances Control Act of 1977 specifically requires the administrator of that act to consider the economic impacts of proposed action and not to "impede unduly or create unnecessary economic barriers to technological innovation" while fulfilling the "primary purpose" of the statute (Toxic Substance Control Act of 1977, 15 U.S.C.A., S 2601, 1978 Supp.). The OSHA legislation of 1970 states that the "feasibility" of standards should be considered relevant to the attainment of the highest degree of health and safety protection for the employee. Here "feasibility" has been interpreted to allow the secretary of labor to take account of economic dislocation in enforcing OSHA regulations.[9]

In addition, recent efforts to modify the Occupational Health and Safety Act and provide for congressional checks on the powers of the Federal Trade Commission (FTC) highlight the extent to which many of these regulatory areas have politicized distinctions between "culpable criminal acts" by corporations and the "social responsibility" of the enterprise. From one perspective, the basic objective of these statutes is "not to punish morally culpable violators but to deter undesirable conduct regardless of culpability" (*Harvard Law Review* 1979, p. 1236). An extreme example of the intrusion of economic criteria into a white-collar regulatory offense is housing-code enforcement. Here strict enforcement is conditioned by the specter of property abandoned by landlords and the dislocation of tenants. There is a belief among officials that the use of sanctions not only will result in noncompliance, but also will encourage such developments (see Galanter, Thomas, and Palen 1976; Ackerman 1971).

Although the enforcement of white-collar/corporate regulatory law traditionally has been bedeviled by the supposed moral neutrality of these offenses (Kadish 1963), this issue of blameworthiness has assumed new relevance with the emergence of "social" regulation. As Keith Hawkins has noted:

> The ambivalence surrounding regulatory deviance . . . is presumably attributable in part to the recency with which new values have been invented and proscribed, and the recognition that economic activity is responsible for the material well-being of the community. . . . [Hawkins 1980, p. 3]

The end result of legislation that accommodates both of these goals is to increase the discretion available to officials in the regulatory agency. Negotiation over the extent and timing of compliance becomes institutionalized. Enforcement is influenced by the way agency officials interpret and resolve conflicts between the moral goals in legislation and pressures for reasonableness represented in the objective of economic efficiency. It could be hypothesized, for example, that to the extent that officials judge a violation to be morally reprehensible, criteria of economic efficiency cannot be taken into account in the enforcement of rules.

In summary, the combination of these trends creates a dilemma for the control of corporate regulatory offenses. On the one hand, there is sentiment for deterrence through the imposition of criminal sanctions; on the other hand, the argument for the moral imperative of many of these offenses has been diluted by the view that enforcement must take economic exigencies into account.

The goal complexity of regulatory legislation also highlights the relationship between the lawmaking process and the exercise of discretion by agency officials who interpret law and apply sanctions. If the criminalization of these offenses is a policy objective, it is important to understand how the regulations influence legislation in ways that can affect the use and impact of criminal sanctions. A study that illustrates this process is Shover's analysis of the enactment of the Surface Mining Control and Reclamation Act of 1977. This research documents how the regulated industry was able to ensure that the final legislation incorporated its perspective on economic considerations and defined enforcement issues as problems to be negotiated with the regulatory agency (Shover 1980, p. 124).

The Nature of the Regulatory Process

The received wisdom of traditional administrative law has been that regulatory agencies are capable of implementing clearly definable, objective goals requiring technical expertise (Freedman 1975). Today, however, it is widely recognized that such a "rational actor" model is misplaced; the regulatory process is more properly conceived as essentially political—a balancing of the competing demands of interests affected by agency decisions. Another contemporary theme is the strong criticism that regulatory decision making is systematically biased in favor of organized interests, most often the regulated firm. As a context for presenting a conceptual framework defining the principal influences on the exercise of discretion in the enforcement process, it is useful to review the reasons that this bias, real or imagined, can occur. First, it is important to recognize that agencies have limited resources and are subject to severe case overloads.[10] Thus, as Richard Stewart notes, "Unremitting maintenance of an adversary posture would quickly dissipate agency resources" 1975, p. 1686). This can result in charges of bias because of a perceived failure to prosecute, and in the view that enforcement favors quiet negotiation and settlement over the virtues of the rule of law.[11]

Second, the nature of the regulatory process is such that agencies confront firms that are what has been termed *repeat players* (see Galanter 1974). The repeat player is that enterprise that has frequent encounters with the regulatory agency either as a violator or as a contestor of rules and policies. In the consumers fraud area and in certain areas of the new social regulation, such firms are often better able than the public, consumers, or victims to learn the rules of the regulatory game—the nature of agency procedures. This familiarity can result in certain advantages that contribute to the perception of agency conservatism and bias.

Finally, the goals of regulation imply that the *deterrence* of future violations goes hand in hand with *obtaining* compliance. Unlike the typical criminal violation, the use of sanctions in regulatory violations is tempered by the realization that the illegal condition may continue unabated, creating further harm to the public and to its victims (see Mileski 1971). Regulatory officials are vulnerable to charges that they are overly conciliatory and that they compromise the law in efforts to bring violators into compliance. In contrast, it has been demonstrated that certain types of regulatory offenses—such as environmental pollution and occupational health and safety violations—require considerable flexibility and adaptability on the part of officials if the objective of real compliance is to be achieved (see Kagan and Scholz, 1980; Hawkins 1980). How, and under what circumstances, compliance should be negotiated poses significant problems of discretion for the regulatory agency. Unfortunately, however, our knowledge of the major influences on this process and its impact on the effectiveness of regulatory sanctions is extremely limited. We now discuss a set of concepts that might usefully guide research in this area. These are classified under two headings: the nature of enforcement policy and constraints on the exercise of discretion.

Policy Formation: Resource Allocation and
Regulatory Priorities

Empirical research on the compliance process and the use of various regulatory sanctions should begin with the simple realization that enforcement is based on explicit or implicit policies. In our framework, policy formation refers to what Diver has termed the "view from the top" of the regulatory agency:

> . . . the enforcement problem is one of structuring and controlling the exercise of choice: what regulated activities to examine, what indicators to monitor, what inferences to draw from observations, which suspected violations to document, whether to initiate formal enforcement proceedings, what concessions to demand or sanctions to seek. A top-down enforcement policy is a set of rules, . . . for allocating resources among, and specifying the content of, various surveillance and prosecutorial tasks. Diver, C.S. 1980 "Modesty and Immodesty in Policy-Oriented Empirical Research," *Administrative Law Review,* 75:261. Reprinted with permission].

In analyzing the nature of the policy-formation task, it is important to note that regulatory organizations face an ever expanding agenda of issues, a problem inherent in the nature of the regulatory process. Because agencies are charged with less-than-precise mandates, officials frequently enlarge the domain and increase the complexity of regulation in an effort to decide what exactly the agency should accomplish (Wilson 1972, p. 152). The current administrator of the Environmental Protection Agency (EPA) recently remarked: ''Only when you try to implement a statute do you find out all the complexity'' (*Business Week*, 26 1980). In addition, the politics of competing demands can create situations in which the agency must respond to an array of legal challenges that forces a revision in priorities and resource allocation.[12] For example, the EPA was recently faced with a deadline of 30 April 1980 imposed by the federal court for the issuance of rules on the handling and disposal of hazardous wastes. This was finally achieved by shifting a large number of personnel from outside the solid-waste division. Apparently, however, fifty-six of these had to come from the office of water-planning standards, which *itself* was falling behind another deadline to regulate toxic prohibitants in wastewater (*Business Week*, 26 May 1980).

The political *and* legal dilemma in the resource-allocation task is the desirability of maintaining fairness and equity. An agency may devise a formal policy based on a sophisticated analysis of where the deployment of resources could achieve the greatest benefits. Such a plan could establish enforcement priorities where the greatest overall reduction in a particular regulatory area of white-collar/corporate illegality would occur for a given expenditure of resources. The problem with these efficiency-driven allocations, however, is that they can lead to inequities. A pattern might be established whereby different violators of offenses regulated by a particular agency would face different probabilities of being caught and sanctioned.[13] The design of formal policies necessarily implies a concept of fairness. If one among several violators must bear a higher burden of being caught or of disproportionate costs to society, the regulatory process can create an incentive not to comply. In general, we need to know more about the way regulatory agencies reconcile conflicts between efficiency-oriented planning and legal criteria of equity.

Agencies structure priorities, either explicitly or implicitly, because they do not have the resources to perform every function delegated by legislation. A formal policy becomes a means of controlling the behavior of lower-level officials who can commit the agency to the investigation and prosecution of specific violations. Thus, an important relationship exists between the task of resource allocation and the exercise of discretion in enforcing actions against particular violators. The impact on enforcement of budgetary policies that restrict resources to certain kinds of activities has been identified by Gifford. He argues that ''complaint-issuance and other decisions within the agency structure ought to utilize the budget decisions as referents." They can do this, however, "only if persons fully acquainted with the implications of the budgeting decisions are involved, either as participants in complaint-issuance and related kinds of decision-making, or participants in the review of those decisions" (Gifford 1972, pp. 32-33). In this sense, communication patterns within an agency can be significant influences on decisions to use sanctions and negotiate compliance in specific cases.

A recent analysis of the IRS (Long 1979) is one of the few studies of the regulatory process that has focused specifically on the relationship of resource allocation to decisions about enforcement. Hypothesizing that "important areas of discretion are exercised not by individual law enforcement officers, but by the law enforcement agency more generally in setting broader policies," this study examined the relationship of resource allocation to (1) choice of sanction—civil versus criminal—and (2) decisions about the auditing of returns. It was found that few criminal sanctions were used and that this was positively correlated with the amount of resources allocated to criminal investigation. In addition, the relatively large allocation of resources devoted to civil investigation (audits) was related to the organizational goal of maximizing total enforcement coverage. The time and, hence, the cost of criminal investigations are substantially higher than for civil, thus "transferring more resources into the criminal area may produce an increase in criminal conviction, but only at the price of greatly reduced enforcement coverage" (Long 1979, p. 11). In this case, allocation priorities were determined by efficiency criteria that arguably bore little relationship to the goal of deterrance. The IRS study has also examined the use of a formal management policy known as the Audit Plan, which incorporates the number of audits within each income class to be carried out the next fiscal year, and allocates this responsibility among geographic regions and districts. As in the case of the choice between sanctions, this pattern of resource allocation was primarily responsive to internal, least-cost pressures. Because higher-income returns are more complex and time consuming, it was found that resources were allocated to the examination of lower-income returns. In addition, there was a "strong inverse relationship between corporate size and audit-intensity" (Long 1979, p. 15).

The IRS project highlights the value of quantitative impact analyses for increasing our understanding of the role of regulatory procedures in the control of white-collar/corporate illegality. In this instance, there would appear to be little, if any, positive relationship between formal resource-allocation policy and the goal of deterring major violators. Such studies need to be combined with inquiries into other factors. For example, what regulatory ideologies determine the choice of a particular policy of resource allocation? How is that policy used to evaluate the performance and to

control the discretion of lower-level officials? What is the relationsh
efficiency objectives to the political process by which an agency obtains it
budget? Do agency officials believe that a resource-allocation policy successfully accommodates both efficiency and fairness criteria? How do
agencies adapt allocation policies to external pressures or to changes in the
agency's general mandate, thus indirectly affecting the exercise of discretion
in individual cases?

Constraints on the Exercise of Regulatory Discretion

Studies of "street-level bureaucrats" have revealed that enforcement
priorities are frequently determined at the field level, despite efforts by
management to implement formal systems of resource allocation and planning. According to Lipsky, street-level bureaucrats, who ostensibly only
apply the formal law, actually make policy. "The policy-making roles of
street-level bureaucrats are built upon two interrelated facets of their positions: relatively high degree of discretion and relative autonomy from
organizational authority" (Lipsky 1980, p. 13). Thus, recommendations
that purport to enhance the capacity of regulatory agencies to control corporate illegality should reflect an understanding of the "dispositions of
implementors—how field level officials exercise discretion" (Van Meter and
Van Horn 1975). The work of Lipsky and his colleagues highlights the
extent to which enforcement officials develop coping mechanisms as a
response to the complexity of enforcement tasks (Lipsky 1976). Officials
respond to resource complaints by enforcing regulations according to their
own assumptions about the basic causes of white-collar/corporate crime.
Violators may be classified as inherently "bad," or as the victims of circumstances beyond their control, regardless of the intent and culpability
that reason would attribute to a specific violation (see Lipsky 1976; Kagan
and Scholz 1979). Our two major problems of discretion—negotiation of
compliance and choice of sanction—are directly influenced by factors that
determine whether regulatory officials are legalistic in the applications of
rules, or flexible—accommodating rules to specific, unique circumstances.
The new areas of social regulation discussed earlier have mandated the use
of professional inspectors who respond to complaints and conduct routine
investigations; it is at the field level of enforcement that critical judgments
about the seriousness of violations and moral culpability of violators
necesarily take place (see Kagan 1990; Hawkins 1980b).

What problems lend themselves to the legalistic, rule-oriented
approach, and why would agencies encourage this approach rather than
flexibility in negotiating compliance? One important constraint is the
legislative mandate of the agency. If the agency is not specifically required

equences into account, then a legalistic approach may
nt. We have argued, however, that this is not the case
:w social regulation that has played a major role in com-
ιing of corporate illegality. Another important aspect of
ates is the extent of regulatory power provided to the
tain white-collar/corporate regulatory offenses, specific
ιn fines and criminal penalties contribute to the norm of flex-
ɔtiating compliance (see Hawkins 1980a). Other important fac-
toι⌣   , the nature of the political support—interest group and media
pressure- surrounding regulatory problems. The presence of these can
create a highly visible enforcement process, and pressure for a less-
accommodative, less-individualized application of the law that is less
vulnerable to perceptions of unfairness and inconsistence (Kagan 1978).[14]

In many respects, the essence of regulatory discretion lies in the nature
of the relationship between field-level officials and the regulated (see
Hawkins 1980; Mileski 1971; Nivola 1978; Lipsky 1976, 1980; and Kagan
1980). The goal of compliance means that officials will make judgments
about the use of sanctions based on the need to maintain access to information and to preserve ongoing relationships, and the cooperativeness of the
regulated (Hawkins 1980b; Nivola 1978). As a consequence, agency
demands for strict enforcement according to the rules can have a negative
impact on the goals of compliance and deterrence. If the requirement of
strict enforcement compromises the official's ability to negotiate, the
ultimate effectiveness of a sanction may be lessened. Kagan's research has
revealed that:

> . . . the inspector's ability to obtain information and evidence that would
> support the use of legal sanctions depends, at least in part, on the implied
> promise that the information supplied will be interpreted fairly and that
> those legal powers will not be employed indiscriminately and
> unreasonably . . . a reputation for reasonableness brings the enforcement
> official more complete access and better information. More information
> increases his legal power, and more legal power gives him more to trade for
> cooperation. [Kagan 1980, p. 21]

The lack of valid information about the nature of violations may be related
to the reluctance of prosecutorial officials to impose criminal penalties for
regulatory offenses (Kagan 1980, p. 20).

An important problem in enforcement policy is the way the law is
mobilized—how cases enter the regulatory process. In the case of housing-
code enforcement, for example, there is a strong tradition of responding to
individual complaints. A major criticism of OSHA regulation has been its
policy of responding to all employee-initiated complaints.[15] This reactive-
proactive dimension of policy formation has important consequences for

the investigation and control of white-collar/corporate illegality (see Edelhertz et al. 1977, pp. 217-219). A complaint-oriented policy is not necessarily congruent with efforts to help specific classes of victims or to understand the underlying causes of problems. According to Black, an inherent limitation of reactive approaches is that, by definition, they operate on a case-by-case basis:

> Cases enter the system one by one, and they are processed one by one. This creates an intelligence gap about the relations agency and between cases. It is difficult to link patterns of illegal behavior to single or similar violators and thus to deal with the sourcs rather than merely the symptoms of these patterns. [Reprinted from "The Mobilization of Law" by D.J. Black in *Journal of Legal Studies* 2:134-135, 1973 by permission of The University of Chicago Press. Copyright © 1973 by The University of Chicago Press.]

There is less incentive for agencies to accumulate knowledge about the underlying causes of illegality if they are dominated by reactive, complaint-oriented inputs. Conversely, the possibility of negotiating compliance and imposing legal sanctions in an individual case on the basis of objective information about recurrent patterns of illegality is enhanced by proactive systems of enforcement. In general, the principal constraints on discretion can be classified according to regulatory task, the needs of the regulatory bureaucracy, and the nature of regulatory ideology.

Task. An important dimension of task has been noted previously—the extent of case overload and the necessity to adapt to conditions of resource scarcity. Officials cope with this problem by controlling the attention devoted to specific cases and by adopting views about the purpose of regulation that are congruent with resources and time constraints. An instructive case study in the consumer-fraud area is Silbey's analysis of the enforcement of the Massachusetts Consumer Protection Act (Silbey 1980). Here it was found that officials handled virtually all complaints through mediation; settlements were negotiated that provided restitution agreeable to both victim and business offender. This extreme strategy of enforcement flexibility was rationalized by officials as being in the best interests of victims. But the end result of this strategy may well have had negative consequences for future compliance and deterrance as violators came to see the enforcement process as relatively costless. Silbey concludes:

> It is not justified to expect that having to make restitution once, or even often, induces purveyors of goods and services to avoid practices that give rise to complaints. . . . The effect is to satisfy the individuals involved, but to fail to protect the anonymous and future consumer. [Silbey 1980, pp. 15-16]

The goals of restitution for victims of regulatory offenses versus retribution against offenders versus deterrence have been recognized as a complicated issue of jurisprudence in defining corporate illegality (see *Harvard Law Review* 1979). Before deciding on any goal or combination of goals, however, it is important to recognize the subtle effects of the nature of the regulatory task on the way discretion is exercised: Problems of case overload can interact with particular values (in this case, concern for the victim), to result in a syndrome of compromise and settlement. If such a pattern becomes an end in itself, real compliance and deterrence will prove increasingly problematic.

A second relevant dimension of regulatory task is the nature of the rules enforced. As Wilson states, "If compliance with a rule is highly visible, costs little, and entails no competitive disadvantage, that rule will be more easily enforced than one with opposite characteristics" (Wilson 1972, p. 163). In these instances, flexibility in individual cases may be dysfunctional and too costly; information about the underlying cause of violations is more readily available, and regulations are less likely to be viewed as unreasonable. The need for a high degree of flexibility in negotiating compliance and the use of sanctions is also lessened to the extent that voluntary compliance is influenced by public sensitivity to the regulatory offense.

Bureaucracy. The problem of discretion in negotiating compliance is further complicated by what can be termed the *maintenance needs* of the regulatory bureaucracy. These are of two types—*political* and *managerial*.

To the extent that an agency must concern itself with a hostile or unpredictable political environment, it will attempt to control the discretion available to officials who must apply rules to individual cases.[16] Whether or not this attempt will be successful, the end result of coping with a volatile regulatory environment can be a proliferation of rules by the concerned agency. As Wilson notes:

> The more visible the agency, the greater the demands on it, and thus the more rules it must produce to assure its security and survival. . . . Critics of regulatory agencies notice this proliferation of rules and suppose that it is the result of the "imperialistic" or expansionist instincts of bureaucratic organizations. Though there are such examples, I am struck more by the defensive, threat-avoiding, scandal-minimizing instincts of these agencies. [From *The Politics of Regulation* by James Q. Wilson (ed.), pp. 377-378. Copyright © 1980 by Basic Books, Inc., Publishers, New York. Reprinted by permission.]

An important consequence of rule proliferation may be an increase in the perceived unreasonableness of regulations and a lower probability of voluntary compliance—a situation that increases the utility of a flexible approach to the negotiation of compliance.[17] Thus, the lower-level official who must exercise discretion against violators is placed in a conflict: On the one hand, the agency will stress the uniform application of rules and risk avoidance; on the other hand, the goals of compliance and deterrence require a greater degree of flexibility and accommodation. If this condition occurs, inspectors may wind up erring in the direction of being too lenient. They will be less inclined to probe the causes of a violation or to monitor progress in remedying it to the extent that a meaningful process of negotiated compliance requires. Diver has described a related phenomenon as follows:

> Efficient risk aversion behavior would therefore involve conducting an extensive, superficial examination for easily detectable violations, rather than an intensive inspection for less visible offenses. [Diver 1980, p. 285]

The political maintenance needs of agencies can disrupt the relationship with those regulated that lower-level officials, such as inspectors, feel is necessary in order to carry out their tasks effectively. A tragic example is Schuck's analysis of meat-packing inspection—a case that also complicates judgments of corruption and unethical conduct on the part of regulatory inspectors. As is the case with many types of regulation, the enforcement of packing regulations has combined the tendency of an agency (the U.S. Department of Agriculture) to overregulate with the propensity of an industry not to want to comply with the law. If all regulations were strictly enforced, no meat processor could remain open; hence, inspectors have had enormous discretion to decide which rules to enforce and how (Schuck 1972). Thus, the Department of Agriculture (USDA) has traditionally allowed inspectors to apply regulations in a flexible manner, recognizing that reasonableness can be important for compliance. Inspectors have been generally assigned to one plant where an informal system of taking gratuities—a system known as "cumshaw"—became accepted and commonplace. Inspectors developed a clear and widely shared morality about the acceptance of gifts: A gratuity becomes a bribe, and therefore off limits, if it will lead to an abnormal enforcement of the regulations. Nevertheless, violating the norm of accepting an occasional bundle of meat, "cumshaw," was also felt by inspectors to jeopardize the ongoing cooperative relationship needed for effective enforcement. As Schuck notes; many elements in a meat inspector's situation—"the pressures of his work routine, temptations by the packer, the job socialization process, the traditions of the industry, the conventional morality of his fellow inspectors, the general bribery statute, and the imperatives of 'getting the job done' "—persuade him that he is blameless in accepting the packer's gratuities (Schuck 1972, p. 83). At the same time, the USDA would adopt a rigidly legalistic position against inspectors and the gratuity system when it occasionally became public and politicized, while recognizing the importance of this system during the normal course of events. In response to the political pressure, the exercise of discretion by inspectors was redefined as corruption.

The managerial type of maintenance need reflects the constant problem of case overload. Efficiency criteria assume greater importance than ambiguous objectives such as compliance and deterrence, which are not easily measurable. This need manifests itself in discretion that is highly legalistic, but is also directed at "closing" cases without the realistic threat of sanctions for noncompliance. Inspectors, investigators, and prosecutors respond to the need to manage case flow—the control system—rather than the unique requirements of individual cases. Cases with the greatest probability of being settled take precedence; evaluations of performance are based on measurable indicators of productivity, creating disincentives to adopt a flexible model of regulatory enforcement.[18] Agencies adopt productivity measures, such as number of violations cited, in the belief that this will inhibit officials from being too lenient. But this can create serious problems for compliance, which depends on the investigation and analysis of the underlying causes of regulatory violations (Kagan 1980). Inspectors subject to such productivity measures will tend to overlook the less obvious, to report violations that are clearly identifiable, and greatly to simplify their procedures of investigation (see Diver 1980). Because regulatory agencies have considerable difficulty in assessing the impact of enforcement on regulated firms, there is a tendency to use sanctions as ends that can be measured with little concern for negotiating compliance or the goal of deterrence. Thus, as Diver notes: "The agency judges its actions by their contribution to the volume and severity of sanctions administered" (Diver 1980, p. 277).

Ideology. Ideological perspectives on the motives of the regulated and the proper goals of regulation are an important influence on the exercise of discretion by officials. Kagan and Scholz, for example, have identified what they term three common "theories of noncompliance" adopted by regulatory officials: the "amoral calculator," who is motivated entirely by profit seeking and who rationally calculates the costs and benefits of breaking the law; the "political citizen," who has principled disagreements with regulations that are considered unreasonable and arbitrary; and the "organizationally incompetent," who violates because of inadequate management procedures and failures in supervision (Kagan and Scholz 1979). Similarly, an important variable in Hawkins's study of water-pollution inspectors in England was the use made by these officials of judgments that classified violators according to moral culpability (Hawkins 1980b). In the Silbey study of the Massachusetts Consumer Fraud Bureau, discussed previously, officials believed that negotiated settlements were the best means of achieving restitution for the injured victim (Silbey 1980).

An important source of regulatory ideology can be the values of top-level professionals in the agency. Kelman's study of OSHA reveals the strong pro-protection values of key officials trained in safety engineering or industrial hygiene, who believe that the costs of regulation should be incidental to the goal of continued risk reduction in the workplace (Kelman 1980). This set of beliefs has exerted a strong influence on definitions of OSHA offenses and the exercise of discretion by inspectors. There is evidence that OSHA inspectors have internalized these values in the enforcement of violations: "There is a cost to infusing this sense of mission. Many American inspectors, armed with their goal of finding violations, appear to be steam-rollers." And a significant percentage of U.S. OSHA inspectors stated that they "took no account when a firm threatened to shut down because they couldn't afford to pay for changes required by the regulations" (Kelman 1979, p. 268).

In the extreme, such an ideology is quite congruent with an excessively legalistic, rigid exercise of discretion by enforcement officials. OSHA, like many regulatory functions, is unable to inspect, investigate, and monitor all regulated workplaces within its jurisdiction; consequently, the legitimacy of its enforcement process is essential as a means of obtaining voluntary compliance. But legitimacy is undermined by ideologies that compromise the discretion required to negotiate compliance and employ sanctions to deter future violations. In this sense, regulatory ideologies are not inherently negative. They incorporate values that, for the most part, are translated into laudable objectives; the ideology of risk reduction and the protection of worker health and safety is unexceptionable and necessary. It is when agency policymakers fail to understand the influence of ideology on enforcement decisions that these values can become disconnected from desired regulatory outcomes. Then the important values are not realized because the impact of sanctions on deterrence and voluntary compliance is undermined.

Perhaps the most-critical ideological factor is the set of beliefs defining the role of sanctions in regulatory offenses. We have emphasized that many regulatory problems are compliance oriented, requiring a flexible enforcement model whereby the threat of sanctions can be instrumental in remedying the problem created by an offender. Notwithstanding the importance of determining the need for flexibility according to the objective circumstances of cases, lower-ranking personnel, who must detect and investigate violations, may still *believe* that compliance should be negotiated. They often place little faith in formal legal processes and the imposition of sanctions. If policymakers are advocates of sanctions as an end in themselves for regulatory crimes, a significant ideological conflict between different levels and roles in the agency can develop.

It is important to recognize the limitations of the flexible appoach. It is vulnerable to the charge of inequity—the failure to treat "like cases alike."

Moreover, the effectiveness of flexibility is highly dependent on the ability and motivation of officials to obtain accurate information relevant to culpability. Another problem is that negotiation may result in failure to achieve changes in corporate policy and/or procedures that would ensure future compliance with the law. Nevertheless, when blameworthiness is highly problematic or the violation is based on rules that are perceived as unreasonable and challenged, a degree of flexibility may be necessary in order to obtain compliance and deter future violations. The policy problem is twofold: (1) What are the key dimensions of competence in the use of this type of discretion? How can we develop the flexible adaptive style? (2) How do task bureaucracy and ideology inhibit capable field-level professionals?

A Research Agenda

A principal theme of this chapter has been the need for more research on the exercise of discretion in controlling corporate illegality through the regulatory process, the negotiation of compliance, and the use of regulatory sanctions. These issues have been the focus of the conceptual framework discussed in the previous section. This concluding section argues for additional, related studies on the criteria for selecting among sanctions and on the impact of administrative remedies such as the consent decree, and for further research on the issue of the "moral neutrality" of regulatory offenses.

Regulatory Sanctions

An important source of discretion available to regulatory policymakers is the choice of sanctions once prosecution has been determined to be necessary for achieving the goals of compliance and deterrence. The decision-making process is complex:

> The decision to proceed at all is complicated by the availability of valid fines, and the decision to proceed criminally is [marked] by the unclear distinction between the two sorts of sanctions. Two decisions must be made: first, whether to seek any sort of sanction, and second, whether to proceed criminality or civilly. [*Harvard Law Review* 1979, p. 1307]

In addition, as stated previously, regulatory agencies have enormous flexibility in fashioning remedies. These include not only criminal and civil penalties, but also administrative proceedings that can result in license revocation or in legal orders to change corporate procedures. As Shapiro notes: "Regulatory agencies differ from traditional criminal justice agencies . . . in the diversity of prosecutorial models available to the former in the disposition of illegality" (Shapiro 1979, p. 2). The selection of criteria governing whether to proceed criminally or civilly is, for the most part, arbitrary; we know little about how criteria are applied in particular cases. With respect to food and drug violations, an associate commissioner for compliance in the FDA has stated that "several" factors are considered in choosing:

> (1) the seriousness of the violation; (2) the evidence of knowledge or intent; (3) the probability of effecting future compliance by the firm in question as well as others similarly situated as a result of the present criteria; (4) the resources available to conduct investigations necessary to consummate the case successfully; and (underlying all of these) (5) the extent to which the action will benefit consumers in terms of preventing recurrence of the violation throughout the industry. [Fine, "The Philosophy of Enforcement," reprinted with permission from the June 1976 *Food Drug Cosmetic Law Journal* published by Commerce Clearing House, Inc.]

The scope for interpreting these guidelines, and for choosing among them in a particular case, is enormous. This subjectivity also creates difficulties for judicial review and the capacity of nongovernmental parties to challenge agency decisions (see Tunderman 1980).

Regulatory statutes leave enormous latitude for judgments about the nature of violations as a basis for applying remedies. For example, the Occupational Health and Safety Act provides for fines according to judgments about the "seriousness" of the violation, and provides that a fine may be "discounted" if the violation demonstrates "good faith." And the FDA has a storehouse of responses to violations, ranging from notices that merely point out "minor violations"; to "regulatory letters" ordering the firm to correct the violation and report back to the agency; to criminal prosecution if the violator is "unresponsive"; and, finally, to court-ordered products if the hazard is considered "imminent" (see Kagan and Scholz 1979). There is broad discretion both in the interpretation of violations at the field level and in the subsequent choice of remedies by higher agency officials.

One method for studying decisions concerning violations and choice of remedies would be to examine instances in which an agency adopted different enforcement procedures in esentially the same factual situations. The infamous Reserve Mining Company case (see *United States* v. *Reserve Mining Co.*) and EPA's suit against Allied Chemical Corporation (*United States* v. *Allied Chemical Corporation*) provide examples suitable for this type of approach (see *Harvard Law Review* 1979). In the *Reserve* case, the EPA chose to pursue civil sanctions, beginning with an injunction to stop the dumping of "tailings" from mining operations into Lake Superior. Later the EPA sued to force Reserve to clean community drinking-water sources that had become contaminated by these tailings. In contrast, the same agency decided to use criminal sanctions against Allied, a case that involved the discharge of the pesticide Kepone into the James River in Virginia. Here the U.S. atttorney succeeded in obtaining numerous indictments against the corporation and several employees. The agency decisions in these cases raise important issues of fairness and equity, as well as of the differential impact of the two strategies on the goals of compliance and deterrence. Organizational case studies of the history of these two decisions, proceeding inductively through interviews and the examination of archives, could provide valuable insights into this aspect of the regulatory process.

A related issue has to do with the fact that many agencies must refer cases for criminal prosecution. The structure of white-collar/corporate crime is such that detection is in the hands of administrative agencies, whereas prosecution rests with the U.S. Department of Justice (U.S. House of Representatives 1978, p. 8). Thus, it can be hypothesized that the informal relationships between regulatory bureaucracies and prosecutorial units are an important factor in decisions about case disposition. Several important questions come to mind in considering the interdependence of two different law-enforcement bureaucracies. For example, are there conflicting expectations and signals that limit referrals? Are referrals governed more by the informal priorities of prosecutors than by the formal policies of agencies? Comparative studies could be conducted of instances in which case referrals were turned down, those in which cases were accepted, and those in which agencies decided not to refer violations for prosecution. The relevance of the agency-prosecutorial relationship has been recognized as an important factor in the effective use of greater personal liability, as in the *Park* case; and efforts to increase the application of criminal fines in areas such as the FDA act and violations of motor-carrier safety legislation. One author has stated, for example:

> Administrative agencies have been reluctant to resort to criminal proceedings for a variety of reasons. Perhaps they fear loss of control over the litigation once it takes on the status of a criminal case. Perhaps they also sense the general reluctance of prosecutors to place prosecutions for such crimes high enough on their list of priorities to receive prompt and appropriate attention. [Tuerkheimer, F.M., 1980, "Corporate Violence Goes Unpunished," *National Law Journal* 2:24. Reprinted with permission.]

Administrative Remedies: The Consent Decree

Given the prominence of administrative remedies for regulatory violations, in contrast to criminal referrals or civil prosecutions, it is important that we learn more about how they are used. The consent decree, for example, is a frequent outcome of administrative action: an agreement between the agency and the violator whereby the violator agrees to no further violations without having to admit guilt. But as the Clinard study points out: "Unfortunately there is no uniformity in monitoring of consent agreements. Some agencies do monitor, some do not, while others, operating in a random fashions [sic], sometimes monitor consent decrees and at other times do not do so" (Clinard 1979, p. 30).[19] We know virtually nothing about the process of implementing consent agreements and their impact on compliance and deterrence. The following questions should be addressed: Are some agencies more prone to adopt consent decrees, or similar remedies? What are the principal influences on the adoption of these methods—the value of regulatory task (overload, resource constraints); belief in their efficacy for compliance and deterrence; or bureaucratic imperatives such as the need to close our case problems? What exactly is the content of these agreements? How are they monitored and enforced? How analogous are consent decrees to the formal bargaining that occurs in the prosecution of nonregulatory criminal offenses?

The Public Perception of Regulatory Crimes:
Moral Neutrality?

Almost twenty years ago, Kadish correctly identified a critical problem in achieving deterrence with respect to white-collar/corporate regulatory offenses. He labeled this the dilemma of "moral neutrality," the fact that the use of traditional criminal penalties is not accompanied by resentment against these types of crimes (Kadish 1963). The perspective we have presented on the nature of the regulatory process indicates that this set of attitudes can figure prominently in agency policymaking and in the exercise of discretion by officials at the field level. Kadish's idea for resolution of this issue, the cultivation of "the sentiment of moral disapproval," deserves systematic analysis (Kadish 1963). Research in this area should focus on the deterrent impact of select prosecutions and their publicity. The larger issue is the role of regulatory agencies in informing public attitudes about the costs to society of corporate offenses. Unfortunately, in many instances this responsibility has been overshadowed by the need to defend against the economic irrationality of regulatory procedures.

In conclusion, it is important to recognize that the regulatory role in white-collar/corporate illegality is a dynamic one—growing and constantly changing. In part this is because of extensive development of the doctrine of judicial review of administrative discretion over the past decade (see Davis 1977). These changes will continue to present significant opportunities for studies of the regulatory process. In particular, impacts of different remedies should be monitored and evaluated. But the design of regulatory policy should also reflect greater knowledge of the enforcement process: the influence of policymaking and of regulatory task, bureaucracy, and ideology on the critical problems of discretion.

Notes

1. For careful assessments of the growth of regulatory bureaucracy, see Lilley and Miller (1977), Bardach (1979), and Weidenbaum (1978).

2. Regulatory agencies make extensive use of what are termed "informal administrative procedures" (see Davis 1977). A vast number of regulatory problems are resolved by these relatively invisible processes. These include various investigations, tests, and inspections conducted in order to detect violations and ensure compliance with rules and standards. In contrast, formal proceedings in administrative law include rule making and adjudicative proceedings and are frequently governed by the provisions of the federal Administrative Procedures Act or its state equivalent. Under rule making, agencies develop policy, which is then applied in the future to all persons and institutions engaged in the regulated activity. Adjudication is somewhat akin to a trial, but applies policy to past actions, resulting in an order against, or in favor of, a named party to the proceeding. These are important dimensions of the regulatory process. But they pale in contrast to the prevalence and impact of informal procedures. A critical problem with informal procedures is the maintenance of important legal norms: for example, the *fairness* of inspections, and the *consistency* and *accuracy* of investigations. Field-level officials responsible for many informal procedures also attempt to maintain considerable autonomy from agency supervision. There is a need for more research on the workings of informal procedures. One respected commentator remarked several years ago, "There have been empirical studies of the accuracy or fairness of informal administrative inspections for thirty years" (Gellhorn 1972). This observation is still accurate.

3. On the nature of economic crimes, see Ball and Friedman (1965). These authors conclude that any assessment of the role of sanctions in economic regulation should begin by distinguishing the types of economic regulation under consideration. More recently, it has been argued that regulatory offenses "show a common label by default, not by theoretical design. For those who seek to examine offenses of this kind, greater discrimination between kinds of violative behavior is necessary" (Shapiro 1979, p. 37). This has become increasingly difficult as more and more regulatory offenses are included in the general category of economic crime.

4. The Department of Justice has recently attempted to assign priorities to classes of white-collar crime according to type of victim. See Report of the Attorney General, *National Priorities for the Investigation and Prosecution of White-Collar Crime*, 1980. Four of the principal categories fall into the regulatory area: "crimes against consumers, crimes against investors, crimes against employees, and crimes affecting the health and safety of the general public." In reviewing recent empirical studies of the regulatory process, this chapter focuses primarily on these issues, including relevant work on the functioning of the Internal Revenue Service.

5. The SEC, for example, functions as investigator, prosecutor, and judge, through a division of authority in the agency structure. See Hazen (1979), p. 431. In a comparative study of corporate illegality, Clinard notes:

> For the most part, corporate lawbreakers are handled by administrative quasi-judicial boards of government regulatory agencies such as the FTC, the NLRC, and the Food and Drug Administration. The government regulatory agencies may impose an administrative remedy or they may ask the civil or criminal court to do so, as for example, to issue an injuction. [Clinard 1979, p. 20]

6. According to James Q. Wilson:

> Regulation on behalf of consumers creates very large problems of discretion among lower-ranking personnel, just as attempts to enforce traffic laws and vice laws create such problems for police departments. How the members of a large organization will manage that discretion depends on a number of factors, of which influence from the affected industry is only one, and may not be the most important. We know very little—indeed next to nothing—about the day-to-day management of these regulatory tasks. [Wilson 1972, pp. 160-161]

7. A recent study of water pollution in Great Britain found that officials were generally unwilling to talk of "crime" when discussing these violations: ". . . sort of language is considered appropriate only where clearly blameworthy conduct exists—where there is a calculated breach of regulation or where the polluting substance is widely known to be dangerous and there was carelessness in handling it" (Hawkins 1980a, p. 3).

8. Proposals have been made to experiment with higher civil penalties. It has been argued: "There are compelling reasons to use civil rather than criminal sanctions in order to deter illegal corporate activity. . . . The basic aim of civil sanctions is deterrence; retribution is the province of criminal law. Therefore, a basic tenet of a system of civil fines should be to ensure that the amount of the fine is a function of deterrence" (*Harvard Law Review* 1979, pp. 1369, 1370).

9. An example of the intrusion of economic criteria into a white-collar regulatory offense is housing-code enforcement. Policies advocating strict enforcement are constantly tempered by the belief that this will lead to the abandonment of property by landlords, the dislocation of tenants, and an erosion of the property-tax base. There is a widespread view among elected officials that the use of sanctions will result in noncompliance and encourage further economic deterioration (see Galanter, Thomas, and Palen 1976; Ackerman 1971).

10. This is a pervasive condition of government bureaucracies whose primary function is the servicing of cases through professionals (see Lipsky 1980).

11. Two significant court opinions that illustrate this perspective on the regulatory process are *Environmental Defense Fund Inc.* v. *Ruckelshaus* and *Moss* v. *Civil Aeronautics Board.*

12. Very few studies have focused on the problem of policy formation in law-enforcement agencies—the way priorities are established and re-sources allocated among competing commitments (see Galanter 1972). In the regulatory area, the FTC has been the focus of both investigative probes and more-academic study. There have been indictments of the agency for its failure to devote resources to the more-important responsibilities of its statutory mandate (see Posner 1969; Edelman 1974). Although subject to criticism on both methodological and theoretical grounds, the Nader group study of the FDA specifically highlighted the problem of resource alloca-tion. This investigation concluded that the agency was ineffective because it failed to go after major firms that routinely broke the law, choosing instead to pursue small violators in order to give an appearance of active regulation (Turner 1970). More recently, the policymaking processes of OSHA have been subjected to careful analysis (see Kelman 1980).

13. Thurow has argued, for example, that there is ample evidence to suggest that large benefits are possible from the use of analytic methods of allocating resources in law enforcement. But such efficiency-oriented tech-niques must be based on a clear notion of equity goals (Thurow 1970, p. 451).

14. On the other hand, regulatory agencies are also aware that political winds can shift rapidly; for this reason, they may attempt to adhere to a general policy of flexibility. Jeffery Jowell has observed: "The tactics of the typical regulatory agency consist of the 'raised eyebrow,' subtle threats and cajolement, and selective enforcement rather than the bludgeon blow of strict enforcement according to defined rights and firm obligations" (1975, p. 197).

15. Recent legislation proposals to amend OSHA would require the agency to attend to only "important" complaints, a change that would clearly increase the discretion available to officials.

16. For a thorough comparative analysis of this dynamic in the FBI and the Drug Enforcement Administration, see Wilson (1980).

17. One effect of the combination of rule proliferation and pressures on enforcement personnel to enforce regulations strictly is to increase the overall legalization of the relationship between regulated and regulator. This can, in turn, lead to delay, game playing with the legal process, and lack of compliance. Kagan has found in studies of various types of inspec-tion processes that:

> When inspection is dominated by official checklists and inspectors stress the documentation and prosecution of rule violations, they are blinded to the novel and fundamental sources of harm that inevitably escape specific rules. . . . In many instances, companies that earlier had been cooperative have become more cautious in giving information to inspectors or discussing

their problems with them. They appeal citations and fines to administrative tribunals or the courts much more often. Inspectorates, in turn, confronted with rising legal contestations and challenges to their authority, respond with enhanced mistrust and legalism. [Kagan 1980, pp. 6-7]

18. This is a phenomenon found in studies of the application of law in nonregulatory settings (see, for example, Ross 1970, p. 237).

19. In the area of antitrust enforcement, the value of consent decrees to the Department of Justice and the FTC has long been advocated. Still, it is recognized that they can create problems. One writer on antitrust law has commented: "A matter of even greater day-to-day concern is the possibility that the Department (or the FTC) may make a poor settlement simply because of the ordinary risks and pressures faced by an overburdened staff. The implication of including or excluding a particular provision may not be fully understood or adequately appraised in the light of the industry context" (Sullivan 1977, p. 758).

References

Ackerman, Bruce. 1971. "Regulating Slum Housing Markets on Behalf of the Poor: Of Housing Codes, Housing Subsidies, and Income Distribution Policy." *Yale Law Journal* 80:1093-1197.

Ackerman, Bruce A.; Rose-Ackerman, Susan; Sawyer, James W., Jr.; and Henderson, Dale W., 1978. *The Uncertain Search for Environmental Quality*. New York: Free Press.

Ball, Harry V., and Friedman, Lawrence, 1965. "The Use of Criminal Sanctions in the Enforcement of Economic Legislation: A Sociological View." *Stanford Law Review* 17:197.

Bardach, Eugene. 1979. "Reason, Responsibility, and the New Social Regulation." In Burnham, W.D. and Weinberg, M.W. eds., *American Politics and Public Policy*. Cambridge, Mass.: MIT Press.

Black, Donald J. 1973. "The Mobilization of Law." *Journal of Legal Studies* 2:125-149.

Brigham, John, and Brown, Don W. 1980. "Introduction: Distinguishing Penalties and Incentives." *Law and Policy Quarterly* 2:5

Caldwell, Robert G. 1958. "A Re-examination of the Concept of White-Collar Crime." *Federal Probation* 22 (March):30-36.

Clinard, Marshall B. 1979. "Illegal Corporate Behavior." Washington, D.C.: Law Enforcement Assistance Administration (LEAA), U.S. Department of Justice.

Davis, Kenneth Culp. 1969. *Discretionary Justice*. Baton Rouge: Louisiana State University Press.

———. 1977. *Administrative Law*. St. Paul, Minn.: West Publishing Company.

Diver, Colin S. 1980. "Modesty and Immodesty in Policy-Oriented Empirical Research." *Administrative Law Review* 32 (Winter):75.

Edelhertz, Herbert. 1970. *The Nature, Impact and Prosecution of White-Collar Crime*. Washington, D.C.: U.S. Government Printing Office.

Edelhertz, Herbert; Stotland, Ezra; Walsh, M.; and Weinberg, M. 1977. *The Investigation of White Collar Crime: A Manual for Law Enforcement Agencies*. Washington, D.C.: LEAA, U.S. Department of Justice.

Edelman, Murray. 1974. *The Symbolic Uses of Politics*. Urbana: University of Illinois Press.

Fine, S.D. 1976. "The Philosophy of Enforcement." *Food, Drug and Cosmetics Law Journal* 31:325-332.

Freedman, J. 1975. "Crisis and Legitimacy in the Administrative Process." *Standford Law Review* 27:1041.

Galanter, Marc. 1972. "The Deployment Process in the Implementation of Legal Policy." Faculty of Law, State University of New York. Proposal, National Science Foundation.

———. 1974. "Why the 'Haves' Come Out Ahead." *Law and Society Review*. 9:95-160.

Galanter, Marc; Thomas, John M.; and Palen, Frank S. 1976. "The Implementation of Legal Policy: Six Case Studies." Unpublished manuscript, Faculty of Law, State University of New York at Buffalo.

Galanter, Marc; Palen, Frank; and Thomas, John M. 1979. "The Crusading Judge: Judicial Activism in Trial Courts." *Southern California Law Review* 52:699.

Gellhorn, Ernest. 1972. *Administrative Law and Process*. St. Paul, Minn.: West Publishing Company.

Gifford, Daniel J. 1972. "Decisions, Decisional Referents and Administrative Justice." *Law and Contemporary Problems* 37:3-48.

———. 1980. "Decision-Making in Regulatory Agencies." Paper presented at the 1980 meeting of the Law and Society Association, Madison, Wisconsin, 5-8 June 1980.

Harvard Law Review. 1979. "Developments in the Law—Corporate Crime: Regulating Corporate Behavior Through Criminal Sanctions." *Harvard Law Review* 92:1227.

Hawkins, Keith. 1980a. "The Use of Descretion by Regulatory Officials: A Case Study on Environmental Pollution in the United Kingdom." Paper presented at conference sponsored by the Baldy Center for Law and Social Policy and Oxford Centre for Socio-legal Studies at the State University of New York at Buffalo, 2-3 June 1980.

———. 1980. "Pollution, Law and Social Control: A Study of the Use of Discretion in a Regulatory Agency." Draft manuscript, Oxford Centre for Socio-legal Studies.

Hazen, Thomas L. 1979. "Administrative Enforcement: An Evaluation of the Securities and Exchange Commission's Use of Injunctions and Other Enforcement Methods." *Hastings Law Journal* 31:427.

Jowell, Jeffrey L. 1975. *Law and Bureaucracy: Administrative Discretion and the Limits of Legal Action.* New York: Dunellen Pub. Co.

Kadish, Sanford H. 1963. "Some Observations on the Use of Criminal Sanctions in Enforcing Economic Regulation." *University of Chicago Law Review* 30:423.

Kagan, Robert. 1978. *Regulatory Justice.* New York: Russell Sage.

————. 1980. "The Positive Uses of Discretion: The Good Inspector." Paper presented at the meetings of the Law and Society Association, Madison, Wisc., 5-8 June.

Kagan, Robert, and Scholz, John T. 1979. "The Criminology of the Corporation and Regulatory Enforcement Strategies." Paper presented at the Symposium on Organizational Factors in the Implementation of Law, University of Oldenburg, 24-25 May.

Kelman, Steven. 1979. "Coercion and Compliance." Ph.D diss., Harvard University.

————. 1980. "Occupational Health and Safety Administration." In J.Q. Wilson, ed., *The Politics of Regulation.* New York: Basic Books.

Lilley, William, III, and Miller, James C., III. 1977. "The New Social Regulation." *The Public Interest* 47:49-61.

Lipsky, Michael. 1976. "Toward a Theory of Street-Level Bureaucracy." In Hawley, D. and Lipsky, M. eds., *Theoretical Perspectives on Urban Politics.* Englewood Cliffs, N.J.: Prentice-Hall.

————. 1980. *Street-Level Bureaucracy.* New York: Russell Sage.

Long, Susan B. 1979. "The Internal Revenue Service: Examining the Exercise of Discretion in Tax Enforcement." Paper presented before the Annual Meeting of the Law and Society Association.

Mashaw, Jerry L. 1979. "Regulation, Logic, and Ideology." *Regulation,* November-December, p. 44.

————. 1980. "Modesty and Immodesty in Policy-Oriented Empirical Research." *Administrative Law Review* 32 (Winter):75.

Mileski, Maureen A. 1971. "Policing Slum Landlords: An Observation Study of Administrative Control." Ph.D diss., Yale University.

Newman, Donald J. 1958. "White-Collar Crime: An Overview and Analysis." *Law and Contemporary Problems* 23:735-753.

Nichols, A.L. and Zeckhauser, R.J. 1977. "Government Comes to the Workplace: An Assessment of OSHA," *Public Interest* 49:39-69.

Nivola, Pietro S. 1978. "Distributing a Municipal Service: A Case Study of Housing Inspection." *Journal of Politics* 40:59.

Posner, Richard. 1969. "The Federal Trade Commission." *University of Chicago Law Review* 37:47.

Rabin, Robert. 1979. "Administrative Law in Transition: A Discipline in

Search of an Organizing Principle." *Northwestern University Law Review* 72:120.

Ross, H. Laurence. 1970. *Settled Out of Court: The Social Process of Insurance Claims Adjustment.* Chicago: Aldine

Schuck, Peter. 1972. "The Curious Case of the Indicted Meat Inspectors." *Harper's*, Nov. 6, 1972:81-88.

Schultz, Charles L. 1977. "The Public Use of Private Interest." *Harper's* 254:43-50.

Shapiro, Susan. 1979. "Thinking About White-Collar Crime: Matters of Conceptualization and Research." Unpublished manuscript, Yale University.

Shover, N. 1980. "The Criminalization of Corporate Behavior: Federal Surface Coal Mining." In Gilbert Geis and Ezra Stotland, eds., *White-Collar Crime: Theory and Research.* Beverly Hills, Calif.: Sage Publications.

Silbey, Susan. 1980. "Mediation: A Means of Cooperating With Business." Paper presented at the meeting of the Law and Society Association, Madison, Wisc., 5-8 June.

Stewart, Richard B. 1975. "The Reformation of American Administrative Law." *Harvard Law Review* 88:1669.

Sullivan, Lawrence A. 1977. *Handbook of the Law of Antitrust.* St. Paul, Minn.: West Publishing Company.

Thurow, Lester. 1970. "Equity versus Efficiency in Law Enforcement." *Public Policy* 18 (Summer):451.

Tuerkheimer, Frank M. 1980. "Corporate Violence Goes Unpunished." *National Law Journal*, 26 May, p. 21.

Tunderman, D.N. 1980. "Constitutional Aspects of Economic Law Enforcement." *Harvard Environmental Law Review* 4:656.

Turner, James S. 1970. *The Chemical Feast.* New York: Grossman.

U.S. House of Representatives. Subcommittee on Crime. 1978. *White-Collar Crime.* Washington, D.C.: U.S. Government Printing Office.

Van Meter, D.S., and Van Horn, C.E. 1975. "The Policy Implementation Process: A Conceptual Framework." *Administration and Society*, February, p. 482. Quoted in Lipsky, *Street-Level Bureaucracy*, p. 216, note 19.

Weidenbaum, Murray. 1978. "The Impacts of Government Regulation." Working paper No. 32, Center for the Study of American Business, Washington University.

Wilson, James Q. 1972. "The Politics of Regulation." In James McKie, ed., *Social Responsibility and the Business Predicament.* Washington, D.C.: Brookings Institution.

———. 1978. *The Investigators.* New York: Basic Books.

———. 1980. *The Politics of Regulation.* New York: Basic Books.

Cases Cited

AFL-CIO v. *Brennan*, 530 F. 2d 109.

Environmental Defense Fund v. *Ruckelshaus*, 439 F. 2d 584 (D.C. Cir. 1971).

Moss v. *CAB*, 430 F. 2d 891 (D.C. Cir. 1970).

U.S. v. *Allied Chemical Corporation*, 1976, *7 Envir. Rep. BNA* at 844.

U.S. v. *Park*, 421 U.S. 658 (1975).

U.S. v. *Reserve Mining Company*, 431 F.Supp. 1248 (D. Minn., 1977).

6 Multidisciplinary Approaches to White-Collar Crime

Simon Dinitz

Introduction

Ford Pinto. Firestone 500. Lockheed payoffs. Equity Funding. Hooker Chemical's Love Canal. A $1.8 billion restraint-of-trade judgment against AT&T. "Reckless endangerment," product-liability issues, corrupt business practices, political payoffs, multinational control and manipulation of vital resources, price fixing, "loss" of pounds of fissionable material, silver-market manipulation, questionable banking practices, auditing "oversights." Computer, welfare, Medicare, and Medicaid frauds.

The Wall Street Journal, Business Week, and *Fortune* all abound with descriptions, allegations, refutations, analyses, and interviews with principals, prosecutors, defense attorneys, and agency regulators. Boardroom decision making is increasingly being litigated in courtrooms and discussed in the mass media. Corporate spokespersons, public-relations staffs, speakers at posh midday luncheons, and academics of all political persuasions are uttering thoughts that reflect the growing disenchantment with and distrust of corporate business practices in today's social climate. The most-important new phrase in today's lexicon on the rubber-chicken circuit is *social responsibility.* Others include *ethical conduct, moral restraint,* and *living with regulations.* Speeches and articles are variously entitled, "An Unscandalized View of those 'Bribes' Abroad," "How I Lost Our Great Debate About Corporate Ethics," "How to Be Ethical in an Unethical World," "Too Many Executives are Going to Jail," "Corporate Social Responsibility: Coming Right With People," and "Business and Accounting: Facing the New Vigilantes."[1] As explained in the 2 July 1979 issue of *Business Week,* people become distrustful of business when corporate officers try to gloss over things that are actually worrying them. The article then explains that corporate leaders are "telling it" as they never did before, speaking both in person and through advertising.[2] But, says *Business Week,* in an understatement worth quoting:

> The real problem is in the credibility of the message and not its communication. . . . It is that over recent years, business appears to have lost a view of itself as a valid social institution—and, in the process, has yielded by default much of the public goodwill upon which social legitimacy is based. In the absence of perceived legitimacy, government

regulation of the corporate sector has become the preferred choice of the public and of the politicians.[3]

What are the policy implications? It may be necessary for executives to speak to the public as they speak to each other.[4] The unwillingness to recognize the importance of institutional norms and social and organizational constraints—the most fundamental of sociological principles—is evident in addresses and articles by men of substance in journals of consequence.

In preparing this chapter I did a content analysis of articles and editorials on white-collar-crime issues appearing in *Fortune, Business Week,* and *The Wall Street Journal* during the years 1976-1979 inclusive. The most interesting were the addresses in *Vital Speeches of the Day,* given chiefly by businessmen, an occasional high-ranking bureaucrat, and a few academics to audiences of business and professional leaders. Apart from specific-subject-matter articles and speeches, the rest fall into one of three broad categories reflecting the prevailing ideologies within the business-professional community. At the risk of sounding insufficiently serious, these ideal-typical perspectives will be labeled in the same fashion as popular rock bands. Thus, the three are:

1. Friedman and His Fundamentalists
2. Arkin and the Persecuted
3. The Responsibles and Ethicals

Friedman and His Fundamentalists

Milton Friedman, the modern apostle of classical economic thought, whose mother worked in a sweatshop as an immigrant girl in the United States, has little patience with anything at all, especially regulation, which diverts the attention of owners, managers, and executives from free-enterprise activities. Friedman, never known for his dulcet tones, argues that executives at all levels in the organizational structure are fiduciaries whose moral obligation is to make as much money as possible for their stockholders and owners. In seeking to maximize profits, businessmen must abide by law and "ethical custom."[5] They must, however, at all costs steer clear of viewing their mission as containing "social responsibility" commitments. To vary from this profit imperative is a form of fraud—the worst kind of wrong-headedness.

Such extremism in defense of profit at the implied and sometimes stated cost of the violation of "ethical custom" (everybody does it, as in the quest for orders by paying off buyers and other influentials) is hardly rare in these speeches. As in a stylized dance or drama, however, the speaker usually concludes his published remarks with a plea for self-regulation, for conformity to "prevailing ethical standards." The divinity is often invoked in support of this moralizing, as are hoary adages.[6] Every so often the speaker openly confesses to the errors of his previous ways, in a manner reminiscent of the testimonials frequently delivered at meetings of various self-improvement groups.

In gathering data for this presentation, I queried in some detail at least twenty colleagues and friends in public administration, accounting, management, law, marketing, and related disciplines. Included also were mechanical and industrial engineers and two nuclear physicists. My approach was to open the dialogue with the Pinto case, asking whether the jury finding of not guilty of negligent homicide was a sound verdict. I then progressed to the Firestone 500 tire recall and the Lockheed overseas bribes. Although these three cases were the central focus, the discussion almost immediately broadened to fundamental issues of crime and morality and, with the physicists and engineers, to nuclear safety and the control of technology.

On the Pinto case, no business-economics-management informant thought the Ford Motor Company and its principal parties were or should have been found guilty as charged. The issue, they said, was a more-technical and noncriminal matter of product liability that should have been dealt with as a civil-damage matter as, indeed, it had been before the Indiana case. As the least-Friedmanesque economist informant and member of eight boards of directors, principally banks and local heavy-equipment companies, told me:

> We [you and I] have been on enough criminology and economic general examinations [for the Ph.D. degree] together so that you know and I know that white-collar crime [concept] is not the real thing [issue]. Ford was balancing the trade-off between redesign of the car at enormous cost versus the cost of rear end collision flame-out payments. In the collisions, the risk of fire was still small. The trade-off was small. Any other calculation [by Ford] makes no economic sense.

Well, how about the deaths involved? His answer: "With the best of equipment, car accidents kill people."

The Firestone 500 tire case was resolved in much the same way. Lockheed, I was told, either did business with payoffs, as is the business ethic in Italy, Japan, the Near East, and Latin America, or it did no business at all. In Friedman's terms, neither law nor "ethical custom" was violated. Finally, this same respondent put his credo in this way: "As a member of a [corporate] board I would never violate the criminal law or permit any such actions by management. Ethical standards were more of a problem, and regulatory constraints were something else again."

Most of the other informants, though less certain, agreed that Ford was noncriminal; that Firestone was culpable on civil grounds; and as for Lockheed, "business is business." Those whose field was law added numerous convoluted arguments, and always "might have been" in favor of a criminal trial but always, for one reason or another, were not. Surprisingly, the scientists were less sanguine about all three key cases, perhaps because it was the faulty engineering by Ford and Firestone that was at issue. In the Lockheed case, for everyone, the issue was meeting the competition.

Arkin and the Persecuted

The December 17, 1979, issue of *Fortune* contains a fascinating interview on business crimes by a defense attorney who specializes in defending clients charged with major economic crimes, for example, Harold Gleason, former chairman of the defunct Franklin National Bank. Although a minority voice, at least publicly, Arkin expressed great concern for the plight of a businessman charged with a criminal offense. In his view such a defendant starts his defense under severe handicaps and may face draconian punishments for relatively minor offenses.[8]

Elsewhere, Arkin argues that (economic-crime) misdeeds should certainly be punished. He goes on to question criminal sanctions as a remedy for business crimes, arguing that they are an excessive response given the nature of the offenses at issue.[9]

Asked to discuss the factors that contributed to the increased number of criminal actions, Arkin cited the civil-rights movement, the attitude that unlike the poor the rich can buy protection from the consequences of their acts, the current economic malaise, and the need for scapegoats for economic problems.

Arkin was also asked by the *Fortune* interviewer to cite the statutes that were being so broadly interpreted as to make businessmen vulnerable to penal sanctions. He mentioned the conspiracy law, which he felt was a catchall snare for the businessman who happened to become involved, even peripherally or inadvertently, in activities that were criminal. Also considered by him to be species of entrapment were the securities laws and the mail-fraud statute. The latter statute, which makes it a federal offense to use the mails in connection with a "scheme or artifice to defraud," was criticized as not always appropriate in an economically complex society where there should be some allowance for an amount of exaggeration in the marketplace.

When asked by the interviewer whether he was arguing that patently illegal acts should be condoned, Arkin denied that this represented his position. His denial, however, was modified by a significant *but*. Arkin argued for more-enlightened responses than imprisonment of white-collar offenders, and for the use instead of injunctions, civil-damage suits, and revocation of licenses. He expressed special concern for the increasing number of "should-have-known" laws and regulations, citing the case of a chief executive officer who was fined and convicted because some of the food products in his warehouse were found to contain rat droppings. The executive's contention that he was unaware of the problem and certainly did nothing to cause the problem was dismissed by the court on the ground that he had a positive duty to see to it that no such contamination occurred. He should have known!

Arkin's lament is that this should-have-known concept is diffusing into many other spheres of business and professional activity. Accountants and auditors, for example, have been held responsible for acts that were heretofore beyond or outside the regulatory purview. There have been indictments for the failure to find something that should have been found rather than for negligent or conscious misdeeds in the accounting or auditing functions. Arkin is incensed that these professionals, and others, have suddenly been endowed with a law-enforcement function that is more significant than their traditional roles. Arkin's plea is that the criminal-justice process not be injected into or, if already injected, that it be removed from everyday business activity and reserved for malicious evildoing. The idea of strict accountability distresses him greatly, as indeed it does many others in the business and professional communities.[10]

The Ethicals and Responsibles

The bulk of the published articles and addresses by elite figures in banking, accounting, auditing, major manufacturing, insurance, petrochemicals, and the professions of law and medicine emphasize the theme of corporate responsibility. For some this means that business must "come right with people."[11] For others, it means being ethical in an unethical world. For a few, it is a religious imperative. For most, however, it is a matter of survival. Social responsibility will ward off further governmental intrusion, roll back hastily conceived legislation like the proposed reckless-endangerment proposal, recover some of the lost public support, and insure corporate no less than societal well-being.[12] This social-responsibility theme, even allowing for Arkin's concept of justifiable puffery, means coming to terms with legal, ethical, and moral constraints; adding people to the equation of profit as the "bottom line"; and dealing with the legitimate worries of consumer and environmental interests.

The social-responsibility advocates are convinced that economic freedom can only be protected by rooting out actors and actions that violate moral strictures in the conduct of their businesses. Ivan Hill, president of American Viewpoint, Inc., in a speech to the National Leadership Conference of the American Medical Association in January 1976, brought his listeners this good news:

Earlier this month, a good event did make the news. It was an unusual event, too, an ethical cannon shot that has been heard throughout the American business community. The board of directors of a big business corporation, America's seventh largest corporation, an oil corporation, divested itself of its chairman and two principal officers. . . .

. . . These men who were forced to resign were men of competence and highly regarded by their peers. But *professional regard and personal friendship among peers, business or professional, should yield to principle—to public interest.* They had to go because the majority of directors apparently believed that their continued presence would weaken the ethical, and, ultimately, the economic underpinnings of the company [Gulf Oil Corporation].[13] [Emphasis added]

The justification for applauding this seemingly draconian measure is this: '. . . when honesty and ethics sink down, centralized authority and coercive regulations rise up. *The further a society moves into the areas of economic controls, the nearer it gets to people controls.*''[14] [Emphasis added]

How utterly at variance with Milton Friedman and his disciples is this emphasis on "social responsibility." Consider, for example, the sentiments of the president of the Equitable Life Assurance Society: "Virtually nothing we do is to be exclusively our own business. We have become quasi-public institutions because of the imperative need to consider always 'coming right with the people' in all we do." The same address contains these "few earnest suggestions":

1. We should make clear our awareness that business must comply with the ground rules society sets.
2. We should make clear our awareness that "generally accepted social principles" must become as controlling as "generally accepted accounting principles."
3. We should make clear our awareness that corporate social responsibility means "coming right with people."
4. We should make clear our awareness that nothing less than corporate survival is at stake.

Further, "Decency, honesty, integrity, legality and justice are fair rules for any enterprise that wants to survive and profit through valued service to society."[15]

The "responsibles" are unanimous in their belief that ethical, moral, and legal practices begin in the innermost sanctum and radiate by deed and example, if they spread at all. The tone, they argue, is set by the superordinates and always, as in Gabriel Tarde's theory of imitation, diffuses down.[16] In addition to competence and all the other necessary business and administrative skills, a deep and abiding commitment to the highest standards of ethical conduct is a vital attribute in a chief executive officer and his staff.

Consensus, however, ends there. Speakers and authors are sharply divided over the creation of a set of ethical guidelines to govern business conduct. The prostandards group looks on such standards and guidelines as a good-faith convenant, whereas the antistandards group views them as either unnecessary, symbolically wrong, or simply a waste of effort. Ethics, said one, is a value system internalized early in life. Ethical conduct cannot be coerced by high-sounding and toothless documents—a position reminiscent of the Etzioni distinction between organizational coercion and compliance.[17] This distinction is also often made by therapeutic-community advocates who believe that treatment cannot be coerced. As the chairman of the board of Union Carbide said in a speech on 5 January 1978:

> I believe we [corporations] have demonstrated a willingness and capacity to respond to society's needs. I believe we can voluntarily correct the abuses of trust that in the long run are also self-defeating. And I see no reason to believe that business cannot respond to and even lead the effort to create an ethical foundation for our commercial life that will restore the position of trust and respect we need in order to serve. We must, because no one can do it for us.[18]

On this matter of company codes of ethics, the Opinion Research Corporation of Princeton, N.J., questioned 650 corporations, 600 trade associations, and all 134 graduate schools of business in the United States.[19] The findings indicated that:

1. The larger the corporation, the greater the likelihood that it had a written code of ethics.
2. Half the codes were developed since 1975.
3. Two-thirds were revised ("updated") since 1977.
4. Five in six corporations thought or assumed that their employees were familiar with the substance of the code.
5. Three in five codes are simply statements of general ethical principles; the others are more specific. Sanctions, in half the codes, are dismissal or possible dismissal. About one-fifth of the codes contain no sanctions at all.
6. Of the codes, 94 percent prohibit conflict-of-interest activities; 97 percent forbid giving or taking bribes; and 62 percent prohibit the abuse of expense accounts and special allowances.
7. Most trade associations, unlike corporations, do not have written codes of ethics.
8. Ironically, only 16 percent of graduate business schools offer separate courses in ethics; 98 percent claim that ethical considerations are included in the treatment of other course material.[20]

The Criminological Perspective

Sutherland and the White Collars

Edwin H. Sutherland, one of the most-inventive minds in criminology in this century, coined the felicitous phrase "white-collar crime" as the title of his presidential address to the American Sociological Association some forty years ago.[21] In this paper, Sutherland discussed the nature and impact of white-collar crime as a violation of criminal law; of interpersonal and entrepreneurial norms; and, above all, of social trust, personal virtue, and the moral imperatives. As a midwestern moralist, Sutherland coined the term "white-collar criminal" as a less-elegant and more-scholarly denunciation of the excesses of laissez faire economics than Theodore Roosevelt's "malefactors of great wealth," Franklin Roosevelt's "economic royalists," Josephenson's "Robber Barons," Ida Tarbell's cruel oil magnets, Upton Sinclair's meat packers (Octopus), or the new rich and the new elite.[22] The concept of white-collar crime lent criminological credence and academic respectability, not to mention a sociological perspective, to the study of what was after all merely the new rules of the economic game. Despite the Sherman and Clayton Acts and the other legislative enactments prohibiting conspiratorial and monopolistic practices, gross fraud and deception, bribery and corruption, and the wholesale violations of even minimal health and safety codes, the new economic morality prescribed building empires, not character. Eventually, the great economic crash the profound social revolution embedded in the New Deal legislation, the loss of business self-confidence, a war or two, the income-tax bite, and other assorted changes on the socioeconomic-political scene soon dampened—but by no means quenched—the unbridled thirst for wealth, status, and power, however achieved.

But Sutherland's goal was not moralizing alone or even translating popular cries for economic justice into criminologic concepts. Instead, Sutherland saw in white-collar crime—concept and behavior—a vehicle for demolishing traditional perspectives about the etiology of crime and delinquency.[23] Surely it was not poverty that drove a railroad tycoon to tell his equally famous colleagues that as men he would trust them with all his material possessions, but as businessmen he would not trust them out of his sight. It was not poor housing, family disorganization, poor schools, unequal opportunity that produced a Fisk, Gould, or Morgan. It was not intrapsychic disabilities caused by maternal deprivation, early weaning, sibling rivalry, or an unresolved Oedipal crisis that made malefactors like Carnegie, Rockefeller, Stanford, and Mellon connive, conspire, and corrupt in order to attain their insatiable economic goals. It is hard to believe that the great scam artist Charles Ponzi had an extra Y chromosome or that the "robber barons" as children suffered from hyperkenesis, dyslexia, or aphasia. The odds are equally great that none of these conspirators (that is, the captains of industry), had high F scores on the Adorno scale or could be differentiated, except for their success, on the projective, pencil-and-paper, or performance tests that were sweeping psychology.[24] The criminal theft, looting, conspiracies, illegal rebates, bribery, corruption, and power struggles associated with our then largely unregulated economy were simply targets of opportunity and not of socioeconomic status, color, ethnicity, or deprivation. To Sutherland, white-collar crime was and is the conventional crime of those in positions of trust and wealth. As Geis has since suggested, the suite is the site of privileged crime.[25]

The demonstration that suite crime is the street crime of the business and professional communities was not, however, the ultimate concern of Sutherland. Indeed, by ridiculing the prevailing etiological conceptions of criminality as class-biased, he was, in fact, offering his genetic theory of crime causation—differential association—as the explanation of crime in boardroom and barroom, in street and suite, of native and naturalized, of winners and losers. Crime is a learned behavior. It is an outgrowth of contact with patterns of deviant conduct and intimate interaction or association with the carriers of these patterns. Thus Sutherland found the concept of white-collar crime eminently useful in documenting and illustrating his differential-association hypothesis.[26]

Under these circumstances, Sutherland was never really forced to deal with the implication of his "discovery" of white-collar crime; he never had to explore the political consequences of his work. He seemed unaware of the need for comparative work to determine whether white-collar crime would surface, in what form, and to what degree, in socialist society; in newly industrializing societies; in transactions that were personal and not simply perfunctory. It is difficult also to determine whether he saw white-collar crime as inevitable. On the control level, Sutherland called for the treatment of white-collar crime as real crime requiring penal rather than civil sanctions. But even here, he never constructed or proposed a theory of justice, of fairness, or punitiveness, of deterrence in dealing with the white-collar offender. Clearly he favored criminal over administrative law. He understood the difficulties inherent in the definition and social control by regulatory agencies over what he perceived to be an occupational variant of ordinary crime involving misrepresentation and duplicity as the chief forms of white-collar crime. In the final analysis, neither Sutherland nor most sociologists who followed in his inventive footsteps fully understood the exquisite problems posed by the emergence of the administrative (regulatory) agency as a rule-making and rule-enforcing body.[27] Nor have the arguments over the "realness" of white-collar crime been resolved since.

Apart from the vexing issue of the definition of white-collar crime and its distinction from Edelhertz's economic crime, Clinard's and Ermann and Lundman's organizational deviance, and Vaughan's organizational crime, various critics have raised objections to the formulation itself.[28] Not only are businessmen, executives, and managers perturbed by the concept, but also criminologists themselves are deeply divided on the issue of the "realness" of such violations. Professional objections are of three kinds: legal, sociological, and statistical.

On the legal front, the concept of white-collar (or economic, corporate, and organizational) crime has been battered by the contention, originally, argued by Paul Tappan, that there can be no crime without criminal proceedings and a criminal conviction.[29] Since nearly all white-collar crime is treated in a civil context, it is specious to describe it as criminal. This attractive proposition was especially congenial to my legal informants, no less than to the businessmen and executives whose speeches I cited earlier. The Sutherland response to this legal assault was that white-collar crime *could* be punished under existing criminal statutes. The issue, he argued, was convictability, not conviction.[30] There is theoretically nothing to preclude criminal sanctions from being instituted against all proven tax evaders, rather than the handful who are currently prosecuted and convicted to dramatize their evil. Violations of state and federal regulatory statutes *can* result in criminal penalties. Indeed, according to Sutherland, the problem was the differential implementation of criminal sanctions in conventional versus white-collar crime.

More serious than the legal attack on the concept was the most-unkind cut of Sutherland's colleague at the University of Chicago, Ernest Burgess.[31] The latter contended that two essential ingredients were absent in white-collar crime, thereby invalidating the idea. First, the public does not react to white-collar crimes, even when it is aware of them, with the moral indignation reserved for the more-conventional personal and property offenses. Federal-agency regulations are so complex that the linkage between victims and perpetrator is obscure. Except for the rare case—the electrical-conspiracy fraud—the public is unpersuaded of the criminal nature of what are currently referred to as "ripoffs." In this context, I was impressed with recent data showing that the public's complaints largely concern personal victimizations by vendors who overcharge, overgrade, fail to make good on ambiguous warranties, and generally cheat the consumer in everyday transactions such as car and appliance repairs. These data are from the Better Business Bureau files over many years.[32] Thus, Burgess is right. The public is hardly perturbed by fraudulent activities, payoffs, conspiracies, and business manipulations traditionally subsumed under the heading of white-collar crime. Moral stigma is lacking except in the eyes of criminologists—the moral entrepreneurs pushing white-collar crime as "real" crime.

Second, not only is the public indifferent to these depradations, except when victimized personally, but the alleged wrongdoers also hardly suffer sleepless nights wracked by guilt and shame. To a man—and that includes the fired Gulf Oil executives who contributed considerable sums to the Nixon reelection campaign—white-collar "malefactors" see themselves as dedicated, loyal, decent managers and executives who were, are, and will continue to be sacrificed when the ordinary and usual ways of doing business become political playthings. To my knowledge, no executive has yet "confessed" his criminal intent to do harm in violation of a criminal statute.

In rebuttal, Sutherland and others have pointed out that guilt is hardly characteristic of conventional offenders either. Either the violation, in Sykes's terminology, has been neutralized or, more recently, a conventional crime becomes a political statement for many offenders.

The third criticism of the Sutherland and subsequent formulations is the argument that white-collar crime (whether by multinations or by the local auto mechanic) is normative. "Everybody" does or is expected to "manipulate" for his own advantage. The distribution of violations is determined chiefly by opportunity. In this connection, the usual citation is to the work of Aubert in Norway on the responses of businessmen to rationing and price regulation.[33] There is also in the United States the research of Hartung on violations in the meat industry during a time of shortage, and Clinard's study of the black market in World War II.[34] The most-compelling statement is that illegality is organizationally required in the world of business. "Whistleblowers" are the deviants of the organization in the same sense that rate-busters are the deviants of the assembly line. To the extent that business and professional organizational practices are based on some types and degrees of fraud and wrongdoing, economic crime is not an ethical, moral, or criminal fact, but a normative activity.

Further, according to the Sutherland disciples, the same is true of delinquency among the underprivileged, which in no way prevents law enforcement from intervening when possible. Both Naderism and investigative reporting in the 1960s and 1970s have been influential in contesting this normative-behavior idea and in forcing some of the eighty-seven separate regulatory agencies and 110,000 or more persons involved in policing the private sector into more-decisive action. The ongoing congressional conflict over the role of the FTC in dealing with "normative" violations reflects the backlash effect of this more-aggressive policing.

Despite these limitations, objections, and criticisms, Sutherland's pioneering ideas met with widespread acclaim among criminologists. His research findings on 70 of the 200 largest nonfinancial enterprises in the United States—980 adverse decisions, 779 involving crimes, a mean of 14 per corporation, the "habitual" criminality of two-thirds—are too well-known to require exposition. Suddenly, reputable journals—both lay and professional—began to raise the issue of ethics in the marketplace and of the honorable men therein.[35] The critical point came, in my opinion, with the electrical-conspiracy case in 1961, in which nearly every major corporation producing heavy generating equipment for the Tennessee Valley Authority (TVA) had conspired in the most ludicrous of ways—a corporate version of the Keystone Kops—to divide the market by rigging bids.[36] The big news, however, was the jailing of the principal General Electric executive involved in the conspiracy—a first in U.S. annals.

The Edelhertz Modification

Despite considerable research, both before and since the electrical-conspiracy case, the ambiguities of the initial concept have made its operationalization extremely difficult. Forty years after Sutherland's initial paper, the definition of white-collar crime is as elusive as ever.

Certain changes have occurred, of course. On balance, they have reduced the muckraking component and increased the possibilities of assessing the problem of white-collar crime with greater incisiveness and specificity. Most of these changes were introduced by legally trained scholars with regulatory-body experience working both ends of the prosecution-defense adversary system. Short on theory, which may be a blessing, they are long on substance and procedure, on classification, and on the rules of evidence. The National District Attorneys Association project is a case in point. With economic-crime units now located in district attorneys' offices in selected cities from coast to coast, economic crime is no longer just an academic concern. It is true, of course, that these units deal chiefly with the white-collar crimes that most resemble conventional crimes, but even that represents a step forward in utilizing the state's strongest medicine, the criminal sanction. More-recent cases indicate a greater willingness to tackle the more-sophisticated and more-difficult white-collar crimes.

One of the most-influential figures in the field is Edelhertz, whose National Institute for Law Enforcement and Criminal Justice (NILECJ) monograph reads more like a legal brief than a criminological piece. Yet this monograph operationalizes the definition and, step by step, leads us through a classificatory system and the entire network of decision points, including detection procedures, investigation techniques and problems, prosecutive evaluations, pleas and plea bargaining, sentencing, diversion, and necessary additional legislation. There are short detours to the cashless society, the impact of civil rights, election-law reforms, environmental problems, and consumer protection. Edelhertz's brief makes it abundantly clear why economic crimes are so difficult to prevent, deter, or even process.

As defined by Edelhertz, an economic crime is "an illegal act or series of illegal acts committed by nonphysical means and by concealment or guile, to obtain money or property, or to obtain business or personal advantage."[37] There is nothing in this definition about occupational role requirements, respectability and high social status, or etiology. In this sense, this legalistic conception is at once superior in being more inclusive and democratic, while lacking Sutherland's principal point—that white-collar crime is an upper-class version of street crime and is, therefore, profoundly more costly in moral and social-integration terms.

Edelhertz, ever the legalist in the best sense of that increasingly derogatory term, presents a four-category classificatory system of economic crime—a term he prefers to white-collar crime. These categories are:

1. Crimes by persons operating on an individual, ad hoc basis (tax violations, credit-card fraud, charity frauds, unemployment insurance, welfare fraud).
2. Crimes committed in the course of their occupations by those operating inside business, government, or other establishments in violation of their duty or loyalty and fidelity to employer or client (computer frauds, commercial bribery, kickbacks, "sweetheart" contracts, embezzlement, expense-account padding, conflicts of interest).
3. Crimes incidental to, and in furtherance of, business operations, but not the central purpose of the business (fraud against the government, food and drug violations, check kiting, housing-code violations, and other forms of misrepresentation).
4. White-collar crime as a business or as the central activity (bankruptcy, land, home improvement, merchandising, insurance, pyramid, vanity, stocks and bonds, and related frauds and schemes.[38]

Although subject to considerable overlap, this assortment of public-bilking schemes and regulatory-agency violations is a considerable improvement over the twin evils of misrepresentation and duplicity identified by Sutherland. Edelhertz finds a great many common elements in the panoply of economic crimes. Among these he identifies:

1. The intent to commit a wrongful act (mens rea), or to achieve a purpose inconsistent with law or public policy.
2. Disguise of purpose or intent.
3. Reliance by violator on ignorance or carelessness of victim. (The same proviso, incidentally, might be applied to conventional criminality as well.)
4. Acquiescence by victim in what he or she believes to be the true nature and content of the transaction.

5. Concealment of the crime by:
   a. Preventing realization of victimization.
   b. Making provision for restitution for small number of complaints.
   c. Creation of some type of dummy facade to disguise the real nature of the illegal activity.[39]

This Edelhertz bread-and-butter formulation represents an improvement over the initial approach of Sutherland. Nevertheless, it still fails to differentiate economic crimes by levels or classes. As I see it, the most-manageable level, both practically and conceptually, is the consumer-fraud level.[40] Here one or more operatives bilk innocent clients in such activities as various repair rackets and in behaviors comparable to petty or grand larceny. The problem can be understood and managed in conventional criminal terms, relying on restitution and public stigmatization including a fine or a short sentence.

One level up, the picture begins to change. Conventional criminal law becomes inadequate, but the regulatory and administrative agencies do not yet fully enter the picture. Cases in point are local price fixing by chain stores, bank interest rates, "competitive" bidding for contracts in the construction industry, and similar economic practices. Misgrading of goods, mislabeling, underweighting, and general misrepresentation, as described by Sutherland, are other illustrations.[41]

At the third level are the economic practices perpetrated by larger, usually national, organizations and bureaucracies in the utility, railroad, airline, food, and almost every other industrial group. These practices, requiring years of litigation to resolve, are so totally unlike conventional criminality that it is a disservice to the discipline to speak to them in the same context as petty frauds and shortweighting. National price fixing, rebates, legislative bribery (as in the ABSCAM scandal), corruption, securities frauds, conspiracies, pension- and welfare-fund raids, incredible bookkeeping practices, false advertising, cost overruns, expense fraud, illegal tax shelters, expensive junkets, industrial espionage, and all the rest of the illegal and unethical methods of doing business are outside the criminal law and beyond the control of the cumbersome bureaucratic machinery designed to control such willful, overt conduct. That the bureaucracies in other countries are even less equal to the task is small comfort to all of us who unwittingly and unwillingly pay the price. Individually and collectively, we are unable to halt the erosion of our personal and social control.

The erosion of public control does not halt at the water's edge. The national conglomerate—horizontal, vertical, or both, with or without computer rigging—is small in comparison with the multinational organizations that are the current equivalents of the feudal nation-states. National controls are no match at all for the unbridled power exercised by the oil-company-OPEC cartel. Apart from the lowest-level defrauders (the embezzlers, the schemers, and the land promoters who defraud the public), *the problem of economic crime is not a crime problem at all but rather an issue of what kind of economic society is to emerge, how it is to be organized and regulated, and by whom.*[42]

To reiterate, it is my contention that, muckraking aside, the issue of economic crime, no matter how formulated, requires an interdisciplinary perspective now alien to criminology, to law, to economics, to psychiatry, and to other social and behavioral disciplines. The assumptions in each discipline are inadequate to cope with phenomena that go beyond conventional legal, political, economic, and sociological boundaries.

Years ago, when I offered my first seminar in white-collar crime, the graduate students were invariably impressed with the problem and with the standard works in the field. Of course, we were unable to resolve some of the issues raised earlier concerning definition, classification, and remedies. The seminar reflected the status of the field, in which most of the work being produced consisted of case histories. Not a single publishable paper emerged from that first exercise. In fact, a good investigative journalist could and certainly should have been able to do as well or better. Since then, I have sponsored two major dissertations and several theses and papers. Still, the same theoretical, substantive, and methodological problems persist.

What, then, is the problem, and why can we not get on with it? I suggest the following special difficulties, which preclude not only significant research but also the management and control of these ethically dubious and legally criminal activities:

1. The concept of economic, white-collar, and corporate crime is based on a nostalgic and erroneous conception of a free-enterprise system in which unfettered competition is a positive good that must be preserved by law, no less than by social consensus and a congenial economic climate. Hence, models based on this conception are, perforce, erroneous, like Becker's economic model of punishment and crime. The corporate economic structure, big labor, big government, and agribusiness operate apart from the wisdom of an Adam Smith, a John Marshall, or even a Milton Friedman. Perhaps if we reversed the conception—that is, assumed that unbridled competition is subject to civil and criminal sanction—the resulting new laws might be more enforceable. In sum, the Baptist-born, midwestern-bred, highly moral Sutherland confused Main Street and Wall Street in his conceptualization of the problem of economic crime. There is, of course, economic crime; but our model of it must be realistic rather than sentimental if white-collar crime is to be dealt with intelligently.

2. For much the same reasons, our thinking about "malefactors" is inadequate. We apply to them the general principles in criminal law—harm,

an overt act or acts, mens rea—as though responsibility can be pinpointed in massive bureaucracies like the conglomerates, the heavy-manufacturing industries, and the multinationals. For most of us, occupational-role behavior is a series of directives rather than a series of responsible judgments involving personal choice. Even the most-powerful executives may be locked into their decisions by external considerations beyond their control.

3. Unfortunately, even the ever tenuous line between legitimate business activity and economic crime is being obliterated. To twist Erasmus, when everything is possible, nothing is wrong. What is the difference, after all, between a $300,000 fund to elect one's supporters to public office and the same amount in a slush fund to raise milk prices. The more we clarify our laws to divide legitimate from illegal activity, the less noticeable becomes the difference. The more regulatory agencies involved, the greater the confusion. Cases that take years to unravel simply do not promote criminological clarity.

4. As a consequence of the complexity of the issues and the subject, we have been forced into several uncomfortable postures: a response of "isn't it terrible that such a thing could happen" to an Equity funding case; a muckraking stance that soon exhausts public patience; the study of the criminally processed violators, as in tax fraud; or reliance on investigative journalism. None of these approaches is designed to generate macrolevel hypotheses, to test those now extant, or to provide more-applicable models based on the actual operation of the marketplace at all levels. Theoretically, therefore, we have moved little since Sutherland's time toward an integrated theory of violations in high and low places, in and out of occupational roles, and by all kinds of offenders—from the tax evader to the well-connected Arizona or Florida land gouger; from the Ford Pinto and Firestone executives to the fraudulent local mechanic.

5. Given these restrictions, suite crime is therefore a more or less nonresearchable area in the conventional sense of research as an analytic and not merely a descriptive enterprise. The reasons, though self-evident on the whole, include some of the following:

a. It is impossible to test hypotheses that have not been formulated.

b. Quantitative analysis is almost impossible. The laundering of money, shredding of records, stonewalling in questioning, and uncommonly high rate of amnesia for specific events make research a near-hopeless cause. Long afterward, when memoirs are written, the safe-deposit boxes emptied, and the unshredded records recovered, it may be possible to reconstruct events more or less as they transpired. But this is hardly the answer, since only the more-famous cases will surface. Almost everything else will have passed from memory.

c. Even qualitative research is difficult at best. Stories are self-serving and contradictory even when obtainable. Since malefactors do not think of themselves as having offended, what is there to discuss? The Equity Funding case, for example, lasted two years in the courts, and $3-billion civil suit was litigated. Two states, three major accounting firms, numerous other corporations and individuals, and 312 separate law firms contested an insurance fraud of elephantine proportions. Over 40,000 policyholders on Equity Funding's books were found to be fictitious, thereby inflating the book value of the company out of all proportion to reality.

No doubt those who perpetrate computer fraud, as Vaughan has shown in her dissertation on the REVCO case (to be discussed later on), continue to manipulate the tapes. But even these small-scale operatives are unreachable by the exceedingly short arm of the law.

d. Few studies—not even one comes to mind—have ever been replicated, even when this would be possible, as in the medical, legal, and other professional spheres. For example, no one ever repeated Quinney's piece on the retail pharmacist. Why not?

e. Difficult as it is to obtain information from the subsystems in the criminal-justice structure, access to the proceedings of regulatory agencies is even harder to obtain. Without cooperation, we are left with the petty crimes that resemble larceny and are processed by economic units or specialists within prosecutors' offices. A major funding center like NILECJ might overcome this defect by supporting a unit in this sensitive area.

f. Similarly, but on a lower level, funding for economic-crime research is almost nonexistent. Picture a "crime in the suites" bill sent up to President Reagan—a bill to establish a research institute to study occupational crime with a view to preventing, managing, and treating the problem; upgrading personnel; speeding court procedures; developing new correctional facilities and diversion alternatives; and specifying compensation and restitution modalities. The proponents of such a measure would not be taken seriously. Yet there are institutes for everything from alcohol abuse to suicidology. Why not for economic crime?

g. Most criminologists with research competency are severely restricted by their traditional training, mostly in the social sciences. Nearly all lack both experience and knowledge of civil, administrative, or business law, not to mention accounting, marketing, and commercial skills. Thus the only hope lies in the creation of an interdisciplinary team or teams that can count on long-term funding and relative freedom of inquiry in carrying out their research mission.[43]

Still, two recent studies give cause for hope that ingenuity, scholarship, and persistence will clarify the problem. The first of the two, by Clinard, is a massive effort. The second, by Vaughan, is a more-limited but equally significant contribution.

Clinard's work on illegal corporate behavior involved a study of the 582 largest publicly owned corporations in the United States.[44] He reviewed all legal actions initiated against these giants during a two-year period by twenty-four federal agencies—an unprecedented feat in itself. In general terms, Clinard found:

1. Of the 582 corporations, 40 percent did not have a single legal action instituted against them during the two-year period; 60 percent, however, had at least one such action.
2. There was an average of 4.8 actions against those manufacturing companies that violated the law at least once.
3. Nearly half of the violations were of a moderate to serious nature.
4. There were 83 corporations (17.4 percent) with five or more violations ("chronics," in conventional crime language); 32, or 6.7 percent, were charged with five or more *moderate to serious* violations.
5. Most actions (more than 75 percent) were for violations in the manufacturing, environmental, and labor-relations areas. The financial and trade areas yielded 5-10 percent of all violations.
6. Large corporations were more likely to be in violation than smaller corporations.
7. Three industry groups accounted for far more than their fair share of violations—the auto, drug, and oil-refining groups.
8. With respect to sanctions, 85 percent of all "penalties" were administrative in character. However, those violations "harming the economy" were likely to receive criminal penalties.
9. As before, large corporations were sanctioned more often then smaller ones; the three most-frequently offending industry groups were, once again, the oil, auto, and drug groups, in that order.
10. Celerity is a key in classical criminological thought, along with certainty and severity. Thus it should be noted that civil cases lasted four months, criminal cases about one year, and minor violations about one month.
11. As to the executives involved (and they were very few in number—only fifty-six in all the corporations studied), over 62 were criminally sanctioned, and only one-quarter of these were given prison sentences.
12. The sixteen executives who did time spent a total of 597 days in confinement. Two of the sixteen did half of the time done by all, and these two were given six months each in the same case. Of the other fourteen, one had a 60-day sentence, another 45 days and a third 30 days. The remaining eleven of the sixteen averaged 9 days of confinement. Of those receiving 60 days or less, 14 of all 16 were involved in the same case—a folding-carton price-fixing conspiracy.

The Clinard study is a macrolevel work that probes broadly but not deeply. Little, for example, is known of the dynamics of the boardroom in any of the major companies studied—both the conforming and the offending ones. The study is clearly a classic in its scope, conception, utilization of sources, and interdisciplinary character-involving lawyers, sociologists, and journalists. It proves that more data are available than are ever mined by criminologists who are concerned with economic crime. This is precisely the point made by a professor of accounting in his interview with me (a self-described maverick in his profession because he accepts the criminological definition of economic crime as a serious matter). He believed that criminological writing reflected ignorance of important source materials and frequently faulty interpretation of those that were unearthed. Parenthetically, he opposed the Pinto criminal prosecution as the wrong way to achieve corporate responsibility.

So much for Clinard's herculean effort. The work of Diane Vaughan is yet another route to the interdisciplinary study of corporate violations.[45] In this case, she worked with lawyers, the journalist who wrote the initial story, and a fiscal analyst to get at the anatomy of a computer fraud.

The case involved the double billing of the Ohio Department of Public Welfare by REVCO, one of the four largest drug discount chains in the United States. In one of the most-improbable sequences yet recorded, beginning with the report of a podiatrist prescribing "unusual" medication for a patient, and a call from a REVCO vice-president to the Ohio State Medical Board to investigate the validity of the podiatrist's prescriptions, the case took a weird series of turns and resulted in a major computer-fraud prosecution of REVCO. The case ended with the resignation of two highly placed (and respected) executives, and a negotiated plea by REVCO. REVCO pleaded no contest to ten counts of falsification and was fined $5,000 per count. In addition, REVCO made restitution of $521,521.12 to the Ohio Department of Public Welfare. The two executives pleaded no contest to two counts of falsification and agreed to pay $2,000 each to the state. No other sanctions were imposed. REVCO stock suffered a limited downturn for a short period of time.[46] Stock trading was halted on 7 July and resumed shortly thereafter. REVCO continued to do as well as or better than its three major competitors despite the fraud and the attendant publicity.

There are several elements to this case that demand further exposition:

1. *The modus operandi.* The Ohio Department of Welfare was in arrears and was questioning the claims submitted by REVCO for prescription drugs under the Medicaid program. For reasons unknown and certainly unstated, the company (under the direction of the vice-president who originally called the Ohio Medical Board to investigate the potentially offending podiatrist) hired six clerks to change case numbers, (for example, *504675*, Valium 10 mg., 50 tabs, $6.83, to *504657* Valium 10 mg., 50 tabs, $6.83). The date of this prescription was altered from 2 October 1975 to 4

October 1975, and the claim resubmitted.[47] In this way, the company rapidly recovered its $521,521.12—without challenge. By accident, a clerk at the Department of Welfare discovered the double billing.

2. *The response.* Before the case was resolved, the Board of Pharmacy, the Department of Welfare, the Ohio State Patrol, and the Economic Crime Unit of the Franklin County Prosecutor's Office devised a network—the first of its kind—to investigate and eventually prosecute. In a scene worthy of a movie thriller, a coordinated raid was staged around the state to determine from the confiscated records whether there was a conspiracy to alter the case numbers or whether this was merely an aberration in one retail outlet. The former was found to be the case and was documented. The altered records were found statewide.

3. *Getting inside the company.* Vaughan made every effort to contact the executives who were fired. One of their attorneys was not only adamant in his refusal but insulting in his comments about this "academic exercise." Even less was achieved with corporate management. Repeated entreaties for interviews, for getting REVCO's side of the story, were stonewalled. The company attorney, at first sympathetic to the point of talking to Vaughan, was apparently instructed to stonewall the project to death. Even the executive secretaries to the president and lesser corporate figures reflected their disdain for both research and researcher. One of the phantom executives—the computer expert—is now in a position of trust in a major hardware-software house servicing the pharmaceutical trade in this region.

Thus, forty years after Sutherland's time, there are more agencies, more regulations, better data, increased interest, and more-sophisticated analytic tools at the macro level, as Clinard's study demonstrates. But the micro level, the task of ferreting out criminal violations in suites, is as punishing as ever. Nevertheless, even the Vaughan study proved extraordinarily fruitful. This is reflected in the first of my recommendations for future interdisciplinary research.

Recommendations

1. It is increasingly clear that no one agency is capable of coping with the economic violations of economic giants whose umbrella shelters many smaller and product-independent subsidiaries. Even the simple REVCO computer-fraud scheme would fall in the interstices between agencies. In this instance, no one state agency—neither welfare, highway patrol, Board of Pharmacy, nor Prosecutor's Office—could muster the skills that could be drawn together from the various agencies. Under current organizational imperatives (protect your turf; add people, not functions; maintain boundaries),

the emergence of effective networks is extremely unlikely. In the REVCO case, the network emerged incidentally and accidentally. The routinization of such "emergences" is a researchable and noble goal. Research should be directed at formulating techniques to encourage network formation as a first priority.

2. Economic crime is no longer to be viewed as the ripoff by large and powerful entities of small, powerless, and inconsequential consumer-user-victims—the elderly, the auto-repair client, or the victims of the new-furnace of bad-roof frauds. In the REVCO case, and in the more-significant electrical-conspiracy case, the crime(s) were perpetrated by the private sector against sector agents. After all, the Tennessee Valley Authority, which lost an estimated $2 billion, is hardly the equivalent of a little old lady in tennis shoes. So far, no one has looked at the implications of private (high-status) on public (usually lower-status) organizational crimes. A study or series of specific studies on "the *routine* management of the military" by private vendors or of capital-improvement projects by architects, engineers, and construction firms would be valuable.

3. New areas of opportunity are daily spawned by changing social needs and emerging technology. Witness computer fraud and industrial piracy, the unbelievable developments in medical technology and especially in the lucrative ethical drug business, vendor fraud involving nursing homes and medical and dental care. Criminologists of all descriptions—legal, clinical, law-enforcement, sociological—are reactive. It is possible to simulate, anticipate, and respond to potentially explosive targets of new opportunity by the equivalent of what, in conventional crime, is known as *target hardening.* Vendor fraud is not new; its diffusion into the health-care area should have come as no surprise at a time when third-party payments have become commonplace.

4. "Thought experiments" are badly needed in promoting a theory of fraud. Fraud is rarely perpetrated on intimates. A basic requirement is "depersonalizing" the victim, whether it be an individual or a private or public organization (including, in the case of embezzlement, one's own organization). U.S. culture thrives on creating norms and developing a consensus to justify them. At the same time, we create normative evasions in order to avoid the very proscriptions we prescribed. If one cheats at school, on one's spouse, in preparing tax returns, and in other traditional ways, then why not on behalf of the organization, or from it, or both? What, in short, is the boundary between normative evasions (socially sanctioned), and fraudulent practices (legally condemned)? Do the boundaries shift? how? under what conditions? In short, I propose the study of fraud, at all levels, as a normative evasion rather than a specifically criminal act. Criminal sanctions are considered harsh and unworkable by nearly everyone connected with the problem of white-collar crime.

5. The "whistleblower" as a deviant. What kind of people jeopardize their futures, risk exposure (at trial at the very least), blacklisting, and personal ostracism by exposing white-collar crimes? Does the "Deep Throat" phenomen represent a personality attribute, a form of revenge, a religious and moral posture, or all of these and more? I suggest a study of the personal and social attributes of Deep Throat—a study of a highly moral deviant type.

6. Most managers, entrepreneurs, and ordinary persons probably avoid involvement in white-collar (fraud) crimes as much as they avoid shoplifting or other forms of larceny. Who engages in economic crimes, and who does not or does so only under the most unusual conditions? I suggest a study of good (clean) and bad (fraud-prone) merchants, executives, owners, managers, and suitemen at the highest levels. The Better Business Bureau might be a fine takeoff point in identifying the cohort of vulnerables.

7. Finally, a cross-cultural study of specific types of economic crime is greatly needed. Fishman and I explored this subject comparing Israeli and U.S. problems, but our work was nonspecific by category of violation and quite tentative.[48] Nearly everything we do or think is culture bound. My impression is that the differences in definition, public attitudes, and social consequences are very different in Italy than in, say, Norway, or in the boardrooms of Silicon Row than in the cartel suites of Tokyo.

Notes

1. Walter Guzzardi, "An Unscandalized View of Those Bribes Abroad," *Fortune,* July 1976, pp. 118-121, 180-182; Eberhard Faber, "How I Lost Our Great Debate About Corporate Ethics," *Fortune,* November 1976, pp. 180-182, 186, 188; Walter F. Beran, "How to Be Ethical in an Unethical World," *Vital Speeches of the Day,* 1 June 1976; "Too many Executives are Going to Jail: An Interview With Stanley S. Arkin," *Fortune,* 17 December 1979, pp. 113-114; Coy Eklund, "Corporate Social Responsibility: Coming Right with People," *Vital Speeches of the Day,* 30 November 1976; William S. Kanaga, "Business and Accounting: Facing the New Vigilantes," *Vital Speeches of the Day,* 21 January 1977.

2. Donald Winks, "Speaking Out—With a Forked Tongue," *Business Week,* 2 July 1979, p. 9.

3. Ibid., p. 9. Reprinted with permission.

4 Ibid., p. 9.

5. See John McDonald, "How Social Responsibility Fits the Game of Business," *Fortune,* 11 February 1980, p. 206.

6. Thomas W. Phelps, "Can We Afford to Be Honest: Christ Was the Greatest Economist," *Vital Speeches of the Day,* 22 September 1976.

7. "Too Many Executives Are Going to Jail," pp. 113-114.

8. Ibid., p. 114.

9. Ibid., p. 113.

10. Ibid., p. 114.

11. Eklund, "Corporate Social Responsibility," p. 168.

12. "A Threat to Crime Code Reform," *Business Week,* 28 January 1980, pp. 106, 108.

13. Ivan Hill, "The Ethical Basis of Economic Freedom," *Vital Speeches of the Day,* 25 January 1976, pp. 345-349; p. 345. Reprinted with permission.

14. Ibid., p. 346.

15. Eklund, "Corporate Social Responsibility," p. 170.

16. Gabriel Tarde, *Penal Philosophy* (Boston: Little, Brown, 1912).

17. Amitai Etzioni, *A Comparative Analysis of Complex Organizations* (Glencoe, IU.: Free Press, 1961).

18. William S. Sneath, "Framework for a Business Ethic," *Vital Speeches of the Day,* 5 January 1978, p. 302. Reprinted with permission.

19. "Company Codes Are Not Uncommon," *Nation's Business,* October 1979, p. 77.

20. ibid., p. 77.

21. Edwin H. Sutherland, "White Collar Criminality," *American Sociological Review* 5 (1940):1-12.

22. Edwin H. Sutherland, *White Collar Crime* (New York: Dryden, 1949).

23. Edwin H. Sutherland and Donald R. Cressey, *Principles of Criminology,* 10th ed. (Philadelphia: Lippincott, 1979).

24. Marshall B. Clinard, *The Black Market* (New York: Holt, 1972).

25. See Gilbert Geis, "Upperworld Crime," in Abraham S. Blumberg, ed. *Current Perspectives on Criminal Behavior* (New York: Knopf, 1974); Gilbert Geis and Robert F. Meier, eds., *White-Collar Crime* (New York: Free Press, 1977).

26. Sutherland and Cressey, *Principles of Criminology.*

27. Sutherland, *White Collar Crime.*

28. Herbert Edelhertz, *The Nature, Impact and Prosecution of White-Collar Crime,* National Institute for Law Enforcement and Criminal Justice, Department of Justice, May 1970; Marshall Clinard, *Illegal Corporate Behavior,* NILECJ, Department of Justice, October 1979; David Ermann and Richard Lundman, *Organizational Deviance* (New York: Oxford University Press, 1978); Diane Vaughan, *"Crime between Organizations"* (Ph.D. diss., Ohio State University, 1979).

29. Paul W. Tappan, "Who Is the Criminal?" *American Sociological Review* 12 (1947):96-102.

30. Edwin H. Sutherland, "Is 'White-collar Crime' Crime?" *American Sociological Review* 10 (1945):132-139.

31. Ernest W. Burgess, "Comment," *American Sociological Review* 56 (1950):32-34.

32. W.H. Tankersley, "The Role of Business Self-Regulation in a Changing World," *Vital Speeches of the Day,* 11 October 1977, p. 127.

33. Vilhelm Aubert, "White-Collar Crime and Social Structure," *American Journal of Sociology* 58 (1952):263-271.

34. Frank B. Hartung, "White-Collar Offense in the Wholesale Meat Industry in Detroit," *American Journal of Sociology* 56 (1950):25-34; Clinard, *The Black Market.*

35. Sutherland, *White Collar Crime.*

36. Gilbert Geis, "The Heavy Electrical Equipment Antitrust Cases of 1961," in Marshall Clinard and Richard Quinney, eds., *Criminal Behavior Systems* (New York: Holt, Rinehart and Winston, 1967), pp. 140-151.

37. Edelhertz, *Nature of White Collar Crime,* p. 3.

38. Ibid., pp. 19-20.

39. Ibid., pp. 12-18.

40. Simon Dinitz, "Economic Crime," in *Criminology in Perspective,* Simha F. Landau and Leslie Sebba, eds. (Lexington, Mass.: Lexington Books, D.C. Heath and Company, 1977), p. 46.

41. Ibid., p. 46.

42. Ibid., p. 47.

43. Ibid., pp. 48-50.

44. Marshall Clinard, *Illegal Corporate Behavior,* pp. xiii-xxxii.

45. Vaughan, "Crime between Organizations," pp. 1-38.

46. Ibid., p. 200.

47. Ibid., p. 179.

48. Gideon Fishman and Simon Dinitz, "White Collar Crime: Conceptual Analysis and Current Status," *Israel Social Science Quarterly* 12-19, (1978):273-288 (in Hebrew).

7

The Interrelationships among Remedies for White-Collar Criminal Behavior

Edwin H. Stier

Introduction

The term *white-collar crime* covers a broad spectrum of illegitimate conduct directed against or arising out of legitimate governmental or commercial activity. Consequently, it falls within the purview of a variety of public and private institutions charged with the responsibility for its containment. For example, bank fraud is the concern of such institutions as law enforcement, banking regulatory agencies and the banking industry itself. Each such institution has available to it remedies through which it controls illegitimate behavior. Therefore, any single species of white-collar crime may be subject to control by numerous institutions employing a wide variety of remedies. Theoretically, at least the enforcement mechanism within these institutions collectively form a comprehensive and effective system of white-collar-crime control. In reality, however, present potential has not been maximized. Efforts to control economic crime have so far been relatively unsuccessful.

The reasons for this failure are manifold. In the first place, the diverse nature of white-collar crime works against conceptual consistency in approach. White-collar crimes range in complexity from relatively simple check forgery to highly intricate and imaginative computer frauds, involving abuse of sophisticated and newly developed technologies. White-collar crime is equally diverse in its victimization patterns. Local, state, and federal government programs are often the targets of fraud, as are shareholders, consumers, and large and small businesses. The nature of the offender will vary as well. White-collar criminals can be found in every socioeconomic group. Offenders range from bank tellers to corporate presidents, from individuals acting alone to large corporations engaged in monolithic conspiracies to restrain free competition. Likewise, motivations differ depending on whether the crime is perpetrated for personal advantage or in furtherance of organizational goals. These variations in form suggest no easy or general solution.

Equally problematic is the covert nature of white-collar crime, which makes it particularly difficult to detect, investigate, and prosecute. Except insofar as denominated "criminal," this type of unlawful behavior is often indistinguishable from the regular commercial and economic transactions of a business or government entity. Indeed, apart from the regulatory or statutory proscription, conduct may closely resemble sharp but tolerable business practice.

This pretense of respectability created by the appearance of normal business transactions explains yet another problem in this area—the ambivalence and moral confusion in the societal response to white-collar crime. Easy moral labels that are readily applied to traditional criminal conduct do not, for the most part, acceptably characterize the various forms of white-collar crime, especially those in which the victim need not be confronted or even identified or where the losses are widely diffused over a large segment of society. Because of the plethora of laws, rules, and regulations relating to businesses' every activity, there has developed a fine line between what is illegal, legal but unethical, and legitimate business behavior.

In part because of this dilemma and in part because of other motivational conflicts, there have emerged gross variations in perspective, priorities, and approach among the system's member institutions once the illicit conduct has been identified. Each institution responsible for white-collar-crime containment has responded to the problem individually and independently of the others. The result has been dramatic differences in enforcement policies and utilization of existing sanctions. This unevenness in approach doubtless reinforces moral confusion. More significantly, however, it suggests an inability to develop societal mechanism(s) to control white-collar crime that have the support of the community as a whole.

This chapter will address problems of fragmentation in the employment of white-collar-crime remedies. Its thesis is that no major white-collar-crime problem can be successfully dealt with absent consistent policies among the institutions that surround the problem. In preparing this chapter, we have read and considered some of the extensive academic literature in the field. This has been highly informative, and we have found the insight gained from our own experience to be of added value. Accordingly, our focus is pragmatic and tailored in ways that should be noted at the outset.

We do not treat all types of white-collar crime in this chapter. Set aside is that class of behavior characterized by the individual fraud operator victimizing other individuals and operating independently, without any corporate or government ties. The flim-flam artist, for example, whose conduct does not usually involve the semblance of legitimate business activity, actually straddles the fence between white-collar crime and conventional criminal activity. In this type of case, law enforcement functions in its traditional role of responding to victim complaints. We also do not address problems of the magnitude of multinational corporate conspiracy involving multiple victims and offenders, as envisioned by the allegation of a possible criminal price manipulation by the oil industry. Because of jurisdictional concerns, the highly complex set of inter- and intracorporate relationships and variables of international proportions, the problem may well be outside the realm of control by state and federal authorities. For present purposes, attention will be focused on those illegal activities directed at, or committed by or within, business, government, industry, or the professions, that is accomplished by breach of trust, fraud, or manipulation of the regular activities of these private or public institutions.

In structuring our response, we have avoided proposals for massive organizational overhaul or sweeping legislative reform. Rather, any reappraisal of approach must first look to the existing framework of control, which we believe to be adequate, and then consider the best means to implement resources and measures already available.

Existing Remedies and Their Use

The criminal sanction is perhaps the most-obvious and most widely employed remedy in the struggle against white-collar crime.

Conventional criminal sanctions against individuals include incarceration and monetary fines, employed primarily for their deterrent potential. In addition, there are a host of compensatory and other remedial measures that can be imposed ancillary to successful criminal prosecutions, usually as a condition of probation. A defendant may be required to make restitution both to the victims whose complaints initiated the prosecution and to all other parties he may have defrauded as well. Where the victim is not specifically identifiable and the impact of the economic crime falls on the public at large, reparation may also take the form of community-service obligations in lieu of prison.

In New Jersey, corporations are also subject to criminal sanctions, which may include heavy fines, probation, and a wide variety of other forms of punishment. The consequences of a criminal conviction may be as slight as a term of probation that requires notification of the criminal conviction to the stockholders or to the general public, and the employment of "supervisors" for key tasks who would be responsible for future compliance with the law. At the other extreme, the attorney general is empowered, subsequent to a criminal conviction, to institute appropriate ancillary proceedings to dissolve a corporation, forfeit its charter, revoke any franchises held by it, or revoke the certificate authorizing the corporation to conduct business in the state. Upon indictment, a corporation can be disqualified from bidding on government contracts, conducting business with public entities, or partaking of other forms of government benefits. Moreover, corporate officers, directors, or managers either individually or collectively responsible for antitrust, consumer-protection, or public-bidding violations may suffer removal from office and debarment from participation in the affairs of any business conducted in the state.

Recent efforts to develop interrelated civil and criminal causes of action are found in Racketeer Influenced and Corrupt Organizations (RICO) legislation. The underlying theory of RICO is that civil and criminal liability will arise out of a criminal business enterprise or a legitimate business taken over or supported by financial resources that are derived from criminal activity. In addition to providing criminal sanctions such as fines, imprisonment, and criminal forfeiture of the defendant's interest in the enterprise, violations of the act may result in civil orders of divestment, prohibitions against business activities, and orders of dissolution or reorganization. Additionally, victims may sue to recover treble damages.

In addition to the broad range of sanctions that may be imposed in conjunction with the criminal remedy, there are a host of civil remedies available that may be employed to combat white-collar criminal activity. State consumer-protection statutes, antitrust laws, and other forms of public-interest legislation often provide for remedies that are farther reaching, more easily employed, and perhaps more effective than the criminal remedy in dealing with some types of economic crime. This is particularly true in those cases where the criminal remedy allows for punishment of the offender but cannot provide for adequate compensation to society in general, or to the aggrieved individual in particular. The scope of civil remedies, however, is not so limited. Under existing consumer-protection legislation, civil actions for recoupment of losses may be enforced either privately or publicly. To overcome difficulties inherent in the class-action suit or other private modes of redress, state attorneys general, under common law or statutory authority, may sue for repayment on behalf of individual citizen-consumers. In New Jersey, the attorney general has taken advantage of this broad power. In one particularly significant case, the New Jersey attorney general instituted a proceeding against a seller of packages of "educational" material for engaging in deceptive practices and misrepresentations. In addition to civil penalties and other relief, the attorney general sought restoration and remedial orders for all persons who were induced to execute purchase contracts with the defendant. The New Jersey Supreme Court upheld recovery not only on behalf of specifically named buyers who testified at the trial, but also for all others similarly situated. Such a class-oriented remedy is clearly preferable to the processing of a myriad of individual complaints.

Recently, courts have granted extraordinary relief that permits continuing law-enforcement scrutiny of the conduct of a defendant's business activities. In a New Jersey antitrust case brought against nine major milk wholesalers, in addition to the traditional injunctive relief and monetary damages, the final judgment contained several innovative provisions. Each defendant is required to submit certifications to the New Jersey Division of Criminal Justice containing detailed reports regarding the basis of internal management decisions pertaining to all aspects of bidding activity. The judgment permits immediate access to all books and records and requires the availability of all employees for purposes of interview by the Division of Criminal Justice. The defendants must submit any additional reports under oath required from time to time by the Division of Criminal Justice. All officers and employees of each defendant must receive personal notification of the terms of the judgment, and each defendant corporation must prepare, with the approval of the Division of Criminal Justice, a memorandum detailing the manner in which it will assure compliance with the terms of the judgment. Additionally, each customer of the defendants must receive a summary of the terms of the judgment written in laymen's language and approved by the Division of Criminal Justice.

Through the exercise of equity jurisdiction, civil courts are also able to supplement and compensate for the limitations inherent in criminal and legal remedies that often prove tragically inadequate to deal with ongoing activity that does not cease with an arrest or the filing of a complaint. Conspiracies that continue to cause damage long after the initial conspiratorial agreement has been detected and investigated exploit the slow pace of most civil and criminal proceedings. Fortunately, equitable and timely relief against these unlawful business practices is available.

In many states, an attorney general acting under a grant of either common law or statutory power may seek and obtain temporary restraining orders and preliminary injunctions in order to halt illegal practices immediately. In cases involving official corruption, equitable remedies may also include the constructive trust and bill of accounting. Usually invoked ancillary to a criminal prosecution or removal proceedings, these types of relief are designed to ensure recovery of ill-gotten gains that public officials have acquired through a proven abuse of public office.

To the extent that economic criminal activity often encompasses conduct that violates various regulatory schemes, the administrative remedy also becomes potentially significant. Administrative agencies created as repositories of specialized knowledge to regulate certain types of commercial activity are often particularly well suited to pursue remedies that may effectively control certain species of white-collar crime. They may be in an excellent position to develop information that may be essential to the successful employment of criminal and civil remedies as well. They almost always set standards for licensing, and often require regular reporting to the agency by the regulated individual or corporation.

Regulatory power may also be used to restructure and supervise the future activities of a business entity found to have engaged in illegal activity.

Consent orders binding management to take certain prospective and remedial courses of action provide another effective means of control. Such agreements may require the institution of internal corporate procedures and controls, the appointment of special receivers or masters to make public disclosure, and reports of corporate transactions or the restructuring of boards of directors or executive committees. License revocation can be an effective deterrent to regulatory abuse that rises to the level of white-collar crime, as can aggressive inspection and investigation of businesses that seem to generate a large volume of complaints.

Finally, extralegal remedies may exist in the activities of professional licensing boards and ethics committees, and in the internal mechanisms of various businesses and corporations. These private and quasi-public bodies are often in the best position to detect white-collar criminal behavior early. Therefore, they have the ability to proceed with haste and thereby to mitigate further damages. Revocation of business or occupational licenses through licensing boards; suspension from active professional practice pending review by an ethics panel; and corporate self-policing through periodic spot checks, internal audits, and tighter enforcement of business-ethics codes all have inherent potential as effective deterrents of illicit economic activity.

The Inadequacy of the Present Approach

When one considers the broad scope of the remedies that are presently available and being used to some extent today, it becomes readily apparent that together they can form the basis of an effective system for the control of white-collar crime in nearly all its forms. Unfortunately, the remedies have rarely, if ever, been intelligently employed as part of an overall system of white-collar-crime control. Herein lies their weakness.

There has been a tendency for the agencies involved in this process to pursue almost exclusively the few remedies that are most convenient and most in conformity with their perception of their own limited roles in the struggle against white-collar crime. Little thought is given to the overall problem, and little emphasis is placed on the rational and intelligent selection of the remedies most likely to accomplish the broader desired results.

Unfortunately, no one remedy can be effectively employed against the broad range of criminal conduct in question; and no group of remedies can be haphazardly pursued by independently operating agencies with any degree of success. For example, although the criminal remedy is perceived by most to afford the most-formidable deterrent to unlawful conduct, it clearly does not appear adequate to deal with every variety of white-collar crime. In the first place, law-enforcement agencies are ill equipped and poorly positioned to detect white-collar crime. The normal channels of information usually relied on by law enforcement to detect other criminal activity are peculiarly ineffective in the detection of white-collar criminal activity. The nature of the unlawful conduct is such that reporting by the immediate victim or witness is the exception rather than the rule. White-collar crime is generally perpetrated by concealment or deception, and is often camouflaged in the legitimate course of business. Cooperative witnesses to such behavior are generally few, and the victims themselves are often unaware of the crimes that have occurred or fail to report them out of a sense of guilt or embarrassment.

Frequently, criminal-justice agencies are dependent for information on private industry or regulatory agencies that, for a variety of reasons, are selective and conservative in their reporting of white-collar criminal activity. Even those white-collar offenses that are eventually reported are often well insulated legally or practically from prosecution because of their complexity and because of the time lapse between their occurrence and their detection.

Added to this are the problems relating to the investigation of white-collar crimes. Virtually concealed in a fabric of complex commercial transactions, crimes such as antitrust conspiracies, stock manipulations, and banking and insurance frauds can take years to unravel. Often it is necessary to review and evaluate extensive financial data in order merely to confirm that criminal activity has in fact occurred. This may prove difficult, given the fact that very few criminal-law-enforcement agencies possess the investigative expertise that may be necessary to complete the investigation of criminal cases referred to them by regulatory agencies. Even those agencies that have such investigative expertise rarely have sufficient resources to undertake more than one complex investigation at a time. Moreover, one large case will sometimes require the division of resources from other assignments for long periods of time. Often, an investigation will continue long past the tenure of the personnel responsible for the case.

Once illegal conduct is successfully investigated, the complex nature of white-collar offenses leads to some substantial difficulties in criminal prosecution as well. A prosecution may involve scores of witnesses and reams of documentary evidence, in order to substantiate the commission of a crime and to prove the guilt of the defendant beyond a reasonable doubt. Just as fraudulent schemes often take years to complete, so the process of detection, investigation, and subsequent trial may take as long. Assuming for the moment a successful result and the imposition of a harsh criminal sanction, one must still doubt the potential deterrent effect of a process so protracted in its application. Of course, neither a successful result nor the imposition of a harsh criminal sanction is to be assumed in the trial of a white-collar criminal. The difficulties in obtaining conclusively proof of complex facts and mental states that are in accordance with rules of evidence and a criminal procedure from a far simpler era are often impossible to overcome. Finally, even if these difficulties are somehow overcome, the sanction imposed may reflect a predisposition toward leniency in sentencing white-collar criminals.

Among the most-plausible explanations for this discord is the moral confusion that attaches to the societal response to white-collar crime. The moral labels so readily applied to those convicted of violent crimes seem, somehow, not to fit this category of statutory violations. The differences between the criminal and the noncriminal become clouded when illegal activity is, at least superficially, indistinguishable from routine, everyday legitimate behavior.

The subtle shadings between legal and illicit conduct are no more obscure than in the investigation of corruption in government. If a government contract is awarded for personal services to a loyal political supporter who otherwise qualifies, then no violation occurs. Even if the intent is to reward past financial contributions or to encourage future support, the conduct is acceptable as a part of the spoils system essential to partisan politics. However, if the contract is awarded as quid pro quo for a political contribution then, a crime has occurred notwithstanding the fact that relationships between the expectations of the parties have not changed perceptibly. Little wonder that a jury may be reluctant to convict on the basis of conduct that appears almost indistinguishable from commonly accepted practice.

Even when criminal sanctions are employed and convictions obtained, the sentence may not be deemed commensurate with the crime or even with the effort of prosecuting in the first place. This only increases the tendency to apply criminal remedies to white-collar offenses inconsistently. Both leniency and disparity in sentencing continue to erode the effect of the criminal sanction.

Perhaps to an even greater degree, civil, administrative, and private remedies also contain significant shortcomings when taken individually. Used as independent enforcement mechanisms, these processes may not be able to reach all those whose actions warrant sanction; among those they do reach, the weight of the available sanctions may be insufficient to deal with certain categories of violations. Clearly, these processes lack criminal-law-enforcement machinery to facilitate detection. Civil and administrative investigations are hampered by certain limitations that do not burden the criminal process. The inability to compel the attendance of out-of-state witnesses or to employ criminal-investigative techniques under appropriate circumstances severely frustrates the administrative agency's effort at information gathering and analysis. In addition to these handicaps, administrative bodies, particularly those charged with *administering* government-assistance programs, often lack the expertise, orientation, and resources that are needed to establish their own internal controls and to identify where the program may be vulnerable to fraud and corruption.

In those instances where regulatory, civil, or private systems are unable to deter the proscribed activity, the reinforcement of the criminal penalty's deterrent effect may be required. Despite the problems mentioned earlier with the deterrent effect of the criminal sanction on white-collar crime, it is still no doubt true that its threat may be important in generating compliance on the part of prospective offenders. In this sense, the potential for criminal penalties may serve as a means to ensure the functioning of the purely administrative process.

All this is to suggest that no single enforcement mechanism—be it criminal, civil, administrative, or private—has wholesale application to white-collar offenses or is able in itself to provide an effective response. Although this interdependence of criminal, civil, administrative, and private remedies would appear to be obvious, this is not reflected in practice. Although the present mix of institutions sharing responsibility for white-collar-crime control is considerable, their efforts so far remain isolated and disorganized. The result is that the present response to white-collar crime is directed only toward those specific remedies that are individually available to the various institutions operating independently of one another. Each institution tends to define the problem from its own limited perspective and to develop its own course of action on an ad hoc basis. Such efforts foster an enforcement environment characterized by a patchwork application of remedies and resources, which emphasize the weaknesses inherent in each, rather than a combined application, designed to capitalize on their collective strength.

Obviously, it would be simple at this point merely to state that this lack of coordination among the involved agencies is the major reason for the ineffectiveness of white-collar-crime remedies and to conclude that all that needs to be done is to foster greater cooperation among these institutions. Such an approach, however, would be overly simplistic. It would fail to give ample consideration to the deep-seated differences in philosophy and approach among these institutions.

Even now, criminal-justice and regulatory agencies, as well as private industry, do not operate in total isolation from one another. However, just as individual utilization of existing remedies and resources is ineffective, current efforts to coordinate their use among institutions also have fallen prey to shortcomings that seriously undermine their joint effectiveness. In order truly to change this situation, it is necessary to understand fully those obstacles that now hinder efforts to combine the most-appropriate available remedies and resources effectively to deal with a particular white-collar-crime problem.

First, the basis for any coordinated effort between criminal-justice agencies, regulatory bodies, and private industry must rest on the free exchange of information among these institutions with respect to matters of mutual concern. This exchange of information is of even greater importance when one considers the relative absence of prompt victim reporting in white-collar-crime offenses. Certainly similar knowledge by all involved institutions of the nature and scope of white-collar-crime activity is vital if optimal use is to be made of existing remedies and resources. Unfortunately, this open and free exchange of information does not appear to be the reality in existing efforts to combat the type of criminal activity in question.

Treatment of the problem of illegal hazardous-waste disposal in New Jersey is a case in point. In 1977, 15,000 manufacturers were producing toxic chemical waste in New Jersey. Of the total produced, 1.2 billion gallons were liquid chemical waste, and 350,000 tons consisted of toxic sludge. The U.S. Environmental Protection Agency (EPA) has estimated that perhaps as much as 90 percent of this toxic material was not disposed of in a legitimate or environmentally sound manner.

Despite the magnitude of this problem and its obvious criminal overtones, neither industry officials nor those responsible for regulating the industry reported the possible widespread criminality to the State Division of Criminal Justice. Indeed, the Division of Criminal Justice became involved in the investigation of this activity only through information received from a municipal fire department. As a result of its investigation, the Division of Criminal Justice discovered incidents of chemicals being dumped into landfill sites and other locations illegally and indiscriminately. These activities were taking place in one of the most densely populated areas of the country and in an area where the potential for pollution and groundwater is extremely high. When the State Department of Environmental Protection (DEP) was advised of the preliminary findings of the division's investigation, there emerged a very serious difference in perception of the problem between the regulators and the criminal-law-enforcement community. The DEP explained that the problem was a temporary one, caused by the closing of the state's largest chemical landfill site, which until 1975 accepted toxic chemical waste. When this dump was closed by order of the DEP, it was thought that the recycling industry—that is, the part of the industry that has developed the technology to dispose of toxic chemical waste legitimately by breaking it down, incinerating it, and so forth—was too young to provide a total outlet for all the generators. As a result, a black market of illegal haulers developed. These haulers ostensibly received chemical wastes and delivered them to a proper disposal site, but in fact they had no such site and were dumping the chemicals illegally.

The DEP was attempting to solve the problem by encouraging the development of the disposal industry. This was primarily accomplished by establishing liberal licensing and inspection standards, thereby giving new recycling companies opportunities to set themselves up in business. The

Division of Criminal Justice was asked to focus its resources on illegal haulers in order to reduce competition from that source. It was thought that once licensed facilities began to develop the capacity to deal with the tremendous volume of chemicals being generated, the problems would be relieved. The division accepted this analysis and so began independent investigation only of the illegal haulers.

During the course of its investigation of the transporters of toxic waste, questions were raised about the DEP's appraisal of the situation. The Division of Criminal Justice surveillances uncovered several licensed waste-disposal facilities that instead of disposing of waste materials properly, were systematically disposing of them illegally. This added a whole new dimension to the problem. In addition to the increased complexity of investigating the recycling level of the industry, the support and protection afforded to licensed companies by the agency charged with their regulation undermined the impact of criminal-law enforcement as a mechanism for controlling behavior. The DEP viewed the division's efforts as an intrusion into an area in which the DEP, by reason of its regulatory responsibilities and technical resources, had primary authority to establish enforcement policy. As disagreement over factual perceptions continued, distrust and personal antagonism deepened the dispute, until developing an objective, consistent understanding of conditions in the toxic-waste industry became secondary to a bureaucratic power struggle.

In analyzing the difficulties illustrated by the example of toxic-waste disposal in New Jersey, we see that the problem resulted in part from conflicting institutional motivations, priorities, and goals. These factors led to the development of a factual perception consistent with the policies that each institution had predetermined for itself.

There were, of course, other factors that created further strains on the relationship between the regulatory and law-enforcement agencies. These must also be recognized. Part of the problem can be easily explained as parochial or jurisdictional pride within each institution. Additionally, each agency was fearful of having its internal policies shaped by others.

The regulatory agency, having decided that the ultimate solution to the toxic-waste problem was the rapid development of the recycling industry, tended to overlook signs that the industry was becoming corrupt. On the other hand, the Division of Criminal Justice, which had no responsibility to find a solution to the toxic-waste problem but which measured its success in terms of criminal prosecution, suspected that the industry as a whole was dishonest and untrustworthy.

In general, a perception on the part of regulatory agencies that criminal-justice institutions will be inflexible in their insistence on prosecution whenever they become involved, notwithstanding that overriding policy consideration, suggests that availability of remedies will increase the former's reluctance to share information. This failure to share information renders coordinated action impossible, and governmental units are thus compelled to rely on the limited resources and remedies to which each has access.

The roles of business, private industry, and government programs are also important in the context of problems in coordination and information exchange. In many cases, evidence of white-collar criminal activity will first be apparent to those actually engaged in the business or program in which the illegal activity occurs. Therefore, a crucial link in the passage of information to a law-enforcement agency is the business or program closest to the criminal conduct. Here again, apart from those who are simply acting to conceal their own illegal activity, diverse institutional goals often militate against an open sharing of information.

Being profit-oriented, private industry, for the most part, may be interested only in eliminating the cause of lost profits. It may be perfectly satisfied with financial recoupment or the termination of an employee deemed responsible. A company may decide against involving regulatory or law-enforcement agencies in white-collar-crime matters out of concern for adverse publicity. Private enterprise may also be reluctant to expose company executives to civil liability. Industry decision makers, who inherit at least the moral ambivalence described earlier, may view economic crime as a technical violation of law, but not as an offense for which someone should be punished. Even in cases in which private industry might be inclined to pursue formal remedies, its perception of the potential delays and procedural difficulties involved in such a process might well dissuade it from doing so. It may feel that the time consumed, the accompanying drain on managerial resources, and the sanctions most likely to be invoked, even if the process were successful, make cooperation with enforcement agencies simply not worth the effort.

Government program agencies have other traditions and goals that may affect their willingness to engage cooperatively with enforcement agencies in dealing with white-collar criminal activity. The law-enforcement agency is primarily involved in ferreting out fraud and criminal conduct, and is ordinarily interested simply in whether an illegal act has occurred. The program agency, by contrast, is generally concerned with providing prompt assistance either directly to the ultimate recipient (as in welfare relief), or with channeling it through a provider (as in Medicaid funding). Given this disposition, the good faith of the recipient or provider is likely to be assumed by the program agency. In this setting, program administrators will generally accept certain levels of fraud as inevitable. The tendency to overlook problems increases as an agency becomes more deeply involved in the development and operation of projects that it funds along with private individuals and businesses. Personal relationships between agency personnel and regulated entities are established, and the agency tends to measure its own success or failure in terms of the success of its projects. In New Jersey, an agency created to provide mortgage money for the construction of low- and middle-income housing was discovered after ten years of operation to have been victimized by flagrant fraud schemes committed by individuals who had developed intimate working relationships with many agency personnel. Those relationships, although not necessarily corrupt, made it impossible for the agency to recognize and respond to indications of fraud, even though adequate auditing and inspection procedures were in place. The response of the program agency when it was confronted with the fraud was defensive, and it was reluctant to cooperate with the investigating agency.

Even when there is a free exchange of information between agencies, disagreement may nevertheless surface as a result of incompatibility between the standards by which those facts are interpreted. In weighing and interpreting facts, the entire range of interest, goals, and motives of the institution come into play most heavily. Again, the toxic-waste example is instructive. The basic judgment on which an institution's decision to invoke its remedies must rest is whether institutional values have been offended by the conduct under review. Put another way, if the DEP remains convinced that a recycling company is sincerely attempting to reach the agency's goal of legitimate toxic-waste disposal, present violations may be tolerated. It is the perception of the character of the recycling company, and not simply the objective facts, that will influence the DEP's enforcement attitude. The Division of Criminal Justice, however, is influenced less by the long-term view of the potential role of the subject of investigation in the industry, and more by its present behavior.

Even when factual disagreement has been resolved and institutional perceptions have been reconciled, there still remains a final impediment to coordination. The ultimate selection of an enforcement strategy will be influenced by a variety of factors, ranging from bureaucratic self-interest to competing social policy. The most-obvious form of self-interest is public credit for enforcement activity. Strong pressure can be generated within an agency to overlook a remedy available to another agency, which will then receive public recognition for having attacked the problem. More difficult, however, are situations in which genuine public-interest considerations are difficult to balance. There is no obvious answer to whether a covert investigation of ongoing illegal toxic-waste disposal should give way to immediate administrative action to prevent further contamination of the invironment.

It is clear that at every step in the enforcement and regulatory process, problems unique to white-collar crime and to the institutions attempting to address such crime have resulted in an uneven and inconsistent containment effort. Any proposal, for upgrading the response to this problem that does take these conditions into account will continue to be of only limited effectiveness. A mechanism must be found to narrow differences in factual awareness, factual interpretation, and policy objectives among institutions involved in white-collar-crime control. In so doing we will begin to attack such problems on the basis of clearly defined and generally accepted moral values, to identify illicit conduct at the earliest possible moment, and to maximize the effectiveness of our remedies.

Development of a Strategy for the Employment of White-Collar Crime Remedies

The ideal system of white-collar-crime control calls for institutional agreement regarding the free flow of information between responsible agencies, creation of joint priorities, and rational employment of the most-effective combination of available remedies. There is no way to achieve this goal, however, in the absence of a certain degree of self-sacrifice and inconvenience to each participating institution and of a means of setting goals that cuts across institutional boundaries.

As already noted, there exists at present an impressive array of resources and sanctions within the system. Although they are not utilized to their fullest potential when operating individually and in isolation, the prospect of their combined and collective deployment is encouraging. For instance, opening up channels of communication between the regulating agency uniquely positioned to detect offensive behavior initially and the agency empowered to prosecute criminal violations will fill extant information gaps and avoid the overlap and duplication of effort inherent in a multijurisdictional system. Not only are time and energy conserved when counterproductive simultaneous investigations into the same behavior are harmonized, but the quality of the overall investigative effort, and hence the prospect of detection and application of the appropriate sanction, is greatly enhanced. The necessary specialization and expert knowledge of the regulating entity may very well be supplemented by the criminal-justice agency in analyzing intelligence data and conducting background investigations or screening of employees. In this manner, the various institutional actors may function to limit their own vulnerabilities, and thereby vastly improve the overall investigative effort.

Coordination of resources and information will also provide a mechanism by which to identify patterns of fraud, as well as operational and policy issues that must be resolved. Most sophisticated fraud schemes are designed to defeat the auditing techniques employed by regulatory agencies and public accounting firms. Intensive law-enforcement investigation will generally penetrate such a scheme, but this requires a heavy concentration of resources. Therefore, the problem for law enforcement becomes one of selectivity, based on a projected likelihood of success and a sense of priority. Non-law-enforcement public and private institutions, however, have the factual information and experience to identify high-priority matters where there exists an adequate factual threshold for intensive investigation.

Collective decision making and evaluation of how a particular white-collar-crime problem can best be handled allow for the most-efficient and most-effective allocation of resources among the already overburdened institutions. They also make it most unlikely that cases will fall into jurisdictional cracks. For instance, efforts to isolate and prioritize the most-serious and most-visible white-collar criminals for selective prosecution will greatly relieve a criminal-justice system already ill equipped to handle its ever-increasing case load. It may be determined for a variety of reasons that other cases can be handled more effectively through the prophylactic actions of a noncriminal remedy. Still others may deserve mutual interest and, accordingly, will be treated on a joint basis.

Furthermore, close cooperation serves to effect a more-forceful and more-imaginative sanctioning policy. With such a broad range of remedies available to combat white-collar crime, reliance can be placed on a combination of sanctions selectively calculated to limit the spread of such crime. For example, the civil and criminal enforcement sections of a state attorney general's office can work together to present a unified solution to a particular problem. Certain situations, such as those involving violations of consumer protection or environmental statutes, may call for the civil branch to initiate an action for the purpose of obtaining a restraining order and injunction, and, subsequently, for the criminal-enforcement agency to seek an indictment after the unlawful practices have been stopped. Here, the system operates at its optimal level of effectiveness by combining both the additional deterrence that penalties of incarceration provide and the emergent and remedial relief that equity secures. In other instances, remedies in addition to the criminal sanctions that flow from conviction by operation of law may be invoked concurrently to attain maximum deterrent effect. An example is the interdict provision of an antitrust statute, whereby a person convicted of violating the criminal portion of the act is barred from conducting any business thereafter in the state. Where noncriminal sanctions are not self-executing, other enforcement mechanisms may be actively implemented and exploited. Ethics committees and administrative licensing boards, on notification of a criminal conviction, have the ability to eliminate the violator from the marketplace, a potentially more-serious threat to the business or professional violator than all but the most-severe sanctions imposed by the criminal process.

The formula for achieving this type of coordinated and cooperative activity, and the benefits that flow therefrom, will vary with the nature of the particular problem presented. It is readily apparent that the dissimilarity of situations presented by white-collar crime generally militates against an across-the-board consistency of approach. Any broad-based strategy for the containment of such crime must necessarily take into account the wide range of offenses and institutional relationships implicit in this variety of criminal and enforcement activity. Where a business may in some instances be the victim and in others the violator, and where a government official may on one day be the regulator and on another the target of an investigation, permanent relationships for white-collar-crime control are difficult to maintain.

Economic forces that give rise to illicit conduct should also influence the appropriate type of institutional response. The situation that prevailed until recently in New Jersey's alcoholic-beverage industry is illustrative. By virtue of a rigid system of control imposed by the Alcoholic Beverage Control Commission, liquor wholesalers could sell their products to retailers only pursuant to fixed prices. The purpose of this regulatory scheme was to reduce price competition, maintain artificially high prices, and thereby discourage alcohol consumption. The practice that developed, however, was quite different. Because the system of regulation would not allow for open price competition, market conditions resulted in widespread illegal activity within the industry. Wholesalers who wished to obtain business from the large retail concerns covertly competed among themselves by offering kickbacks of a portion of the purchase price to those concerns. Periodically, these practices were exposed and heavy fines imposed; yet they continued. The solution was to relax regulatory control that no longer served a useful public policy, and thereby to relieve the pressures on the industry to engage in this type of illegal activity. Once deregulation occurred, competition that had previously taken an illicit form was transformed into legitimate economic behavior.

The variety of institutional actors charged with the responsibility for white-collar-crime control further compounds the analysis. Government administrative agencies, alone, run the gamut from completely regulatory to competitive with private business. Differences in the internal dynamics of these entities should influence the nature of the relationship that they can maintain with other agencies. For example, law-enforcement authorities should strive for close personal contact with those administrative agencies that are solely regulatory in nature or with those providing either direct or indirect assistance to the ultimate beneficiary. Such contacts break down institutional competition. On the other hand, it may be advisable for law-enforcement agencies to establish a more-distant relationship with government agencies that are involved in the development of funding applications, opting instead to maintain direct contact with agency supervisory boards and oversight committees. Such a policy recognizes that an agency of the latter type will be subject to overriding self-interest in the success of its projects, which will inevitably disrupt any close dealings with law enforcement.

Another way to analyze the impediments to full cooperation between institutions is in terms of whether they derive from differences in the perception of facts; from divergent interpretations of and standards applied to the facts, once these are mutually understood; or from disagreement about the appropriate sanction for commonly characterized behavior. Where the first variety of problem is found, it is essential to establish information networks to guarantee a full and shared collection of data and facts. This can be accomplished largely through regular meetings among specially designated agency representatives, during which information is exchanged and measures are taken to exhaust all possible avenues of fact gathering. For instance, arrangements can be made to share computer time and resources for the analysis of data. In addition, valuable input can be routinely provided by the appropriate administrative agency through its compliance-reporting function, by the criminal-justice authority through its network of informants and intelligence practices, and by the private sector through annual corporate internal audits and industry-wide investigative and education programs.

Once such a data-collection system has been established, techniques for identifying and investigating suspect activities can be analyzed and implemented. In certain situations, the agency primarily responsible for ferreting out and dealing with a white-collar offense can draw on the collective experience and expertise of other institutions to augment its traditional law-enforcement activities. Where this may not be possible, active recruitment of trained auditors, accountants, and other specialized personnel will be necessary. In cases of mutual responsibility, multiagency investigatory teams staffed by qualified technical and investigative personnel can be formed. In most instances involving complex and voluminous documentary evidence, the success of the investigatory effort entails coordinated and effective teamwork, even if only in the form of increased backup and support activities.

Where the impediment to cooperation arises from inconsistent interpretation of facts by the institutions involved, the problem must be attacked by mutually defining the goals and standards by which factual information is analyzed and judged. The means to this end are necessarily intangible. As in those cases plagued by differences in perception of facts, problems arising out of factual analysis require close and direct interagency relationships; here, however, there must be higher-level contact among the concerned institutions. Regular and frequent consultation and communication can be maintained through creation of a formal committee under the guidance of a high-level executive and comprising senior-level representatives from appropriate government agencies, as well as from the business sector. This committee would be responsible for identifying patterns of fraud, corruption, waste, and other forms of system abuse; for enunciating clear policy and operational guidelines; and for shaping priorities.

The solution to the problem arising out of New Jersey's toxic-waste enforcement efforts presents a prototype of such a cooperative endeavor. The New Jersey Inter-Agency Hazardous Waste Task Force was created after exhaustive individual efforts proved futile. The task force is composed of representatives from the civil and criminal-justice divisions of the State Attorney General's Office, the U.S. Attorney's Office, the State Department of Environmental Protection, and the U.S. Environmental Protection Agency. Other agencies, such as the New Jersey State Police (which provides air surveillance and disaster expertise) and the Office of the Medical Examiner (which analyzes samples of chemical wastes), are also involved. The stated objectives of the task force are the free exchange of information among the agencies involved, the joint setting of priorities, and the selection of appropriate remedies to deal with the problems as defined by the task force.

Each of the units that make up the task force function and interrelate through a series of operating procedures established by the task force. Task-force representatives realized that communication was the key to a successful program in cases in which multiple units are geographically separated, having different functions and operating under a variety of statutes, regulations, and administrative procedures. It also became apparent that a regular monthly meeting was needed, at which responsible members of each unit would have an opportunity to present an overview of the investigations being conducted by their units, and the anticipated results. At this monthly meeting, the task force identifies problem areas for intensified concern of its investigative personnel. A determination is then made as to the proper remedy to pursue, whether it be administrative, civil, or criminal. Additionally, the task force is responsible for identifying procedural problems within the regulatory agencies that are highlighted by its investigations.

This monthly forum serves as a means of reducing the probability of duplication of effort or interference among the member groups. It also provides an opportunity for one agency to transfer an investigation or case pending prosecution to some other agency that is in a better position to obtain the desired results. For example, if it is determined that the evidence cannot be used for a criminal proceeding because of legal infirmities, or if a critical environmental problem requires immediate action, then the case may be referred by the Division of Criminal Justice to the Department of Environmental Protection and the Division of Law for the appropriate civil or administrative action.

In the case of an environmental disaster, such as that of the Chemical Control Corporation in Elizabeth, New Jersey, where the DEP was attempting to remove 60,000 drums of hazardous chemical waste illegally stored at the site, the Divisions of Law and Criminal Justice were pursuing violations of state laws and federal agencies, such as Alcohol, Tobacco, and Firearms; and the Federal Bureau of Investigation was pursuing federal violations along with the U.S. attorney. Only because of the established lines of communication was serious interference among these investigations averted.

The process of consensus building, however, entails a certain accommodation to the needs and interests of participating institutions, a realistic recognition of their relative strengths and deficiencies, and an adjustment of traditional roles. In dealing with a regulatory agency, the criminal-justice agency may have to relax its opposition to including outside agencies in its investigations and consider permitting administrative action to begin before its criminal case is concluded. Likewise, the administrative agency must recognize the needs of law enforcement in entering a case early, develop a reward system for agency personnel to encourage cooperation with criminal-law enforcement, and recognize the experience of criminal investigators as a primary resource in developing internal program controls. Government agencies must recognize the disincentives in private institutions to cooperate with government, and must work toward overcoming them. Such simple measures as consciously avoiding inconveniencing employees of a business during an investigation will, in the long run, tend to break down the barriers to cooperation between enforcement agencies and the private sector.

All involved institutions should be made to feel integrally responsible for a broad social program of substantive control, regardless of the respective roles each may play in any given instance. Simply put, credit for success must be shared. Regulatory-agency personnel who painstakingly comb through business records, financial statements, and similar documentation for evidence of unlawful economic activity should be considered full-fledged members of the prosecutorial team that ultimately secures the conviction. Likewise, the use of private sanctions by corporations, business, and professional associations should be encouraged and publicized by law-enforcement authorities as a necessary component in a larger network of social control.

Basically, the approach just outlined also applies where disagreement focuses on the balancing of fundamental social policies among institutions, rather than on differences in the perception or interpretation of facts. Practically speaking, however, there can be no effective resolution of such basic differences without the active intervention of those at the highest level of decision making. Such sensitive and crucial issues require bypassing department operational levels and dealing directly with the ultimate policymakers. Thus, the forum for the airing of these differences could take the form of a gubernatorially appointed advisory commission, council, or other cooperative structure comprising the heads of all concerned institutions or their high-level designees. Representing diverse public and private interests, this body can provide an organizational arrangement that will expedite the coordination of agencies and groups that have previously acted independently, and often at cross-purposes, in the formulation and implementation of sanctioning policy. By drawing on the collective knowledge and experience of its membership, such an advisory committee would be in a unique position to provide meaningful guidance as well as specific recommendations to the governor, attorney general, or legislature.

An example of such an endeavor is provided by the New Jersey Governor's Arson Task Force. Preliminary study of New Jersey's arson problem revealed a wide variety of institutions, each becoming more active in arson control from its own limited perspective. Police, fire officials, prosecutors, banking institutions, insurance companies, and numerous regulatory agencies were all beginning to formulate more aggressive antiarson policies, independent of one another. Analysis of these efforts reflected that they were often duplicative, and sometimes even in conflict. Attempts to resolve these differences in approach were futile because the various institutions rigidly pursued policies consistent with their own limited charters.

Finally, a task force consisting of high-level representatives from these institutions and agencies was created for the purpose of rectifying the situation. The results were extremely positive. The conflicting policies that had been formulated were easily identified by the group and, within a short time, were integrated into a uniform statewide strategy for arson prevention and control. The process of blending the unavoidable pursuit of alternative arson remedies into one statewide strategy was so well received that plans to institutionalize the Arson Task Force are now underway.

In another instance, as part of the solution to New Jersey's toxic-waste-disposal problem, the governor created the Hazardous Waste Advisory Commission, consisting of industrial, academic, environmental, and governmental leaders. This high-level committee has been charged with the responsibility of recommending long-term solutions that take into account the technological complexity and economic risks inherent in the waste-disposal industry, as well as the environmental concerns and control mechanisms required to prevent the corruption that presently exists in that industry.

Although the restructuring of institutional relationships described earlier requires additional energy and commitment, there are growing indications that the time is right for such efforts. In the first place, public awareness of both the pervasiveness and the damaging effects of white-collar crime appears to be growing. As a result of the inflationary pressures of the 1970s, the fiscal troubles of government, and the rapid depletion of essential energy resources, there is a growing realization of the economic impact of white-collar crime. Higher levels of education and sophistication in society explain the presence today of a consumer movement more vocal in its demands, determined in its expectations, and persistent in its objectives than ever before.

Aggressive investigative reporting by the communications media also has contributed immeasurably to the public perception of the problem. Recent exposures in the news of such crimes as environmental pollution and frauds by nursing-home administrators emphasize the seriousness of the resultant social and physical harm. In New Jersey, for instance, the news media waged a large-scale campaign targeting the toxic-waste-disposal industry. By stressing the hazardous consequences of rampant illegal and indiscriminate dumping of toxic chemicals in the state, this series of articles was responsible for stimulating government concern that agencies operating independent of one another were ineffective. This concern spurred the development of cooperative governmental action.

The strength of the public's concern has spawned calls on civil and criminal enforcement agencies, as well as on the courts, for prompt and vigorous enforcement of the laws governing economic activity and more-stringent punishment for white-collar offenders. Legislators have responded by enacting statutes extending criminal accountability to the corporate entity on the basis of strict liability, and to individual officers on the theory of vicarious liability for negligent acts or omissions by subordinate employees. It is hoped that these events, in turn, will facilitate private executive consciousness raising about the public considerations implicated by corporate policies. Indeed, private businesses have already responded by augmenting internal-security forces, mounting investigative and educational programs designed to ferret out and control fraud within the corporation, and initiating complaint-handling mechanisms to deal with consumer grievances. Increased societal pressure will ensure that these measures continue and that additional ones are undertaken.

However, we remain convinced that concerted effort is the key to any major future success in white-collar-crime containment. Strategic planning must occur immediately to take advantage of present public interest and support. We must evaluate our alternatives carefully. For example, RICO statutes may be counterproductive if they broaden law-enforcement remedies and thereby discourage interagency cooperation. With such planning, much can be accomplished in the immediate future without massive new resources and complex legislative reforms.

8

A Research and Action Agenda with Respect to White-Collar Crime

Gilbert Geis

The fundamental focus of this book has been on the generation of information and ideas about suitable strategies for further study of white-collar crime. The various chapters have offered a number of ideas about different approaches that were deemed likely to be fruitful. Generally, the authors have concentrated on a segment of the problem and on detailed methods by which that portion might better be addressed; they have pinpointed the gaps in our knowledge and told how such gaps might be filled. In this concluding chapter, I will attempt to coordinate and extend the bounds of the foregoing chapters, and to build on elements of the free-wheeling discussions that took place after each of the colloquium presentations from which these chapters are drawn.

Unlike persons concerned with more-traditional forms of crime, scholars and practitioners working on the problems of white-collar crime happily avoid at least one matter of moral perturbation: They do not need to deal with accusations that their work is but a thin camouflage of an unappetizing effort to keep the deprived in their downtrodden condition, or that it is part of a racist scheme to define as mere criminals persons who truly are political offenders. There was complete agreement—and perhaps this itself ought to arouse suspicion—that white-collar crime is bad, even evil, and that those seeking to understand and to combat it are enrolled in a worthy cause.

Beyond this, however, the subject matter itself, as the chapters of this book attest, is inordinately complex, its roots beyond altogether clear comprehension, its definition in great dispute. Indeed, efforts to pin down the issues associated with white-collar crime seem at times much like those of Stephen Leacock's fabled horseman who was seen riding off frantically toward all four points of the compass.

The Primary Postulation

In my opinion, one issue takes precedence above all others with respect to research and action bearing on white-collar crime. That issue, which will inform the largest part of this chapter and the suggestions that are offered, has to do with the public definition of white-collar crime and the attitudes

175

that are manifested toward the phenomena that constitute such crime. By this, I do not mean what the public thinks about diverse aspects of white-collar crime—that is, whether it regards offenses producing certain kinds of harms as seriously as it regards so-called street crimes that bring about equivalent degrees of injury. Work directed toward the further resolution of that very important issue has been outlined in some detail earlier in the book.[1] For me, the implicit policy question underlying such research holds the key ingredient for the direction of a consideration of white-collar crime. The issue, briefly put, is this: *How do we best produce a social and political atmosphere in which the matter of white-collar crime is regarded as of high importance?*

Unless such a state of mind comes to prevail, white-collar crime is apt to be neglected as a matter of paramount concern, regardless of its inherent traits. On the other hand, if the public and the authorities come to see white-collar crime as a subject in urgent need of attention and remediation, then funds and personnel will be made available to carry out the kinds of work suggested in this book. The issue is one that Becker has labeled "moral entrepreneurship."[2] By this he means that situations are taken up by certain groups, which, on the basis of one or several of a very wide range of considerations, are able to convince others—particularly others who can exert social suasion—that what they are advocating is important.

At times, evils call attention to themselves spontaneously. This is particularly true if they come to be associated with a notorious incident, such as a coal-mine catastrophe; a Thalidomide scandal; a blatant and easily understood antitrust violation; or a situation involving infants, widows, or other stereotypically sympathy-arousing victims. But a more-sensible path, and perhaps in the long run a more-satisfactory one, is to have dedicated persons embark on an impassioned crusade in behalf of this or that reform. Such a crusade is most apt to encounter success, I believe, if it possesses intrinsic worth and is well fortified by impregnable persuasive evidence. It is toward the establishment of such conditions with respect to white-collar crime that the present blueprint is directed.

To carry the point a bit further, let us note that life is replete with indecencies and injustices. For diverse reasons, some are ignored and some downplayed, whereas others arouse enormous indignation and result in much enterprise being directed toward their amelioration. The concentration of resources and attention on highlighted issues often serves to lessen the ills associated with them. In recent times, we have seen a federal focus on racial injustice, street crime, poverty, women's rights, and a number of other issues that came to be defined as demanding close attention and effective resolution. But each of these problems had been around for a long time, and each was no worse (and in some respects was actually more benign) than it had been in earlier periods. None "cried out" for attention, despite the rhetoric commonly employed by those who demand that their concerns take precedence over matters others deem more important.

Most of the issues likely would not have come to the forefront if they did not contain some element of merit, some wrong needing redress—that is, if the fundamental logic of their appeal to the minds and hearts of the constituency they desired to create was not relatively persuasive. At the same time, it is obvious that they sought the advantage of one group at the expense of another, usually on the ground that such a rearrangement would more justly achieve fairness. On the other hand, numerous matters have come to command public attention that later judgment declared to be mindless or at least ill considered in terms of the achieved results. The successful campaign for the prohibition of the sale of alcoholic beverages is a prime example.[3]

In this respect, it is of primary importance to document that proposed solutions to problems said to emerge from white-collar crime will leave things in a better state than they were earlier. This can raise arguable issues: There are, for instance, those who believe that the "harassing" of business operations by government regulations that carry heavy penalties produce, on balance, more undesirable than beneficial results.[4] They insist, for instance, that there should be incentives for things such as satisfactory occupational-safety records, rather than fines or prison sentences for violations. They argue that the cost of the marginal degree of protection that the regulations afford workers against such "iffy" things as workplace-"caused" cancer can prove so fiscally prohibitive that it will force plants to close and throw a large number of employees out of work.[5] Similar kinds of objections are raised against many other kinds of white-collar crime enforcement strategies.

Resolution of issues such as the foregoing should assume a very high priority on the agenda of research on white-collar crime. Part of the effort ought to include monitoring meticulously the consequences of attempts to control by law the abuses of power that are classed as white-collar crime. I believe that no legislated program ought to proceed without a sum of money being appropriated for an independent group that is given a long-term mandate to follow the career of the new program. The report of this group ought to go back to those who decided to try the new approach, so that its members may, if necessary, amend their original ideas, and so that they may learn in what ways their earlier views proved to be incorrect. Presumably they will use such information as a basis for their subsequent decisions.

Documenting Developments

The fact that white-collar crime has, in the past five years, assumed considerable importance on the political and social scene in the United States should not be taken as a true testament to the growing seriousness of the problems the term embraces. Some things—such as crimes associated with the profusion of nuclear materials—could not have occurred earlier, since the technology was not at hand.[6] In this sense, the occurrence of more white-collar crime merely reflects additional technology and more-complicated life patterns. Indeed, it is not unlikely that there is less of the serious kinds of white-collar crime today than in earlier times—or, at least, less of the kinds of offenses that could have been committed both then and now, such as bribery and antitrust violations. Certainly most of the phenomena that constitute "white-collar crime" have been with us in some form as far back as memory and archives extend.

Nor is it likely that the emergent concern with white-collar crime is a function of the burgeoning social-science and legal research directed at the subject. The reverse is more likely to be true—that as the subject assumed public and political importance, scholars more often turned their attention to it. Why white-collar crime came forth as a major issue is a matter of considerable importance, because understanding the dynamics of the situation offers an opportunity to continue to fuel the flame—presuming, of course, that the question of white-collar crime is reasonably deemed to be one that needs and will benefit from increased attention.

It is, perhaps, worthwhile to pin down a few of the signposts that signify the recent movement of white-collar crime into the limelight as an issue of importance. This colloquium itself certainly is one item of evidence documenting the trend. No such meeting ever had been held until a few years ago, despite the introduction of the concept of white-collar crime into the social-scientific literature almost four decades ago.[7] In the past eighteen months, there have been colloquia dedicated specifically to white-collar crime at the Temple Law School;[8] at the State University College of New York, Potsdam;[9] at the Battelle Human Affairs Research Center in Seattle, Washington;[10] and in Glen Cove, New York, under the sponsorship of Peat, Marwick, Mitchell, and Co.[11] Simultaneously, sessions on white-collar crime are now routinely incorporated into the programs of meetings of scholarly associations of sociologists, criminologists, and persons interested in issues of law and society. The 1980 national conferences of the Law and Society Association, held in Madison, Wisconsin; the American Sociological Association, in New York City; and the American Society of Criminology, in San Francisco, all included such panels. Two of the twelve sessions of the February 1981 meeting of the Western Society of Criminology in San Diego were devoted to white-collar crime, one under the heading of "Corporate Crime," and the other of "Government Crime." In 1980 at Caracas, Venezuela, white-collar crime, under the generic heading of "abuse of power," was for the first time a major agenda item at a United Nations Congress on criminology. The subject also has come to the fore in the work of the Council of Europe, headquartered in Strasbourg, France.

In the U.S. Congress, hearings on white-collar crime currently are

underway in the subcommittee on crime of the House Comm
the Judiciary.[12] At the same time, academic writing on the subject ha
almost geometrically. The bibliography at the end of this book p
some indication of the large amount of material about white-collar
that has been published recently.

Perhaps the surest sign of this development has been the decision by
authorities at the Federal Bureau of Investigation (FBI) to downgrade the
bureau's efforts to solve offenses such as bank robbery, in order to concentrate more intensively on a spectrum of frauds, corruption, and violations
of federal statutes that largely are designed to control the behavior of members of the more "respectable" elements of society. The enforcement priorities established by the Department of Justice now give preeminence to acts
such as "crimes against the government by public officials, including federal,
state, and local corruption" and "crimes against consumers, including
defrauding of consumers, antitrust violations, energy pricing violations, and
related illegalities."[13] In fiscal 1979, 21 percent of the FBI investigative
resources was reported to have been allocated to efforts to combat white-
collar crime or organized crime, compared with less than 10 percent each for
crimes against the person and crimes against property.[14] Similarly, the Law
Enforcement Assistance Administration (LEAA) has assiduously increased
its attention to white-collar crime in terms of research and action grants.

Finally, the work of Ralph Nader and his colleagues merits special mention.[15] It is likely that Nader's campaigns spearheaded priority reconsidera-
tions with respect to white-collar crime. The fact that Nader, although he
continues his muckraking with undiminished efficiency, appears to have
less support today than in past years may be a reflection of a short public attention span and/or of a need for new heroes and new issues. If so, this too
should be analyzed to derive lessons about the methods needed to avoid and
overcome public cynicism with respect to efforts toward reform.

It is evident that white-collar crime has become defined in the United
States—and, indeed, in most western countries—as a matter of consummate importance. How can that definition of the situation be solidified and
turned to its most productive ends?

Programmatic Underpinnings

There are two basic dimensions involved in penetrating and holding fast
public and political consciousness with respect to white-collar crime. Research and action programs ought to be directed to the enhancement of
these dual conditions.

1. *The first has to do with convincing persons that white-collar crime is a
   serious matter and that it is to their advantage to do something about it.
   This involves a joint appeal to conscience and to self-interest.*

2. *The second is related to the need to establish that there exist reasonable
   potentialities for resolution of problems of white-collar crime in a satisfying and satisfactory manner.*

People have little patience with irresolvable issues. There is not much
hope for sustaining interest very long if persons do not believe there is some
hope for improvement, a hope best sustained by demonstrated evidence.

The issue of crime illustrates this point. Crime has always been with us,
but only in 1964 in the United States did it surface as a paramount political
issue. Both presidential candidates that year concentrated on convincing the
electorate that they possessed the will and the expertise to protect us from
the outrages of street offenses. In 1966, President Johnson appointed a
Commission on Law Enforcement and Administration of Justice to study
the problem of crime and to formulate a national approach to the matter.
Subsequent presidential elections saw opponents vying to convince the
public that they would deal with matters of crime skillfully. In 1972, President Nixon stressed in his campaign that he now was winning the war
against crime, noting that during the first six months of the year the crime
rate *increase* was "only" one percent, lower than for any period during the
previous decade.

The denunciation of crime in presidential politics is well known. Crime
continues to be a matter of great public anxiety: In fact, it is likely that
such anxiety is now greater than ever before in U.S. history. A September
1980 report, subtitled *America Afraid*, indicated that "fear of crime in the
United States far outstrips the rising incidence of crime and is slowly
paralyzing society."[16] But national office seekers have totally abandoned
the issue; it was not mentioned by either major presidential nominee in his
acceptance speech. Candidates were perfectly aware that federal policies at
best could have only a marginal impact on the amount and kind of crime
occurring. But such realities did not dissuade rhetoric. The abandonment of
the issue probably is a function of the fact that it seems like a no-win
situation, apt to haunt an incumbent in later years. It is noteworthy that
the abandonment of crime as a national political issue has been accompanied by a severe reduction in the amount of federal funds allotted to
research and action. The moral seems clear: Not only the significance of
an issue, but also its potential resolution must inform research and policy
devoted to it. It is with such a goal in mind that the present blueprint is being set forth.

It follows from the foregoing observations that a step of overarching
importance is to determine with respect to white-collar crime its biography
both as a scholarly endeavor and as a matter of public concern. It was noted
during one colloquium session that the civil-rights movement, the unequal
treatment of rich and poor, and the current economic malaise afloat in the

United States (the last carrying with it a need for scapegoats) may lie at the core of the increase in attention to white-collar crime. I can offer no better explanatory roster, but I suspect that the matter is a good deal more complicated, particularly if it is examined historically and cross-culturally. It might be worthwhile to try to pinpoint both social conditions and personal attitudes as they relate to views—and to the intensity of such views—with respect to different forms of white-collar crime. Are feelings about the need for economic equality related closely to indignation about illegal forms of exploitation of others? Or are general economic conditions better bases for predicting the level of concern about this or that kind of white-collar crime? Who believes what about the subject, and what do people do, and what do they say they are willing to do about white-collar crime? A clearer mapping of the nature and behavior of the constituency is needed.

It would, of course, be particularly valuable to be able to document longitudinally the drift of public opinion on a wide spectrum of issues, and to relate these views and their alteration to changes in attitudes about white-collar crimes. It would have been useful to have followed carefully developments in the Watergate scandal in order to determine how these bore on attitudes about upper-class illegalities in general and how they related to the level of confidence in politics and business throughout the nation. Was it those who were most loyal to the president who later became the most cynical? Or did these people—and, if so, which of them?—take refuge in explanations and rationalizations of the kind that protect all of us from some of the discomfiting aspects of life?

Documenting the ebb and flow of public opinion on white-collar crime has two particularly important policy ingredients. First, it allows a determination of how people's feelings about different aspects of the situation are related to their own situation and to external events. Second, the tapping and circulation of such views tends to legitimize and strengthen them. The indignation of many people about street crime led others, who had not given the problem much thought, to become indignant themselves when the problem was effectively called to their attention. It may be that, in truth, people have trouble summoning up much indignation about most aspects of white-collar crime. If so, this is worth knowing. It does not follow—even, or especially, in a democracy—that the prevailing positions should determine policy. The results only indicate (presuming that those who form policy themselves believe white-collar crime to be a serious problem) that ways must be found to persuade others of the accuracy of views contrary to their own. It is always easier to do this if the nature of public opinion is thoroughly known and appreciated.

I particularly favor institutionalizing the monitoring of sentiments over a continuing period of time. Short-term surveys tend to have only a short-lived impact, and this transience defeats the purpose of keeping the subject and the temperature of feelings about it continuously in the limelight. The census bureau or a Gallup-type organization with an ongoing mandate would be particularly valuable in carrying out work that spotlights attitudes and the conditions that affect such attitudes with respect to white-collar crime.

The Definitional Dilemma

In this section I will consider the much-addressed matter of settling on a "proper" definition of the bounds of the realm of white-collar crime. This matter has preoccupied many persons since the birth of the concept. Some argue that without precision of definition, generalizations float and lack adequate anchorage. Others insist that some common-sense guidelines ought to suffice until more information is at hand to allow sophisticated distinctions to be drawn between the diverse kinds of behavior that are being studied as part of the work on white-collar crime. These persons believe that there is a general understanding of what kinds of acts clearly constitute white-collar crime, with some acceptable fuzziness at the interstices. Things such as anti-trust violations and Medicaid fraud by physicians would be well within the ambit of white-collar crime. Some other illegalities can only arguably be regarded as falling within the definitional confines of the category—for example, organized schemes to cheat home owners by pretending to do roof repairs after the customers have been gulled into believing that their homes require such work. Cheating on applications for food stamps or welfare payments by persons in the lower socioeconomic strata also is not a clear contender for classification as white-collar crime. Why such acts should (or should not) be regarded as white-collar crime is debatable, and the decision will go to whoever makes the most-persuasive case in terms of the utility of one or another classificatory scheme for the purpose of insight and action.

The task of defining white-collar crime is in many ways wearisome, perhaps best left to those with a predilection for medieval theological debates. What is required for the moment is taxonomy, based on:

1. Existing law (note, for instance, the U.S. Department of Justice's precise listing of each of the statutes it enforces that it considers as falling within the category of white-collar crime.[17]
2. Determinations of forms of harm.
3. Categorization of the traits of offenders, especially their position in the occupational structure, as such position bears on their illegal behavior.
4. Modus operandi.
5. Types of victims of the offenses, whether customers, competitors, the general public, or the offender's own organization, among others.

Each of these delineations would have its particular value, depending on the task it is called on to perform; each could form the basis for additional discussion and refinement.

There remains also the possibility of discarding the term *white-collar crime* on the ground that it is too imprecise—even, perhaps, too inflammatory. There is a tendency, particularly outside the United States, to employ terms such as *economic crime* and *occupational crime* for the kinds of acts regarded here as white-collar crime. I would resist such a temptation, despite its greater intellectual purity, on the basis of the argument that pervades this chapter—that it is essential for satisfactory resolution of problems associated with white-collar crime for a forceful constituency to dedicate itself to this end. However metaphorical and imprecise, the term *white-collar crime* conjures up a real set of ills, and is particularly satisfactory in solidifying an emotional and intellectual concern about such ills. I take seriously Gordon's speculation that it is not that the police and the public show greater concern about working-class crime because greater interpersonal violence is involved, but, rather, that working-class crime is seen to involve greater interpersonal violence because the police show greater concern about it.[18]

The Sense of Seriousness

It is argued that the idea of "harm" remains the "most underdeveloped concept in our criminal law."[19] The concept of harm is by no means a simple one. An elaborate philosophical discussion by Kleinig of the ramifications of harm argues that "there is not much mileage to be gained by explicating harm in terms of loss, damage, or injury," because these are nothing but synonyms for most crime; therefore, they lack analytical power. Kleinig advocates as more promising the characterization of harm as "interference with or invasions of a person's interests"; but he grants that the idea of "interests," if it is to be the basis of testable propositions, poses some heady definitional problems.[20]

Nonetheless, the need to establish with some precision the parameters of real and perceived harm from a variety of forms of white-collar crime seems to me to carry a very high research priority. Recently, many white-collar-crime research veterans have been put in our place by a number of writers who regard as inaccurate our conclusions about what we consider a mood of public indifference toward most varieties of white-collar offenses.[21] The tradition of castigating the public for its inertia about white-collar crime, well established by the Biblical prophets, traces its social-science origins to Ross, who in the early 1900s bemoaned the fact that white-collar offenses "lack the brimstone smell."[22] Kadish built policy on presumed public position, noting that the offenses were perceived as "morally neutral," and arguing that punitive sanctioning was untoward when the matter at issue involved no more than the redistribution of fiscal resources.[23] I was pleased to note that one of the colloquium speakers fell back on this position by suggesting that the absence of public outrage was one of the major conditions that handicapped effective prosecution of white-collar-crime cases in his jurisdiction. C. Wright Mills agreed, too. He thought that the basis of our tolerance of despicable and illegal behavior by persons in the upper echelons of our social system stemmed from the fact that we were envious of them, that in our secret hearts we applauded the exploits of the latter-day robber barons, that we hoped some day to have our own chance to do the same.[24]

But the conclusion of the most-recent work—Mills, Kadish, Ross, and the rest of us notwithstanding—is that if harms resulting from white-collar offenses are congruent with those resulting from street crimes, then the public will regard such offenses as equivalently serious and dangerous, and will call for equally stern, if not sterner, punitive measures against the per-petrators of such offenses. This conclusion stems largely from a reworking of data gathered by Rossi and his colleagues as part of a general sampling of public opinion about a variety of criminal activities.[25]

This is an extraordinarily important line of research. It demands further exploration and fine tuning. It is important because, if true, it provides a firmer basis for more-effective action against white-collar crime, action that this chapter constantly suggests is essential if the nascent concern is not to flag and ultimately to disappear. Of course, there is also a subtler agenda that lies behind such work. By establishing a priori the idea that measure-ment of stipulated harms is an important area to be examined, such equi-valence then assumes that very importance: The connective link becomes set in place. It thereafter becomes difficult to argue that a victim is less dead if killed by pollution than if killed by an intrafamily homicide. But the equivalence of the deaths—in a society attuned to cause and effect and to locating blame—must be documented and highlighted if the comparison is to be manifest and effective.

In chapter 2, Meier and Short underlined some of the deficiencies of the existing data on which the conclusion about similar public responses to traditional and white-collar offenses producing the same harm is based. There was, for instance, the problem of drift in responses. That is, when the same question was twice put to the same respondent group, the answers tended at times to be significantly different. This undercuts the credibility of the results.

Obviously, there is a vital need for a study that moves beyond obtaining simple public responses to questionnaire items in which the rich details of the various white-collar offenses are presented in shorthand as truncated, brief items. Although similarly truncated queries are used as interview items

for both traditional street offenses and white-collar crimes,
much broader repertoire of affect. Mention a mugger, and ?
of stereotypes that excuse and/or aggravate the offense co₁
The fact is that the behaviors about which the questions are as
much more complicated matters than the item the respondent
with. For the white-collar crime, we have not only the objectiv₁
finds its way into the questionnaire inquiry but, among other thin₁
defendant of good manners and amiable mien, who has purchaseᴅ a lawyer
who can, articulately and persuasively, put the very best light on sometimes
fuzzy and arguable factual situations. Indeed, as the Ford Pinto case so well
illustrated, the fundamental issue of the defendant's criminal responsibility
for the harm—assumed out-of-hand in the questionnaire studies—often is
much more problematic in white-collar crime cases than in the usual street
offenses.[26] (That is, there has been a death; a gunshot caused it; did the
defendant or did someone else produce that death by firing the gun? Contrast this with: There has been a death caused by cancer; was the cancer,
which did not show up until years later, induced by the asbestos dust that
the worker inhaled? Was the defendant responsible for the site conditions
that produced the asbestos-fiber-level violations? Did he know that he was
acting in a criminally negligent manner?)

On these lines, I would advocate strong support of extensive research
seeking to plumb the range of public attitudes toward white-collar offenses
and offenders, and the nuances of such attitudes. A variety of videotaped
trials, with their components varied along important dimensions, could be
employed as stimuli. Respondents should not only be members of the general
public and specialized publics (such as prosecutors and corporate officials),
but also persons gathered into jury-like groups. English researchers have
evolved a procedure in which they employ "shadow juries"—persons on
the regular jury panel who at the moment are not being pressed into active
duty.[27] These persons then witness an actual or simulated trial, and
thereafter reach their decision under the unobtrusive scrutiny of the
criminal-justice research team.

There is also much to be learned from follow-up inquiries with members
of juries who sat through trials of persons prosecuted for white-collar
crimes. There is a growing literature suggesting that most lay persons do not
readily comprehend the often complicated and abstruse evidence that such
trials may entail.[28] They are said to reach their verdicts in terms of spurious
consideration, often in a so-called *mumpsimus* manner.[29] There is a belief
that such juries, failing to appreciate the state's evidence, are apt to decide,
more readily than they should, that there is a benefit of a doubt working for
the white-collar-crime offender. Other commentators, on the contrary, believe that regular jury members are best suited for *all* kinds of criminal
trials, because the integrity of the jury system guarantees things that would

be lost under a system of blue-ribbon juries made up of persons particularly competent to weigh white-collar-crime evidentiary matters. This is a testable proposition, and it ought to be tested.

The aim of the suggested public-opinion and jury probes should be to determine and to circulate widely the state of responsiveness to diverse aspects of white-collar crime. In the course of such statements, it would not be remiss to point out discrepancies that come to be perceived between different forms of death-dealing behavior, and to suggest reasons for this situation, if it proves to be so. It should also prove valuable if we were able to secure satisfactory evidence of the relationship between white-collar crime and other forms of criminal behavior. It is believed by many persons that the existence of upper-class lawbreaking impels other kinds of violations—that is, those within their domain—by persons with less power and fewer resources.

Additional Activist Inquiries

There are a number of other noteworthy paths to better understanding and advertising of white-collar crimes. Their value is to be judged in terms of their likely impact on the behavior.

Statistics

There exists a pressing need for a continuing statistical series that addresses the extent of white-collar crime. Most authorities concede that, for starters, it would be necessary to confine the reporting system to offenses that come under the jurisdiction of the federal regulatory agencies and the U.S. Department of Justice. There now exists an outstanding review of possible data sources on white-collar crime and a sophisticated critique of their shortcomings and potentialities if certain reforms were introduced.[30]

I would take a first step toward further research and action in this realm by inaugurating as quickly as possible, either within the Department of Justice or externally, what for now would have to be a primitive centralized reporting procedure. It would rely on information supplied by the agencies that enforce white-collar-crime laws. Such agencies would be given guidelines for reporting, but it would be appreciated that by and large the information they would provide would not be comparable from one agency to another in any serious way. Comparison would require an array of interpretative aids and suitable reservations about what the reports mean.

The annual document that would emerge from this operation would serve as a research-action-propaganda mechanism. For one thing, it would draw the attention of the public to the work in the criminal arena of the federal agencies, and to some of the results of that work. In so doing, it would reinforce incentives of the agencies to do this part of their job particularly effectively. Like the Uniform Crime Reports, the document would provide a source for continuing public enlightenment and agitation.

Presumably, in the long run the proposed project, by its very existence, would exert continuing leverage on the agencies for more-equivalent kinds of reporting, and for a better rationalization of their procedures, where such reforms are appropriate. It would force the agencies to explain publicly any striking changes either in their activities or in their reporting systems from one year to the next, by putting their crime-related work under closer scrutiny. And it would provide research workers with a readily available source of information for use in hypothesis testing and other kinds of research work for which some statistical baseline is essential.

Costs

The statistical inventory just proposed could provide a basis for some tentative attempt to gather cost figures for white-collar crime. No person who has even dabbled in the subject of white-collar crime is immune to the recurring question from media and political sources: Just how much does white-collar crime cost the public? Some of the less gun shy, or more reckless, of us in the field have attempted to attach numerical quantities that they maintain reflect the cost of white-collar crime. Such persons in general are not notably careful to employ any precision in designating exactly what their figures cover. Indeed, once a set of numbers receives prominent display, future commentators are apt to seize on it, perhaps add an inflation factor to bring it up to date, and carry on from there.

Obviously, cost figures are believed to be an important element of the study of white-collar crime. It probably is foolhardy to take the high-minded position that the numbers now in circulation are totally meaningless, except as part of a scare tactic or part of an effort to call attention, somewhat raucously, to the significance of white-collar crime as a national issue. I have no objection to tactics of spotlighting, which, indeed, seem to me, basic at present in the area of white-collar crime. But it seems both important and responsible to base the attention on information that has true meaning, and on results that can be obtained—or rebutted—by others who follow the same data-gathering processes. At the moment, the situation with respect to cost estimates for white-collar crime meets neither of these criteria.

The cost issue, then, deserves some research priority, but probably only to the extent that probes are directed scrupulously to carefully specified kinds of issues. This work should not be done by other than highly skilled economists, preferably persons with considerable training in the matter of placing financial consequences of particular behaviors within relevant categories.

Media

The media represent the catalyst by means of which attitudes toward white-collar crime and white-collar criminals are crystallized. I believe there is no arguing that the media in the United States have not, to date, been notably attentive to matters of white-collar crime, except when they involve notoriously "newsworthy" figures or dramatic illegal actions. At the same time, it was observed during our colloquium that *The Wall Street Journal*, the voice of the business community, abounds with reports of frauds, extortions, violations, and sundry other white-collar crimes. The amount of space devoted by that newspaper of the corporate world to law violations within the ranks of its major subscribers seems a bit surprising to a constant reader. This may offer a clue to the fact that an untapped source of important information and action about white-collar crime lies within the business world itself. If businessmen could be convinced that rectitude pays—both in terms of public relations and by eliminating corrupt competitors—the fight against white-collar crime would have enrolled some powerful allies. The domain of business attitudes toward white-collar crime, then, needs thorough exploration.

To return to the media, it should be noted that there never has been a good counting of what they say and how much they report about white-collar crime. Content analyses and line counts comparing papers such as *The Wall Street Journal* with other dailies, with the weekly news magazines, and with the television networks and local stations could provide valuable information. The items that appear in these outlets could be compared with the news releases from regulatory agencies and from the prosecutorial offices from which a large part of such information is gleaned. In addition, it would be interesting to relate public opinion about white-collar crime to particular news stories about its occurrence. There now exist excellent mass-communication techniques that could be employed to determine the things that newspaper readers see and how much and what they retain—or distort. These techniques should be brought into play for research on white-collar crime.

There is a further need to compare the perceptions of the parties involved in news stories with the facts that are transmitted to the public. It is commonplace among virtually all persons who recieve media attention that what they say and do is distorted, or at the least is placed in an inaccurate, or perhaps an unflattering, light. Do white-collar offenders feel that they get a fair deal when their cases are covered? Do prosecutors? What distortions do they believe are inserted into the reports of their activities? How do they handle the press and the television crews? And what implications does all of this have for basic issues in white-collar crime: its detection, the framing of public opinion about it, and its control?

The best-known commentary on this issue of media handling of white-collar crime is the examination of media response to the General Electric anti-trust conspiracy in 1961, which concluded that because of the "negative and emasculated reporting of this issue by the bulk of the nation's press [the] reaction of the American public to the largest antitrust suit in our history has generally been that of mute acquiescence."[31] Harris Steinberg, an attorney who defends white-collar persons accused of crimes, disagrees, maintaining that trials of white-collar offenders are subject to extensive reports in the media and that they produce acute discomfort among defendants because they influence their standing with colleagues whose good opinion they value.[32] Certainly, the response of one General Electric conspirator disclosed grave anxiety. "There goes my whole life. Who's going to want to hire a jailbird? What am I going to tell my children?" he was quoted as saying.[33] Note, however, the following courtroom interchange:

> Federal District Judge Barrington D. Parker told Mr. Helms [the former director of the CIA, accused of lying under oath about the agency's contributions to undermine the Allende government in Chile] before sentencing: "You dishonored your oath and now you stand before this court in disgrace and shame."
>
> "I don't feel disgraced at all," Mr. Helms later told reporters outside the courtroom after sentencing.[34]

It may be noted that Helms's attorney, Edward Bennett Williams, had told the judge in the courtroom that Helms would "bear the scar of a conviction for the rest of his life." Following the trial, Williams told newspaper reporters that his client would "wear his conviction like a badge of honor."[35]

Another particularly fine source on the subject of white-collar crime involves the trade publications of the business community. These outlets often express much more frankly and openly—since they are oriented toward the in-group—the opinions that permeate the industries that are served by the publications.

Case Studies

Differences continue to exist among persons working in the area of white-collar crime about the need to accumulate, to a much greater extent than we have to date, elaborate case studies of individual offenses. A contrary view is that a more-pressing task is to take what we now have and attempt to generalize about it. There are also those who believe that there has been too much free-floating investigation of white-collar crime, and that the basic requirement now is to have such work guided by theoretical notions of some sophistication and pressed into service to test such notions.

The simplest answer—and, I believe, the truest one at this time—is that all these kinds of work require attention and resources. There is no need to exhort persons to concentrate on the latter two research areas—they have deep disciplinary support—but I think that a strong case should be made for the continuing accumulation of detailed examinations of individual cases of white-collar offending, particularly those employing the corporate form to carry out the lawbreaking. Such studies should fuel grander theoretical explorations and, in particular, can provide sparks of insight that otherwise would be overlooked by persons who started with predetermined questions that exclusively occupied their attention.

It is correctly maintained that case-study work has a tendency toward the journalist. But journalism itself is not an unencumbered exercise; it too is directed by a set of postulates that determine what a reporter will or will not see, and what he or she will report. In that sense, case studies of white-collar crime conducted by trained criminal-justice research workers inevitably will be responsive to the kinds of issues that are stressed in the education that the research workers have received, an education most usually in sociology, economics, criminal justice, or law. It usually is a good idea to have as large as possible an accumulation of factual information before venturing too far theoretically. It is the little facts, the elder Huxley once remarked, that break the back of the grand theories (Huxley also cynically noted that, though moribund, such grand theories have a tendency to carry on as if they were viable).

Case studies, with their particularity and their drama, make interesting and appropriate targets of inquiry. Throughout this book there has been constant reference to this or that case in order to support a more-general position. At the colloquium, we heard both informally and in the prepared papers about the Ford Pinto case, the Lockheed overseas bribes, and the Firestone 500 scandal, among many others. Detailed examination of episodes such as these refines, expands, or contradicts our current beliefs, and points to new areas in which productive insights might lie.

Again, longitudinal probes tying the cases to public attitudes might well prove valuable. I recall Charles Winick's rather ingenious little study, in which he asked a group of persons what the Mad Bomber (as the newspapers had dubbed him), then at work blowing up pieces of New York, would prove to be like when and if he or she finally was apprehended. The responses provided an intriguing glimpse of how stereotypically such persons are viewed, although they were almost totally awry in describing the mild-mannered old man with a grudge against the electric company who had committed the offenses.[36] How did people view the culpability of the Ford Company in the Pinto case? What did they think of the Indiana statute? Did their views change as the evidence in the trial unfolded? Did they agree with the verdict, and did it produce any alteration of their original position? How did Ford personnel see the prosecution, and what, if any, behavior and attitudinal changes did it introduce into their ranks and those of their competitors?

A research approach in this vein that I have always favored—although it has its problems—involves the monitoring on diverse sites of essentially similar kinds of cases. How is Medicaid fraud handled in California, New York, North Dakota, and Georgia? The work of different researchers at different sites often can produce complementary materials that illuminate an issue much more brightly than do uncoordinated kinds of examinations.

Organizational Studies

Undoubtedly, the most-important recent surge in white-collar-crime work has been the movement toward a focus on organizational function and structure as these bear on the amount and types of violations.[37] Most fundamentally, this work replaces emphasis on the individuals involved in the offenses with a focus on the organizational climate. It considers matters such as the interaction of executives, the ethos of the bureaucratic structure, the play of the market, business demands, and ethical codes as forming the roots of white-collar crime. A particular advantage of such work is that it brings to bear concepts that have been tested and refined in a well-established field of inquiry on an area of work where they largely have been overlooked. The title of an article by Gross quintessentially delineates the nature of this newer work; it is called "Organizations as Criminal Actors."[38]

In this article, Gross demonstrates how an organizational focus can prove fruitful for pinpointing imperatives pressing toward illegal behavior when he notes a study that examined data on violations of antitrust laws and FTC rules by private firms and found an inverse relationship between the "munificence" of an organization's environment and the likelihood of its being cited for unfair market practices and restraint of trade.[39] This conclusion duplicates an earlier result obtained by Lane, and is in line with some of the findings of Clinard's updating and refinement of the pioneering study of corporate crime by Sutherland.[40] Further pursuit of organizational analysis in the area of white-collar crime should enjoy a high research priority. Also, the vast accumulation of materials by Clinard offers a corpus of data for reanalysis in terms of a number of particularistic hypotheses that are implicit or suggested in the more-general study. Finally, there is a need to integrate the large body of literature on the delinquent activities of juvenile gangs with the study of white-collar crime. Theoretical and empirical work on gangs stands out as probably the best large and cumulative collection of materials in criminology, and it has a direct bearing on how groups organize in terms of their behavior vis-à-vis the law.[41]

What I particularly would like to see in organizational studies of white-collar crime would be on-site investigation—that is, participant-observer work carried out by persons who obtain employment within the corporate world and report on the basis of ethnographic field study about the day-to-day job climate and activities, and the manner in which these bear on attitudes and behaviors with respect to the laws requiring the company's activities.

Various chapters of this book also have discussed the possible value of ethical codes in containing business behavior that otherwise might violate the criminal law. Generally, outsiders are skeptical about the utility of such codes, suggesting that they look good on paper but are by and large ineffective. They are often seen as placating exercises designed to quiet external criticisms of a business or trade. But the matter seems worth more-detailed scrutiny. How are such codes generated, what do they say (and not say), and how seriously are they taken by those who promulgate them and those to whom they are directed—indeed, how well are their contents known to the relevant parties?

More generally, the absorption of behavior standards with respect to the law, as these standards penetrate an organizational structure, demands close investigation. Again, longitudinal study appears likely to produce particularly worthwhile information, especially continuing study of a panel of junior executives from the time they enroll in business school through the period when they move up (if they do so) into the ranks of management. Becker and his associates have provided a model in his study of the socialization of medical students into the role of practicing doctor, but we lack a good study that duplicates this kind of investigation for the business schools, and beyond their doors.[42] At what point does the young career person begin to identify with goals that involve violation of the law, and in what manner does he come to this position? Cressey's study of embezzlers suggests that a triad of conditions has to be in place before a person will commit a defalcation; are these and/or other items involved in violations of laws regulating corporate behavior?[45] And how about the whistleblowers? What takes place within themselves or in their corporate experience that pushes them to inform on their employer?

Similarly, we ought to know more precisely the nature of the rationalizations that permit violators in the world of white-collar crime to carry out their illegal acts. We suspect that virtually all offenders against the criminal law incorporate a set of "explanations" of their behavior that redefines it in a light that they find comfortable to live with. "The law was inexact," they might say. Or, "We never knew we were violating any law." "We did what we did for the best interest of our employees." Or, "Nobody lost anything through our actions." These are among the innumerable responses of accused white-collar law violators. The nature of such responses, their distribution by offense and offender, is worth examination. It has been suggested in one investigation that the most-effective manner

for dealing with "respectable" lawbreakers—shoplifters,
stance—is to penetrate the shell of their structure of rationa
force them to redefine their behavior in more meretricious term
seem especially important to compare offenders with nonofl
respect to a large number of factors that must illuminate the di:
tween law-abiding and lawbreaking acts.

Miscellaneous Matters

A number of other matters merit passing attention as promising research
realms. Interviews with incarcerated white-collar offenders could yield
material parallel to that which we have derived from studies of other kinds
of inmates: The offenders could reflect on their past behavior, inform us
about their presumed future, and give us ideas about their perception of the
suitability of sentence. More than most personnel involved in white-collar
crime, these people represent an available study population, literally one
with time on its hands, and probably one that would prove reasonably
cooperative. Similarly, retired business executives with no existing stake in
their careers probably could provide valuable ideas about the acts and attitudes of the workplace while they were involved in it that could bear on
our understanding of white-collar crime. Courtrooms also offer outstanding research sites, since the Sixth Amendment allows untrammeled access to
their environs; an astute observer, watching a series of white-collar-crime
trials, could add greatly to our knowledge of their dynamics. Similarly, the
Freedom of Information Act offers an unequaled opportunity to obtain
data that long has been denied researchers and that could prove invaluable
for more-informed studies of white-collar crime.[45] Finally, there is a need to
launch and evaluate programs designed to incorporate awareness of white-
collar crime in students at the secondary level, in colleges and universities,
and in professional schools.

Controlling White-Collar Crime

The ultimate goal of concomitantly increasing concern and encouraging
research about white-collar crime is to enhance the quality of life for the
general public and for those who currently are harmed by such behaviors.
There is a need in this context to determine the effectiveness of existing and
proposed methods for dealing with white-collar crime and those who
perpetrate it.

As in most aspects of criminological work, the issue of *deterrence* is a
crucial issue with respect to white-collar crime. Considerable controversy

exists about the fairness and efficacy of a panoply of punishments that are suggested for white-collar-crime offenders. The penal sanction is sometimes said to be notably useful in deterrence terms because white-collar criminals in general are believed to be rational planners and persons particularly responsive to the shame and degradation of incarceration.[46] Other writers feel that the focus on criminal enforcement and penal sanctions so emasculates efficiency—largely because of the complex nature of the cases—that is it counterproductive.[47] There also is a strong belief that penal sanctions usually are much too harsh for white-collar crime, and that there are other enforcement consequences that would prove more effective in terms of both specific and general deterrence.

Equal-protection laws seem to inhibit any truly experimental designs that might definitively test some of the basic propositions surrounding these disparate viewpoints. But there are naturalistic conditions that can be scrutinized closely; that is, we can concentrate on monitoring carefully the apparent consequences of one or another method that is employed for dealing with specific instances of white-collar crime. In terms of consent decrees, for instance—a subject that has aroused some controversy—it would appear worthwhile to determine how businesses feel about the severity of such decrees, and how their future behavior appears to be influenced by the entering of a consent decree against them. Certainly, the effectiveness of the sanction of publicity, strongly recommended in some well-argued papers by Fisse, should be looked at along a variety of exploratory dimensions.[48] Anthony Sampson, for instance, noted in anecdotal fashion that a suit against ITT was followed by a boom in business for the Sheraton Hotels, which ITT owned, because, he thought, any publicity—even bad publicity—created name awareness, an essential element in consumer appeal.[49]

It needs to be considered also that some punishments can result in behaviors worse than those they were designed to alleviate. An illustration is provided in the area of sex offenses by Graham:

> In Scotland, even more feared than the pillory was the punishment of having to appear in church every Sunday for a given number of weeks . . . to be harangued for half an hour in front of the congregation by the minister—for which, in some churches, offenders were fastened to the wall in iron collars, or jougs. This was the penalty for adulterers and fornicators of both sexes, and was greatly feared. So much so, that it caused a sharp rise in the infanticide rate, for women who had illegitimately become pregnant preferred to risk the capital penalty for infanticide rather than admit the facts and suffer such extreme humiliation.[50]

The range of penalties proposed for white-collar crimes involving corporations has included suspension of corporate managers and board members, temporary bans on corporate advertising because of deceptive practices, required publication of violations to inform consumers, and imposition of corporate bankruptcy.[51] Determining the comparative utility of such sanctions is not a simple matter, but it is one that requires considerable attention. In the area of probation, too, the idea that a white-collar offender, as a condition of his probation, must submit to a reasonable audit of his financial dealings and must provide periodic statements of his income and expenses, is another innovative measure—among many others proposed—that ought to be given a trial and subjected to evaluation.[52]

A detailed analysis of the role of statutory requirements as they bear on the effective delineation and control of white-collar crime also must receive a high priority on any research agenda. The Library of Congress recently completed a review of laws dealing with the liability of corporate officials for the negligence of persons who are supposed to be under their supervision.[53] We could use further inventories of laws and their implications for dealing with white-collar offenses and offenders. August Bequai, for example, records what he regards as the archaic nature of the legal and administrative arrangements in the federal government today for dealing with complex white-collar crimes. First, he refers to consumer-fraud cases:

> Prosecuting consumer fraud cases, as with other white-collar crimes, is seriously hampered by various drawbacks. It is difficult, for example, to prove that, in fact, the outcome has been the product of a willful intent to defraud the public rather than an error in business judgement. In addition, the felons in these cases argue that their agents, and not they, were behind the scheme. Proving that both agent and principal acted jointly is rarely an easy task. Felons also argue, in defense, that it is merely salesmanship, that in every business there concededly is an element of "puffing." Liability is difficult to attach to the actual manipulators, and as a consequence, prosecution usually takes the form of an injunction or consent agreement. Criminal actions are rare and hampered by a judiciary that metes out lenient sentences against those convicted of frauds.[54]

There recently have been some fine detailed studies of the sentencing practices and dynamics behind them in white-collar-crime cases.[55] As the implications of this work are absorbed, they undoubtedly will suggest fruitful follow-up investigations. But how do we deal with Bequai's sweeping allegation that:

> In large part, white-collar crime prosecutions have been hampered by bureaucratic redtape, absence of a firm commitment, the politicized nature of the present U.S. Attorney's Offices, and a hesitancy to shift prosecutorial strategies. The entire federal prosecutorial apparatus is in need of review and revision.[56]

This appears rather broad, but it does suggest that we could probably benefit from an organizational study of the prosecution of white-collar crime on both federal and state levels. In fact, the determination of the proper roles of state as compared with federal authorities in the field requires closer attention. My initial recommendation would be for the identification of particularly effective organizational arrangements, which then will be regarded as model programs, and for the subsequent reporting and dissemination of information about the arrangements and tactics that appear to be the foundation of their achievements.

With respect to prosecutorial tactics, the matter of whether white-collar-crime cases are pursued as civil suits or moved against under criminal law is another issue worthy of study. Instances that appear to me to merit criminal prosecution may well not be so treated because the persons involved, whatever desire for "revenge" or "justice" they may hold against the depredators, harbor an even greater desire to get a money settlement or reward. They would rather sue than see a crime prosecuted. State and federal attorneys are apt either to be overloaded with work or moved by a spirit that dictates that they will not do anything more than they absolutely must. There was a common-law doctrine, since fallen into disuse, that might well be reexamined as part of a general research probe into the whole issue of sanctions against white-collar crime. It required that:

> Where injuries are inflicted on an individual under circumstances which constitute a felony, that felony could not be made the foundation of a civil action at the suit of the person injured against the person who inflicted the injuries until the latter had been prosecuted or a reasonable excuse shown for his non-prosecution.[57]

There remains a dearth of useful information from other societies with respect to the enforcement procedures and sanctions that they employ for white-collar-crime violations. Such materials might well suggest more-effective ways we could marshal our resources for the same purposes. Chambliss has argued that, overall, socialist societies manifest less crime than capitalist societies. He believes that the seemingly striking variations in crime rates between places such as China and the Soviet Union are primarily a function of their degrees of commitment to the "true" principles of Marxist doctrine.[58] Criminologists working in communist societies like to point out that they have no corporate crime; but this is a bit of semantic sleight-of-hand, since they have no corporations. There is ample evidence that violations of the laws regulating their employment behavior by managers and employees of communist collectives is not at all uncommon,[59] and it may be that the extent of such crime provides support for Smigel's thesis that people find it easier to steal from impersonal organizations than they do from individuals or from small, more-intimate business enterprises.[60]

The vast array of cross-cultural information on white-collar crime that barely has been tapped to date might inform us about why some societies seem to produce a cadre of relatively honest and trustworthy political officeholders, whereas others are plagued by dishonesty among their officials.[61] In Japan, theorists speculate that custom and structural variables insist that officeholders engage in often illegal practices, largely as a function of fiscal demands placed on them by their constituents.[62] We might well learn more about our own society by distancing ourselves a bit to look at what happens elsewhere.

A Concluding Caveat

To take on the task of establishing some research and action priorities, in the manner that has been attempted in this chapter, itself implies an understanding of the elements of the process that will prove most effective in reaching preordained goals. That we possess such an understanding is, of course, arguable. We do not truly know whether the most-effective approach to stipulated success is to make available "suitable" sums of research money and to allow the imaginations and interest of those seeking such funds to dictate what they propose to accomplish, or whether the outcome is likely to be more satisfactory if preestablished, detailed blueprints are drawn up and workers forced to toil only within these set boundaries. There are strong arguments on both sides. Note, for instance, Cottrell's conclusion about the same problem and its consequences for the quality of the wall paintings and artifacts that are found in the tombs of early Egyptian pharoahs:

> In art the freedom of the craftsman was restrained by a rigid religious convention, but within the limits set by this convention, perhaps because of them, the Old Kingdom sculptors produced work of an austere beauty and majesty; work which . . . was never equalled by Egyptian craftsmen of later centuries.[63]

Cottrell's thesis regarding the enabling aspects of set boundaries finds support in Proust's remark that the "tyranny of rhyme" often forces poets "into the discovery of their finest lines."[64] These arguments for rigid structure and explicit guidelines, so that the worker does not flounder because of an overly amorphous assignment, are seconded by Riesman with respect to matters closer to our work here. Riesman suggests that superior results often are achieved in response to a mundane pragmatic issue, compared with the work done when grander concerns underlie the effort:

> [W]hen I examine the work done by scholars in universities in comparison with the applied work done in answer to some client's need, I cannot argue that the track of the discipline produces in general more seminal research than the quest of an answer to an extra-academic problem. Only a very rare person will be an intellectual self-starter.[65]

On the other side, the unbridled play of curiosity, the freedom to think in an unrestricted manner, is believed by some to be likely to yield the highest dividends. Indeed, arguments might be set forth that the basic thrust of our work here is counterproductive, since it formalizes too much, and in a collaborative manner, things that best should be individual enterprises. Let it be remembered that, in large measure, we all are present today because Edwin H. Sutherland, a lone scholar, working by himself with only library resources, came (by means of an obscure process that he called "differential association") to produce the classic work on a topic virtually ignored theretofore, a topic that he labeled "white-collar crime."[66] I have recently, with a colleague, traced in some detail the personal and intellectual sources that constituted Sutherland's patrimony; it seems that he chose his subject largely because it was one that interested him, and one about which he had strong feelings.[67] Most assuredly, the roots of his concern did not emerge from a preconstituted agenda. In short, like our subject, our purpose too contains many contentious components. At the very least, its efficacy should not be taken for granted. Indeed, even the commitment to a more-decent world, the commitment that I suggested lies behind work on white-collar crime, does not go unchallenged. Note the observation made by a character in a novel written by a law professor at the University of Michigan: "One receives only imperfect justice in this world; only fools, children, left-wing Democrats, social scientists, and a few demented judges expect anything better."[68] If so, our work here enlists us as part of a motley group, indeed.

Notes

1. The key article on the subject is Laura Shill Schrager and James F. Short, Jr., "How Serious a Crime? Perceptions of Organizational and Common Crimes," in Gilbert Geis and Ezra Stotland, eds., *White-Collar Crime: Theory and Research* (Beverly Hills, Calif.: Sage Publications, 1980), pp. 14-31.

2. Howard S. Becker, *Outsiders* (New York: Free Press, 1963), pp. 147-163.

3. Joseph R. Gusfield, *Symbolic Crusade* (Urbana: University of Illinois Press, 1966).

4. James Q. Wilson, *The Politics of Regulation* (New York: Basic Books, 1980); James Greene, *Regulatory Problems and Regulatory Reform: The Perceptions of Business* (New York: Conference Board, 1980).

5. Compare Seymour Martin Lipset and William Schneider, "The Public View of Regulation," *Public Opinion* 2 (January-February 1979):6-13.

6. Herbert Edelhertz and Marilyn Walsh, *The White-Collar Challenge to Nuclear Safeguards* (Lexington, Mass.: Lexington Books, D.C. Heath and Company, 1978).

7. Edwin H. Sutherland, 'White-Collar Criminality,'' *American Sociological Review* 5 (February 1940):1-12.

8. Symposium on White-Collar Crime, *Temple Law Quarterly*, 53, no. 4, 1980.

9. Proceedings, edited by Phillip Wickerman, to be published in 1981.

10. Herbert Edelhertz and Charles Rogovin, *A Strategy for Containing White-Collar Crime* (Lexington, Mass.: Lexington Books, D.C. Heath and Company, 1980).

11. See Robert K. Elliott and John J. Willingham, *Management Fraud: Detection and Deterrence* (New York: Petrocelli, 1980).

12. See U.S. Congress, House of Representatives, Committee on the Judiciary, Subcommittee on Crime (95th Congress, 2nd Session), *White-Collar Crime* (Washington, D.C.: U.S. Government Printing Office, 1979); Ibid. (96th Congress, 2nd Session), *Corporate Crime* (Washington, D.C.: U.S. Government Printing Office, 1980).

13. U.S. Attorney General, *National Priorities for the Investigation and Prosecution of White Collar Crime: Report of the Attorney General* (Washington, D.C.: U.S. Government Printing Office, 1980).

14. Ibid.

15. There is a small library of work produced by this group. See, for example, James S. Turner, *The Chemical Feast* (New York: Grossman, 1970); John C. Esposito, *The Vanishing Air* (New York: Grossman, 1970).

16. A-T-O Inc., *Figgie Report on Fear of Crime: America Afraid* (New York: Ruder and Rinn, 1980). See *Los Angeles Times*, 19 September 1980.

17. U.S. Attorney General, *National Priorities*, note 13.

18. David M. Gordon, "Capitalism, Class and Crime in America," *Crime and Delinquency* 19 (April 1973):163-186.

19. G.O.W. Mueller, "Criminal Theory: An Appraisal of Jerome Hall's Studies in Jurisprudence and Criminal Theory," *Indiana Law Journal* 34 (Winter 1959):220.

20. John Kleinig, "Crime and the Concept of Harm," *American Philosophical Quarterly* 15 (January 1978):27-36.

21. Schrager and Short, Jr., "How Serious a Crime?"; Marilyn E. Walsh and Donna D. Schram, "The Victim of White-Collar Crime: Accuser or Accused," in Gilbert Geis and Ezra Stotland, *White-Collar Crime: Theory and Research*, pp. 32-51 (Beverly Hills, Calif.: Sage Publications, 1980).

22. Edward Alsworth Ross, "The Criminaloid," *The Atlantic Monthly*, January 1970, pp. 44-50.

23. Sanford H. Kadish, "Some Observations on the Use of Criminal Sanctions in Enforcing Economic Regulations," *University of Chicago Law Review* 30 (Spring 1963):423-449.

24. C. Wright Mills, *The Power Elite* (New York: Oxford University Press, 1956), pp. 343-344.

25. Peter H. Rossi, Emily Waite, Christine E. Bose, and Richard E. Berk, "The Seriousness of Crimes: Normative Structure and Individual Differences," *American Sociological Review* 39 (April 1974):224-237.

26. See, generally, Ronald C. Kramer, "The Ford Pinto Homcide Prosecution: Criminological Questions and Issues Concerning the Control of Corporate Crime," Paper presented to the American Society of Criminology, Philadelphia, 1979.

27. Sarah McCabe and Frank Sutcliffe, *Defining Crime* (Oxford: Blackwell and Mott, 1978).

28. See, for example, "Now Juries Are on Trial: 'Big Cases' Call Into Question Their Ability to Do Justice," *Time*, 3 September 1979. A few federal judges have refused to allow jury trials in such cases, relying on a footnote in a 1970 Supreme Court decision that suggests that the Seventh Amendment right to a jury may be limited by "the practical abilities and limitations" or jurors.

29. In dictionary definition, *mumpsimus* refers to "an error or prejudice obstinately clung to; the term is supposedly taken from the story of an illiterate priest who, in his devotions, had for 30 years used *mumpsimus* for the proper Latin word *sumpsimus*, and who, on his mistake being pointed out to him, repied, 'I will not change my *mumpsimus* for your new *sumpsimus*. . . .' "

30. Albert J. Reiss, Jr., and Albert Biderman, *Data Sources on White-Collar Law-Breaking* (Washington, D.C.: U.S. Government Printing Office, 1980).

31. *The New Republic*, 20 February 1961, p. 7.

32. Harris B. Steinberg, "The Defense of the White-Collar Accused," *American Criminal Law Quarterly* 3 (Spring 1965):129-138.

33. Richard A. Smith, "The Incredible Electrical Conspiracy," *Fortune*, April 1961, pp. 132-137; *Fortune*, May 1961, pp. 161-164.

34. Quoted in Joseph Heller, *Good as Gold* (New York: Pocket Books, 1980), p. 357.

35. Ibid.

36. Charles Winick, "How People Perceived the 'Mad Bomber,' " *Public Opinion Quarterly* 25 (Spring 1961):25-38.

37. A key article is M. David Ermann and Richard J. Lundman, "Deviant Acts by Complex Organizations: Deviance and Social Control at the Organizational Level of Analysis," *Sociological Quarterly* 19 (Winter 1978):55-67.

38. Edward Gross, "Organizations as Criminal Actors," in Paul R. Wilson and John Braithwaite, eds., *Two Faces of Deviance* (St. Lucia: University of Queensland Press, 1978), pp. 199-213.

39. Barry M. Staw and Eugene Szwajkowski, "The Scarcity-Munificence Component of Organizational Environments and the Commission of Illegal Acts," *Administrative Science Quarterly* 20 (September 1975):345-354.

40. Robert E. Lane, "Why Businessmen Violate the Law," *Journal of Criminal Law, Criminology, and Police Science* 44 (July 1953):151-165; Marshall B. Clinard, *Illegal Corporate Behavior* (Washington, D.C.: U.S. Government Printing Office, 1979); Edwin H. Sutherland, *White-Collar Crime* (New York: Fryden, 1949).

41. Among the best known works are Albert K. Cohen, *Delinquent Boys* (New York: Free Press, 1955); Richard A. Cloward and Lloyd Ohlin, *Delinquency and Opportunity* (New York: Free Press, 1960); James F. Short, Jr., and Fred L. Strodtbeck, *Group Process and Gang Delinquency* (Chicago: University of Chicago Press, 1965); and Walter B. Miller, "Lower Class Culture as a Generating Milieu of Gang Delinquency," *Journal of Social Issues* 14 (April 1958):5-19.

42. Howard S. Becker, Blanche Geer, Everett C. Hughes, and Anselm L. Strauss, *Boys in White: Student Culture in Medical School* (Chicago: University of Chicago Press, 1961).

43. Donald R. Cressey, *Other People's Money: The Social Psychology of Embezzlement* (New York: Free Press, 1953).

44. Mary Owen Cameron, *The Booster and the Snitch* (New York: Free Press, 1964).

45. Susan Long, *The Internal Revenue Service: Measuring Tax Offenses and Enforcement Response* (Washington, D.C.: U.S. Government Printing Office, 1980).

46. Gilbert Geis, "Deterring Corporate Crime," in Ralph Nader and Mark J. Green, eds., *Corporate Power in America* (New York: Grossman, 1973), pp. 182-197.

47. Christopher D. Stone, *Where the Law Ends* (New York: Harper and Row, 1975).

48. See, for example, Brent Fisse, "The Use of Publicity as a Criminal Sanction Against Business Corporations," *Melbourne University Law Review* 8 (June 1971):107-150.

49. Anthony Sampson, *The Sovereign State of ITT* (New York: Stein and Day, 1973), p. 15.

50. Henry G. Graham, *The Social Life of Scotland in the 18th Century* (London: A&C Black, 1899), p. 43.

51. Morton Mintz and Jerry S. Cohen, *America, Inc.* (New York: Dial, 1971).

52. Elsie L. Reid, "Looking at the Law," *Federal Probation* 41 (June 1977):50.

53. See U.S. House of Representatives, *Corporate Crime.*

54. August Bequai, *White-Collar Crime: A 20th-Century Crisis* (Lexington, Mass.: Lexington Books, D.C. Heath and Company, 1978), p. 53.

55. See Kenneth Mann, Stanton Wheeler, and Austin Sarat, "Sentencing the White-Collar Criminal," *American Criminal Law Review* 17 (Spring 1980):479-500; Ilene Nagel Bernstein, John L. Hagan and Celesta Albonetti, "Differential Sentencing of White-Collar Offenders in Ten Federal Courts," *American Sociological Review* 45:802-820.

56. Bequai, *White-Collar Crime*, p. 151. See also Suzanne Weaver, *The Decision to Prosecute* (Cambridge, Mass.: MIT Press, 1977).

57. *Smith* v. *Selwyn*, 3 K.B. 98 (1914).

58. William Chambliss, Paper presented at Conference on Crime in Developing Countries, Ibadan, Nigeria, July 1980.

59. Walter D. Connor, *Deviance in Soviet Society* (New York: Columbia University Press, 1972).

60. Erwin O. Smigel, "Public Attitudes Toward 'Chiseling' With Reference to Unemployment Compensation," *American Sociological Review* 18 (February 1953):59-67.

61. Ronald Wraith and Edgar Simkins, *Corruption in Developing Countries* (London: Allen, 1963).

62. Mamoru Iga and Morton Auerback, "Political Corruption and Social Structure in Japan," *Asian Survey* 17 (June 1977):556-564.

63. Leonard Cottrell, *The Last Pharoahs* (London: Pann, 1977), p. 21.

64. Marcel Proust, *Swann's Way*, trans. C.K. Scott Moncrieft (New York: Modern Library, n.d.), p. 28.

65. David Riesman, "Law and Sociology," in William Evan, ed., *Law and Sociology* (New York: Free Press), p. 41.

66. Edwin H. Sutherland, "Crime of Corporations," in Albert Cohen, Alfred Lindesmith, and Karl Schuessler, eds., *The Sutherland Papers* (Bloomington: Indiana University Press, 1956), pp. 78-96; idem, "White-Collar Criminal."

67. Gilbert Geis and Colin Goff, "Edwin H. Sutherland: A Biographical and Analytical Commentary," Paper presented at Conference on White Collar and Economic Crime, Potsdam College of Arts and Sciences, Potsdam, New York, February 1980.

68. Walter F. Murphy, *The Vicar of Christ* (New York: Macmillan, 1979), p. 93.

Appendix:
Colloquium Authors
and Participants

Authors

Simon Dinitz, professor of sociology, Ohio State University, Columbus, Ohio   43210

M. David Ermann, associate professor of sociology, University of Delaware, Newark, Delaware   19711

Gilbert Geis, professor, Program in Social Ecology, University of California, Irvine, California   92717

Richard J. Lundman, associate professor of sociology, Ohio State University, Columbus, Ohio   43210

Robert F. Meier, associate professor, Social Research Center, Washington State University, Pullman, Washington   99164

James F. Short, professor, Social Research Center, Washington State University, Pullman, Washington   99164

Edwin H. Stier, director, Division of Criminal Justice, State of New Jersey, Princeton, New Jersey   43210

Ezra Stotland, director, Society and Justice Program, University of Washington, Seattle, Washington   98195

John M. Thomas, director, Center for Policy Studies, State University of New York, Buffalo, New York   14214

Participants

Bernard Auchter, program manager, National Institute of Justice, Washington, D.C.   20531

Richard Barnes, director, Center for the Study of the Correlates of Crime and Criminal Behavior, National Institute of Justice, Washington, D.C.   20531

W. Robert Burkhart, director, Office of Research Programs, National Institute of Justice, Washington, D.C.   20531

Herbert Edelhertz, director, Law and Justice Study Center, Battelle Human Affairs Research Centers, Seattle, Washington   98105

Donald Foster, director, Economic Crime Enforcement Unit Program, Criminal Division, U.S. Department of Justice, Washington, D.C. 20531

John Gardner, director, Office of Public Policy Research, University of Illinois at Chicago Circle, Chicago, Illinois   60680

Fred Heinzelmann, director, Community Crime Prevention Division, National Institute of Justice, Washington, D.C.   20531

Steven Hitchner, director, Office of Policy and Management Analysis, Criminal Division, U.S. Department of Justice, Washington, D.C. 20531

Barbara McClure, analyst in social legislation, Congressional Research Service, Library of Congress, Washington, D.C.   20540

Thomas D. Overcast, research scientist, Law and Justice Study Center, Battelle Human Affairs Research Centers, Seattle, Washington   98105

Mark Richard, deputy assistant attorney general, Criminal Division, U.S. Department of Justice, Washington, D.C.   20531

Miriam Saxon, analyst in social legislation, Congressional Research Service, Library of Congress, Washington, D.C.   20540

Joseph B. Tompkins, Office of Policy and Management Analysis, Criminal Division, U.S. Department of Justice, Washington, D.C.   20531

Stanton Wheeler, director, Yale/NIJ Research Agreements Program to Study White-Collar Crime, Yale University, New Haven, Connecticut 06520

National Institute of Justice Staff

Richard Laymon
Lois Mock
Richard Rau
Winifred Reed

Bibliography

Books

American Enterprise Institute for Public Policy Research. *Government Regulation: Proposals for Procedural Reform*. Washington, D.C.: American Enterprise Institute, 1979.

Anderson, Jack, and Boyd, James, *Confessions of a Muckraker*. New York: Random House, 1979.

Anderson, Kent, ed. *Television Fraud: The History and Implications of the Quiz Show Scandals*. Westport, Conn.: Greenwood, 1979.

Arnold, Thurman W. *Folklore of Capitalism*. Northford, Conn.: Elliots' Books, 1937 ed. reprinted 1979.

Aronoff, Craig. *Business and the Media*. Santa Monica, Calif.: Goodyear Publishing Company, 1979.

Auchter, Bernard, Katz, Jonathan; and Graham, Mary. *Crime and the Abuse of Power: Offenses and Offenders Beyond the Reach of the Law?* United States Discussion Paper for the Sixth United Nations Congress on the Prevention of Crime and the Treatment of Offenders Washington, D.C.: National Institute of Justice, 1980.

Austin, M.M., and Vidal-Naquet, P. *Economic and Social History of Ancient Greece: An Introduction*. Berkeley: University of California Press, 1978.

Bakal, Carl. *Charity U.S.A.: An Investigation into the Hidden World of the Multi-Billion Dollar Charity Industry*. New York: Times Books, 1979.

Barry, Vincent. *Moral Issues in Business*. Belmont, Calif.: Wadsworth, 1979.

Barth, Peter S., and Hunt, H. Allan. *Workers' Compensation and Work-Related Illnesses and Diseases*. Cambridge, Mass.: MIT Press, 1980.

Bartsh, Thomas; Boddy, Francis M.; King, Benjamin F.; and Thompson, Peter N. *A Class-Action Suit That Worked*. Lexington, Mass.: Lexington Books, D.C. Heath and Company, 1979.

Beauchamp, Tom L., and Bowie, Norman, eds. *Ethical Theory and Business*. Englewood Cliffs, N.J.: Prentice-Hall, 1979.

Becker, Robert A. *Revolution, Reform and the Politics of American Taxation, 1763-1783*. Baton Rouge: Louisiana State University Press, 1980.

Berman, Daniel M. *Death on the Job*. New York: Monthly Review Press, 1979.

Boardman, Fon W. *America and the Robber Barons, 1865 to 1913*. New York: H.Z. Walck, 1979.

Borkin, Joseph. *The Crime and Punishment of I.G. Farben.* New York: Free Press, 1978.

Braxton, Bernard. *Sexual, Racial and Political Faces of Corruption: A View on the High Cost of Institutional Evils.* Washington, D.C.: Verta Press, 1977.

Bridbord, Kenneth. *Toxicological and Carcinogenic Health Hazards in the Workplace.* Park Forest South, Ill.: Pathotox, 1979.

Bringhurst, Bruce. *Antitrust and Oil Monopoly: The Standard Oil Cases, 1890-1911.* Contributions in Legal Studies, vol. 8. Westport, Conn.: Greenwood, 1979.

Brintnall, M. "Police and White Collar Crime." Department of Political Science, Brown University, 1978.

Brown, E. Richard. *Rockefeller Medicine Men: Medicine and Capitalism in America.* Berkeley: University of California Press, 1979.

Brown, James K. *This Business of Issues: Coping with the Company's Environments.* New York: Conference Board, 1979.

Bryant, Clifton D. *Khaki-Collar Crime: Deviant Behavior in the Military Context.* New York: Free Press, 1979.

Burt, Robert. *Taking Care of Strangers: The Rule of Law in Doctor-Patient Relations.* New York: Free Press, 1979.

Calabrese, Edward J. *Pollutants and High Risk Groups: The Biological Basis of Increased Human Susceptibility to Environmental and Occupational Pollutants.* New York: Wiley Interscience, 1977.

Campbell, Alastair. *Medicine, Health, and Justice.* New York: Churchill Livingstone, 1979.

Caris, Susan. "Community Attitudes toward Pollution." Department of Geography, University of Chicago, 1978.

Church, Roy, ed. *The Dynamics of Victorian Business: Problems and Perspectives to the 1870's.* Boston: Allen and Unwin, 1980.

Clement, Wallace. *Continental Corporate Power: Economic Elite Linkages Between Canada and the United States.* Tortonto: McClelland and Stewart, 1977.

Clinard, Marshall B. *Illegal Corporate Behavior.* Washington, D.C.: U.S. Government Printing Office, 1979.

Connell, Jon, and Sutherland, Douglas. *Fraud: The Amazing Career of Dr. Savundra.* Briarcliff Manor, N.Y.: Stein and Day, 1979.

Coxon, Anthony P., and Jones, Charles L. *Class and Hierarchy: The Social Meaning of Occupations.* New York: St. Martin's Press, 1979.

DeGeorge, Richard T., and Pichler, Joseph A., eds. *Ethics, Free Enterprise, and Public Policy.* New York: Oxford University Press, 1978.

De Mott, Deborah. *Corporations at the Crossroads.* New York: McGraw-Hill, 1980.

Dobb, Maurice H. *Capitalist Enterprise and Social Progress.* Westport, Conn.: Hyperion, 1925 ed. reprinted 1979.

Dodd, Lawrence, and Schott, Richard L. *Congress and the Administrative State.* New York: Wiley, 1979.

Domhoff, G. William. *Power Structure Research.* Beverly Hills, Calif.: Sage Publications, 1980.

————. *The Powers That Be: Process of Ruling Class Domination in America.* New York: Random House, 1979.

Donaldson, Thomas, and Werhare, P. *Ethical Issues in Business: A Philosophical Approach.* Englewood Cliffs, N.J.: Prentice-Hall, 1979.

Dorman, Michael. *Dirty Politics: From 1776 to Watergate.* New York: Delacorte Press, 1978.

Dunn, S.W.; Cahill, M.F.; and Boddewyn, J.J. *How Fifteen Transnational Corporations Manage Public Affairs.* Chicago: Crain, 1979.

Edelhertz, Herbert; Stotland, Ezra; Walsh, Marilyn; and Weinberg, Milton. *The Investigation of White-Collar Crime: A Manual for Law Enforcement Agencies.* Washington, D.C.: U.S. Government Printing Office, 1977.

Eisenstadt, Abraham S., Hoogenboom, Ari, and Trefousse, Hans L. (eds.) *Problems of Corruption before Watergate.* New York: Brooklyn College Press, 1979.

Elliott, Robert K., and Willingham, John. *Management Fraud: Detection and Deterrence.* Princeton, N.J.: Petrocelli, 1980.

Engelbourg, Saul. *Power and Morality: American Business Ethics, 1840-1914.* Westport, Conn.: Greenwood, 1980.

Fletcher, Thomas; Gordon, Paula; and Hentzell, Shirley. *An Anti-Corruption Strategy for Local Governments.* Washington, D.C.: U.S. Government Printing Office, 1979.

Gardiner, John; Lyman, Theodore; and Waldhorn, Steven. *Corruption in Land Use and Building Regulation: Case Studies of Corruption.* Washington, D.C.: U.S. Government Printing Office, 1979.

Geis, Gilbert, and Meier, Robert F., eds. *White-Collar Crime: Offenses in Business, Politics, and the Professions.* New York: Free Press, 1977.

Geis, Gilbert, and Stotland, Ezra, eds. *White-Collar Crime: Theory and Research.* Beverly Hills, Calif.: Sage Publications, 1980.

Getzels, Judith, and Thurow, Charles. *An Analysis of Zoning Reforms: Minimizing the Incentive for Corruption.* Washington, D.C.: U.S. Government Printing Office, 1979.

Girvan, Norman. *Corporate Imperialism: Conflict and Expropriation. Transnational Corporations and Economic Nationalism in the Third World.* New York: Monthly Review Press, 1978.

Goff, Colin, and Reasons, Charles. *Corporate Crime in Canada: A Critical Analysis of Anti-Combines Legislation.* Englewood Cliffs, N.J.: Prentice-Hall, 1978.

Gomez, Manuel; Duffy, Richard; and Trivelli, Vincent. *At Work in Copper: Occupational Health and Safety in Copper Smelting*. 3 vols. New York: Inform, 1979.

Green, Mark, and Massie, Robert, Jr., eds. *The Big Business Reader*. New York: Pilgrim, 1980.

Greene, James. *Regulatory Problems and Regulatory Reform: The Perceptions of Business*. New York: Conference Board, 1980.

Greer, Edward. *Big Steel: Black Politics and Corporate Power in Gary, Indiana*. New York: Monthly Review Press, 1979.

Haeger, John, and Weber, Michael. *The Bosses*. St. Louis, Mo.: Forum Press, 1979.

Hagen, Roger. *The Intelligence Process and White-Collar Crime*. An Operational Guide to White-Collar Crime Enforcement of the National Center on White-Collar Crime. Washington, D.C.: U.S. Government Printing Office, 1979.

Hammond, Edward C., and Selikoff, Irving J. *Public Control of Environmental Health*. New York: Academy of Science, 1979.

Held, Virginia. *Property, Profits, and Economic Justice*. Belmont, Calif.: Wadsworth, 1980.

Hessen, Robert. *In Defense of the Corporation*. Stanford, Calif.: Hoover Institution Press, 1979.

Hopkins, Andrew. *The Impact of Prosecutions under the Trade Practices Act*. Canberra, Australia: Australian Institute of Criminology, 1978.

Ingraham, Barton L. *Political Crime in Europe: A Comparative Study of France, Germany, and England*. Berkeley: University of California Press, 1979.

Jaspan, Norman. *Theft in the Health Care Industry*. Germantown, Md.: Aspens Systems Corporation, 1978.

Kanwit, Stephanie. *Federal Trade Commission*. Colorado Springs, Colo.: Shepard's, 1979.

Karchmer, Clifford L. *Model Curriculum and Trainer's Guide for Programs to Combat White-Collar Crime*. An Operational Guide to White-Collar Crime Enforcement of the National Center on White-Collar Crime. Washington, D.C.: U.S. Government Printing Office, June 1980.

———. *Enforcement Manual: Approaches for Combatting Arson-for-Profit Schemes*. Part II: *Tactical Guides*. Prepared for LEAA by Battelle Human Affairs Research Centers, Seattle, Wash., July 1980.

Karchmer, Clifford L., and Greenfield, James. *Enforcement Manual: Approaches for Combatting Arson-for-Profit Schemes*. Part I: *Strategic Approaches*. Prepared for Law Enforcement Assistance Association (LEAA) by Battelle Human Affairs Research Centers, Seattle, Wash., November 1980.

Karchmer, Clifford L., and Randall, Donna. *Compendium of Operational and Planning Guides to White-Collar Crime Enforcement*. Report of the National Center on White-Collar Crime. Seattle, Wash.: Battelle Human Affairs Research Centers, August 1979.

Karchmer, Clifford.; Walsh, Marilyn E.; and Greenfeld, James. *Enforcement Manual: Approaches for Combatting Arson-for-Profit Schemes*. Part I: *Strategic Approaches*. Prepared for LEAA by Battelle Human Affairs Research Centers, Seattle, Wash., July 1980.

Katzman, Robert A. *Regulatory Bureaucracy: The Federal Trade Commission and Antitrust Policy*. Cambridge, Mass.: MIT Press, 1979.

Kaufman, Burton I. *The Oil Cartel Case: A Documentary Study of Antitrust Activity in the Cold War Era*. Westport, Conn.: Greenwood, 1978.

Kelbley, Charles A., ed. *The Value of Justice: Essays on the Theory and Practice of Social Virtue*. New York: Fordham University Press, 1979.

Kennedy, Tom, and Simon, Charles E. *An Examination of Questionable Payments and Practices*. New York: Praeger, 1978.

Kennis, Kenneth G. *Competition in the History of Economic Thought*. New York: Arno, 1977.

Kitch, Edmund W., and Perlman, Harvey S. *Legal Regulation of the Competitive Process*. Mineola, N.Y.: Foundation Press, 1979.

Kloman, Erasmus H., ed. *Cases in Accountability: The Work of the GAO*. Boulder, Colo.: Westview, 1979.

Knepper, William E. *Liability of Corporate Officers and Directors*, 3rd ed. Indianapolis: Allen Smith, 1979.

Krauss, Leonard, and MacCahar, Aileen. *Computer Fraud and Countermeasures*. Englewood Cliffs, N.J.: Prentice-Hall, 1979.

Kripke, Homer. *The SEC and Securities Disclosure: Regulation in Search of a Purpose*. New York: Norton, 1979.

Kwitny, Jonathan. *Vicious Circles*. New York: Norton, 1979.

Kyd, Stewart. *A Treatise on the Law of Corporations*. 2 vols. New York: Garland, 1794 ed. reprinted 1979.

Lamden, Charles W. *The Securities and Exchange Commission: A Case Study in the Use of Accounting as an Instrument of Public Policy*. New York: Arno, 1978.

Lange, Andrea, and Bowers, Robert. *Fraud and Abuse in Government Benefit Programs*. Washington, D.C.: U.S. Government Printing Office, 1979.

Lasko, Keith Alan. *The Great Billion Dollar Medical Swindle*. Indianapolis: Bobbs-Merrill, 1980.

Lippman, Morton, and Schlesinger, Richard B. *Chemical Contamination in the Human Environment*. New York: Oxford University Press, 1979.

Liu, Joseph C. *Computer Crime, Security, and Privacy*. Monticello, Ill.: Vance Bibliographies, 1979.

Long, Joseph C. *Expanding Enforcement Options: The Securities Fraud Approach*. An Operational Guide to White-Collar Crime Enforcement of the National Center on White-Collar Crime. Washington, D.C.: U.S. Government Printing Office, June 79.

Long, Susan. *The Internal Revenue Service: Measuring Tax Offenses and Enforcement Response.* Washington, D.C.: U.S. Government Printing Office, 1980.

Louise, Francis D. *Malpractice—The Doctor's Delinquency.* Port Washington, N.Y.: Ashley Books, 1978.

Lunt, Richard D. *Law and Order vs. the Miners, West Virginia, 1907-1933.* Hamden, Conn.: Shoe String Press, 1980.

Lydenberg, Steven. *Minding the Corporate Conscience: Public Interest Organizations and Corporate Social Accountability.* New York: Council on Economic Priorities, 1978.

Lyman, Theodore. *Corruption in Land Use and Building Regulation: An Integrated Report of Conclusions.* Washington, D.C.: U.S. Government Printing Office, 1979.

Lyman, T.; Fletcher, T.; and Gardiner, J.A. *Prevention, Detection, and Correction of Corruption in Local Government.* Washington, D.C.: LEAA, 1978.

Manikas, Peter, and Protess, David. *Establishing a Citizens' Watchdog Group (re: anti-corruption).* Washington, D.C.: U.S. Government Printing Office, 1979.

Margolis, Diane R. *The Managers: Corporate Life in America.* New York: William Morrow, 1979.

McAleer, Gordon, and DeJager, George. *Salaries and Attitudes: A Profile of the Internal Auditing Profession.* Altamonte Springs, Fla.: Institute of Internal Auditors, 1979.

McMenamin, Michael, and McNamara, Walter. *Milking the Public: Political Scandals of the Dairy Lobby from L.B.J. to Jimmy.* Chicago: Nelson-Hall, 1980.

Mendeloff, John. *Regulating Safety: A Political and Economic Analysis of the Federal Occupational Safety and Health Program.* Cambridge, Mass.: MIT Press, 1979.

Michaels, L., and Chissick, S.S. *Asbestos: Properties, Applications, and Hazards.* New York: Wiley-Interscience, 1979.

Mitford, Jessica. *Poison Penmanship: The Gentle Art of Muckraking.* New York: Knopf, 1979.

Mitnick, Barry M. *The Political Economy of Regulation: Creating, Designing, and Removing Regulatory Forms.* New York: Columbia University Press, 1980.

Modelski, George, ed. *Transnational Corporations and World Order: Readings in International Political Economy.* San Francisco: Freeman, 1979.

Mosher, Frederick D. *The GAO: The Quest for Accountability in American Government.* Boulder, Colo.: Westview, 1979.

Moss, Ralph. *The Cancer Rebellion*. New York: Grove Press, 1979.

National District Attorneys Association. "Fighting the $40 Billion Rip-Off: An Annual Report from the Economic Crime Project." Washington, D.C., 1976.

New South Wales (Australia), Parliament. *Report of the Criminal Law Review Division on Summary Prosecution in the Supreme Court of Corporate "White-Collar" Offenses of an Economic Nature*. New South Wales: Government Printer, 1979.

Nossen, Richard A. *Determination of Undisclosed Financial Interest*. An Operational Guide to White-Collar Crime Enforcement of the National Center on White-Collar Crime. Washington, D.C.: U.S. Government Printing Office, June 1979.

Olins, Wally. *The Corporate Personality: An Inquiry into the Nature of Corporate Identity*. New York: Mayflower, 1979.

O'Neill, Robert O. *Investigative Planning*. An Operational Guide to White-Collar Crime Enforcement of the National Center on White-Collar Crime. Washington, D.C.: U.S. Government Printing Office, June 1979.

Parker, Donn B. *Crime by Computer*. New York: Scribners, 1976.

Perez, Jacob. "Corporate Criminality: A Study of the One Thousand Largest Industrial Corporations in the U.S.A." Ph.D. diss., University of Pennsylvania, 1978.

Petersen, Dan. *The OSHA Compliance Manual*, rev. ed. New York: McGraw-Hill, 1979.

Reams, Bernard D., Jr., and Ferguson, J. Ray. *Consumer Protection: Basic Documents and Laws, Federal and States*. 4 vols. Dobbs Ferry, N.Y.: Oceana, 1978.

Recommendations of the American Bar Association Section on Criminal Justice, Committee on Economic Offenses. Final Report. Washington, D.C.: American Bar Association, 1977.

Reiman, Jeffrey H. *The Rich Get Richer and the Poor Get Prison: Ideology, Class, and Criminal Justice*. New York: Wiley, 1979.

Reisman, W. Michael. *Folded Lies: Bribery, Crusades, and Reform*. New York: Free Press, 1979.

Reiss, Albert, and Biderman, Albert. *Data Sources on White-Collar Law-Breaking*. Washington, D.C.: U.S. Government Printing Office, 1980.

Report on the National District Attorneys Association Economic Crime Project: Fifth Grant Period. Report to the National District Attorney's Association Economic Crime Project by Battelle Human Affairs Research Centers, Seattle, Wash., August 1980.

Rider, Barry, and French, Leigh. *The Regulation of Insider Trading*. Dobbs Ferry, N.Y.: Oceana, 1979.

Ritter, Gerhard. *The Corrupting Influence of Power*, trans. F.W. Pick. Westport, Conn.: Hyperion, 1952 ed. reprinted 1979.

Roebuck, Julian, and Weeber, Stanley C. *Political Crime in the United States: Analyzing Crime by and against Government.* New York: Praeger, 1978.

Rose-Ackerman, Susan. *Corruption: A Study in Political Economy.* New York: Academic, 1978.

Rosen, Charles. *Scandal of '51: How the Gamblers Almost Killed College Basketball.* New York: Holt, Rinehart and Winston, 1978.

Rowe, Richard H. *Handling an SEC Investigation.* New York: Practising Law Institute, 1979.

Saxon, Miraim S. *White-Collar Crime: The Problem and the Federal Response.* Report No. 80-84 EPW, Library of Congress, Congressional Research Service, Washington, D.C., 14 April 1980.

Schmertz, Herbert. *Corporations and the First Amendment.* New York: American Management Association, 1978.

Schnapp, John B. *Corporate Strategies of the Automotive Manufacturers.* Lexington, Mass.: Lexington Books, D.C. Heath and Company, 1978.

Schubert, Jane, and Krug, Robert. *Consumer Fraud: An Empirical Perspective—Summary Report.* Washington, D.C.: U.S. Government Printing Office, 1979.

Schur, Edwin M. *The Politics of Deviance: Stigman Contests and the Uses of Power.* Englewood Cliffs, N.J.: Prentice-Hall, 1980.

Selekman, Sylvia, and Selekman, Benjamin. *Power and Morality in a Business Society.* Westport, Conn.: Greenwood, 1956 ed. reprinted 1978.

Selikoff, Irving J., and Lee, Douglas H. *Asbestos and Disease.* New York: Academic Press, 1978.

Selznick, Philip. *Law, Society, and Industrial Justice.* New Brunswick, N.J.: Transaction Books, 1980.

Shapiro, Eileen C., and Lowenstein, Leah M. *Becoming a Physician: Development of Values and Attitudes in Medicine.* Cambridge, Mass.: Ballinger, 1979.

Shapiro, Susan P. *Thinking about White-Collar Crime: Matters of Conceptualization and Research.* Washington, D.C.: U.S. Department of Justice, 1980.

Sheldon, Jonathan, and Zweibel, George. *Survey of Consumer Fraud Laws.* Washington, D.C.: U.S. Government Printing Office, 1978.

Shepherd, William G., and Clair, Wilcox. *Public Policies Toward Business*, 6th ed. Homewood, Ill.: Richard D. Irwin, 1979.

Sherman, Roger. *Antitrust Perspectives and Issues.* Reading, Mass.: Addison-Wesley, 1978.

Siebert, Horst. *The Political Economy of Environmental Protection.* Greenwich, Conn.: JAI, 1979.

Siegan, Bernard H. *Regulation, Economics, and the Law.* Lexington, Mass.: Lexington Books, D.C. Heath and Company, 1979.

Simons, Howard, ed. *The Media and Business.* New York: Random House, 1979.

Sinkey, Joseph F., Jr. *Problems and Failed Institutions in the Commercial Banking Industry.* Greenwich, Conn.: JAI, 1979.

Sittig, Marshall. *Hazardous and Toxic Effects of Industrial Chemicals.* Park Ridge, N.J.: Noyes Press, 1979.

Smith, Peter, and Swann, Dennis. *Protecting the Consumer: An Economic and Legal Analysis.* London: Martin Robertson, 1980.

Sobel, Lester. *The Disaster File: The Seventies Post Watergate Morality.* New York: Facts on File, 1979.

Spagnole, John A., Jr., and Rohner, Ralph J. *Consumer Law: Cases and Materials.* St. Paul, Minn.: West, 1979.

Stans, Maurice. *The Terrors of Justice.* Edison, N.J.: Everest House, 1978.

Stewart, Charles T. *Air Pollution, Human Health, and Public Policy.* Lexington, Mass.: Lexington Books, D.C. Heath and Company, 1979.

Stich, Rodney. *The Unfriendly Skies: An Aviation Watergate.* Alamo, Calif.: Diablo Western, 1978.

Stinson, Robert. *Lincoln Steffens.* New York: Frederick Ungar, 1979.

Stroman, Duane F. *The Quick Knife: Unnecessary Surgery, U.S.A.* Port Washington, N.Y.: Kennikat, 1979.

Suffer the Children: The Story of Thalidomide. London Sunday Times. New York: Viking, 1979.

Sufrin, Sinden C. *Management of Business Ethics.* Port Washington, N.Y.: Kennikat, 1979.

Thompson, George, and Brady, Gerald P. *Text, Cases, and Materials on Antitrust Fundamentals,* 3rd ed. St. Paul, Minn.: West, 1979.

Tobin, Richard J. *The Social Gamble.* Lexington, Mass.: Lexington Books, D.C. Heath and Company, 1979.

United States Attorney General. *National Priorities for the Investigation and Prosecution of White-Collar Crime: Report of the Attorney General.* Washington, D.C.: Department of Justice, 1980.

U.S. Congress, House Judiciary Committee. *Corporate Crime* Washington D.C.: U.S. Government Printing Office 1980.

United States Congress. Senate Committee on Governmental Affairs. Subcommittee on Investigations. *Arson in America.* 96th Congress, 1st Session. 20 December 1979.

———. Senate, Committee on Governmental Affairs. Subcommittee on Investigations. *Arson-For-Hire.* 95th Congress, 2nd Session, August-September 1978.

U.S. Congress, House of Representatives. Committee on the Judiciary. Subcommittee on Crime (Conyers committee). 95th Congress, 1st Session, 1977.

———. House of Representatives, Committee on the Judiciary. Subcommittee on Crime. *Corporate Crime.* 96th Congress, 2nd Session. Washington, D.C.: U.S. Government Printing Office, 1980.

Vaughan, Diane. "Crime between Organizations: A Case Study of Medicaid Procedural Fraud." Ph.D. diss., Ohio State University, 1979.

Villano, Clair E. *Complaint and Referral Handling*. An Operational Guide to White-Collar Crime Enforcement of the National Center on White-Collar Crime. Washington, D.C.: U.S. Government Printing Office, May 1980.

Viscusi, W. Kip. *Employment Hazards: An Investigation of Market Performance*. Cambridge, Mass.: Harvard University Press, 1980.

Vogel, David. *Lobbying the Corporation: Citizen Challenges to Business Authority*. New York: Basic Books, 1979.

Wadden, Richard A. *Energy Utilization and Environmental Health: Methods for Prediction and Evaluation of Impact on Human Health*. New York: Wiley-Interscience, 1978.

Walsh, Diana Chapman. *Industry's Voice in Health Policy*. New York: Springer-Verlag, 1979.

Weidenbaum, Murray L. *The Future of Business Regulation: Private Action and Public Demand*. New York: American Management Association, 1979.

Weinstein, Deena. *Challenging Abuses at the Workplace*. Elmsford, N.Y.: Pergamon Press, 1979.

Westin, Alan, and Salisbury, Stephan. *Individual Rights in the Corporation: A Reader on Employee Rights*. New York: Pantheon, 1980.

White-Collar Crime, Proceedings of the Institute of Criminology No. 37. Sydney, Australia: Sydney University Law School, 1979.

White-Collar Crimes 1978. Litigation and Administrative Practice Course Handbook, vol. 100. New York: Practising Law Institute, 1978.

Wilson, James Q. *The Politics of Regulation*. New York: Basic Books, 1980.

Wilson, Paul, and Braithwaite, John, eds. *Two Faces of Deviance*. St. Lucia: University of Queensland Press, 1979.

Winter, Ralph K. *Government and the Corporation*. Washington, D.C.: American Enterprise Institute, 1978.

Wolfgang, M. *National Survey of Crime Severity*. Philadelphia: Center for Studies in Criminology and Criminal Law, University of Pennsylvania, 1980.

Wrong, Dennis. *Power: Its Forms, Bases, and Uses*. New York: Harper and Row, 1979.

Zavaterro, Janette. *The Sylmar Tunnel Disaster*. New York: Everest House, 1978.

Zweibel, George. *Federal Law on Consumer Deception: An Agency by Agency Analysis*. Washington, D.C.: U.S. Government Printing Office, 1979.

Collected Articles

Benham, T.W. "Trends in Public Attitudes Toward Business and the Free Enterprise System." In *Business in 1990: A Look to the Future*, A. Starchild, ed., pp. 39-52. Seattle: University Press of the Pacific, 1979.

Braithwaite, John. "An Exploratory Study in Used Car Fraud." In *Two Faces of Deviance*. Paul R. Wilson and John Braithwaite, eds., pp. 101-122. St. Lucia: University of Queensland Press, 1978.

Braithwaite, John, and Condon, Barry. "On the Class Basis of Criminal Violence." In Wilson and Braithwaite, *Two Faces of Deviance*, pp. 232-254.

Braithwaite, John, and Wilson, Paul R. "Introduction: Pervs, Pimps, and Powerbrokers." In Wilson and Braithwaite, *Two Faces of Deviance*, pp. 1-14.

Bright, Robin Anne. "Dole Bludgers or Tax Dodgers: Who Is the Deviant?" In *Two Faces of Deviance*, Paul Wilson and John Braithwaite, eds., St. Lucia: University of Queensland Press, 1979.

Carson, W.G. "The Institutionalization of Ambiguity: Early British Factory Acts." In *White-Collar Crime: Theory and Research*, Gilbert Geis and Ezra Stotland, eds., pp. 126-141. Beverly Hills, Calif.: Sage Publications, 1980.

Endres, Michael. "Social Response to White-Collar Crime." In *Critical Issues in Criminal Justice*, R.G. Iacovetta and Dae H. Chang, eds., pp. 95-109. Durham, N.C.: Carolina Academic Press, 1979.

Gorring, Pam. "Multinationals or Mafia: Who Really Pushes Drugs?" In Wilson and Braithwaite, *Two Faces of Deviance*, pp. 81-100.

Gross, Edward. "Organizational Crime: A Theoretical Perspective." In *Studies in Symbolic Interaction*, vol. 1, Norman Denzin, ed., pp. 55-85. Greenwich, Conn.: JAI, 1978.

———. "Organizations as Criminal Actors." In Wilson and Braithwaite, *Two Faces of Deviance*, pp. 199-213.

———. "Organizational Structure and Organizational Crime." In Geis and Stotland, *White-Collar Crime*, pp. 52-76.

Hodge, Pat. "Medibank Fraud." In Wilson and Braithwaite, *Two Faces of Deviance*, pp. 123-131.

Hopkins, Andrew. "The Anatomy of Corporate Crime." In Wilson and Braithwaite, *Two Faces of Deviance*, pp. 214-231.

Hundroe, Thor. "Heads They Win, Tails We Lose: Environment and the Law." In Wilson and Braithwaite, *Two Faces of Deviance*, pp. 132-160.

Katz, Jack. "The Social Movement Against White-Collar Crime." In *Criminology Review Year Book*, vol. 2, Egon Bittner and Sheldon L. Messinger, eds., pp. 157-160. Beverly Hills, Calif.: Sage Publications, 1980.

Madden, Carl. "Forces Which Influence Ethical Behavior." In *The Ethics of Corporate Conduct*, Clarence Walton, ed. Englewood Cliffs, N.J.: Prentice-Hall, 1977, pp. 31-78.

Maltz, Michael, and Pollock, Stephen M. "Analyzing Suspected Collusion Among Bidders." In Geis and Stotland, *White-Collar Crime*, pp. 174-198.

McGuire, Mary V., and Edelhertz, Herbert. "Consumer Abuse of Older Americans: Victimization and Remedial Action in Two Metropolitan Areas." In Geis and Stotland, *White-Collar Crime*, pp. 266-292.

Meier, Robert F., and Geis, Gilbert. "The White-Collar Offender." In *Psychology of Crime and Criminal Justice*, Hans Toch, ed., pp. 427-469. New York: Holt, Rinehart and Winston, 1979.

Parker, Donn B. "Computer-Related White-Collar Crime." In Geis and Stotland, *White-Collar Crime*, pp. 199-221.

Reasons, Charles E., and Goff, Colin H. "Corporate Crime: A Cross-National Analysis." In Geis and Stotland, *White-Collar Crime*, pp. 126-141.

Roebuck, Julian, and Weeber, S. "Political Crime in the United States." In *Studies in Symbolic Interaction*, vol. 2, Norman K. Denzin, ed., pp. 307-330. Greenwich, Conn.: JAI, 1979.

Schrager, Laura Hill, and Short, James F., Jr. "How Serious a Crime? Perceptions of Organizational and Common Crimes." In Geis and Stotland, *White-Collar Crime*, pp. 14-31.

Shover, Neal. "The Criminalization of Corporate Behavior: Federal Surface Coal Mining." In Geis and Stotland, *White-Collar Crime*, pp. 98-125.

Sorensen, James E.; Grove, Hugh D.; and Sorensen, Thomas L. "Detecting Management Fraud: The Role of the Independent Auditor." In Geis and Stotland, *White-Collar Crime*, pp. 221-251.

Stotland, Ezra; Brintnall, Michael; L'Heureux, Andre; and Ashmore, Eva. "Do Convictions Deter Home Repair Fraud?" In Geis and Stotland, *White-Collar Crime*, pp. 252-265.

Sutton, Adam, and Wild, Ronald. "Corporate Crime and Social Structure." In Wilson and Braithwaite, *Two Faces of Deviance*, pp. 177-198.

———— . "Investigating Company Fraud: Case Studies from Australia." In Geis and Stotland, *White-Collar Crime*, pp. 293-316.

Vaughan, Diane. "Crime between Organizations: Implications for Victimology." In Geis and Stotland, *White-Collar Crime*, pp. 77-97.

Walsh, Marilyn E., and Schram, Donna D. "The Victim of White-Collar Crime: Accuser or Accused?" In Geis and Stotland, *White-Collar Crime*, pp. 32-51.

Articles

Allera, Edward J. "Warrantless Inspections of the Food Industry." *Food-Drug-Cosmetic Law Journal* 34 (June 1979):260-270.

Atkeson, T. "The Foreign Corrupt Practices Act of 1977." *International Lawyer* 12 (Fall 1978):703-720.

Austin, Arthur D. "Negative Effects of Treble Damage Actions: Reflections on the New Antitrust Strategy." *Duke Law Journal* 6 (January 1979):1353-1374.

Bartrip, P.W.J., and Fenn, P.T. "The Administration of Safety: The Enforcement Policy of the Early Factory Inspectorate, 1844-64." *Public Administration* 58 (Spring 1980):87-104.

————. "The Conventionalization of Factory Crime—A Reassessment." *International Journal of the Sociology of Law* 8 (May 1980):175-186.

Beilock, Richard P. "The Economics of Jailing Executives for Violations of Health and Safety Regulations." *Journal of Consumer Affairs* 13 (Winter 1979):386-392.

Bequai, August. "White Collar Crimes, The Losing War." *Case and Comment* 82 (September-October 1977):3-10.

Bernstein, P.W. "Prison Can Be Bad for Your Career," *Fortune*, 28 July 1980, pp. 62-67.

Blakey, G. Robert, and Goldstock, Ronald. " 'On the Waterfront': RICO and Labor Racketeering." *American Criminal Law Review* 17 (Winter 1980):341-366.

Bookholdt, J.L., and Horvitz, Jerome S. "Prosecution of Computer Crime." *Journal of Systems Management* 29 (December 1978):6-11.

Bradley, P. "Henry George, Biblical Morality and Economic Ethics." *The American Journal of Economics and Sociology* 39 (July 1980): 209-214.

Braithwaite, John. "Transnational Corporations and Corruption—Towards Some International Solutions." *International Journal of the Sociology of Law* 7 (May 1979):125-142.

Brintnall, Michael A. "Police and White-Collar Crime." *Policy Studies Journal* 7 (1978):431-435.

Carson, W.G. "The Other Price of British Oil—Regulatory Safety on Offshore Oil Installations in the British Sector of the North Sea." *Contemporary Crises* 4 (July 1980):239-266.

Cerullo, Vincent. "Criminal Investigation Techniques as Applied to the Investigation of White-Collar Crime." *Police Chief* 46 (May 1979):32-34.

Clark, Glenn A. "Corporate Homicide: A New Assault on Corporate Decision-Making." *Notre Dame Lawyer* 54 (June 1979):911-924.

Coffee, John Collins, Jr. "Corporate Crime and Punishment: A Non-Chicago View of the Economics of Criminal Sanctions." *American Criminal Law Review* 17 (Spring 1980):419-478.

Committee on Corporate Law Department Forums. "Recent Developments in EEO, EPA, and OSHA." *Business Lawyer* 35 (January 1980):573-604.

"The Consumer and Antitrust Law" [Symposium]. *Congressional Digest* 59 (February 1980):33-59.

Conyers, John, Jr. "Criminology, Economics, and Public Policy," *Crime and Delinquency* 25 (April 1979):137-144.

———. "Corporate and White-Collar Crime: A View by the Chairman of the House Subcommittee on Crime." *American Criminal Law Review* 17 (Winter 1980):287-300.

Crane, E. "Crime at the Top." *Fortune* 24 September 1979, p. 144.

Cullen, Francis T.; Link, Bruce G.; and Polzani, Craig W. "The Seriousness of Crime Revisited: Have Attitudes toward White-Collar Crime Changed?" Unpublished paper, Department of Sociology, Western Illinois University, Macomb, 1980.

Davies, J.J. "Acountants' Third Party Liability: A History of Applied Sociological Jurisprudence." *Abacus* 15 (December 1979):93-112.

Dean, Peter; Keenan, Tony; and Kenney, Fiona. "Taxpayers' Attitudes to Income Tax Evasion: An Empirical Study." *British Tax Review* 1 (1980):28-44.

de Lone, Sandy. "Contribution Among Antitrust Violators." *Catholic University Law Review* 29 (Spring 1980):669-696.

"Developments in the Law—Corporate Crime: Regulating Corporate Behavior through Criminal Sanctions," *Harvard Law Review* 92 (April 1979):1227.

Devlin, Patrick. "Jury Trial of Complex Cases: English Practice at the Time of the Seventh Amendment." *Columbia Law Review* 80 (January 1980):43-108.

Dick, N.D., and Cavanaugh, R.S. "A Hard-Hitting White-Collar Crime Unit of the United States Government." *Police Chief* 47 (May 1980):26-29.

Dickenson, Thomas A. "Travel Consumer Fraud: Rip-offs and Remedies." *Syracuse Law Review* 28 (1977):847.

Ellington, R. "Pitfalls of Payoffs in Indonesia." *Asia Magazine*, January-February 1970, pp. 6ff.

Engel, David. "An Approach to Corporate Social Responsibility." *Stanford Law Review* 32 (November 1979):1-98.

Ermann, M. David, and Lundman, Richard J. "Deviant Acts by Complex

Organizations: Deviance and Social Control at the Organizational Level of Analysis." *Sociological Quarterly* 19 (Winter 1978):55-67.

Felman, Yehudi M.; Corsaro, Maria C.; and Jones, Julia Rivers. "Laboratory Compliance with Syphillis Reporting Laws—The New York City Experience, 1972-77." *Public Health Reports* 95 (January-February 1980):53-57.

Fox, Karla Harbin. "The Right to Say 'No': The Fourth Amendment and Administrative Inspections." *American Business Law Journal* 17 (Autumn 1979):283-312.

Friedman, Howard M. "Some Reflections on the Corporation as a Criminal Defendant." *Notre Dame Lawyer* 55 (December 1979):173-202.

Garber, Charles A. "Letters—White-Collar Crime." *Dun's Review* 112 (December 1978):14.

Gardiner, Hilliard A. "OSHA and the Fourth Amendment: Corruptissima Republica Plurimae Leges?" *American Business Law Journal* 17 (Autumn 1979):405-412.

Garvey, George E. "The Sherman Act and the Vicious Will: Developing Standards of Criminal Intent in Sherman Act Prosecutions." *Catholic University Law Review* 29 (Winter 1980):389-426.

Geis, Gilbert. "White-Collar Crime: It Pays." *Washington Post*, 16 September 1977, p. 11.

Gondelman, Larry. "False Claims Against the Government: Defense Tactics in a False Claims Prosecution." *American Criminal Law Review* 17 (Winter 1980):399-408.

Goodwin, Stephen T. "Individual Liability of Agents for Corporate Crimes under the Proposed Federal Criminal Code." *Vanderbilt Law Review* 31 (May 1978): 965-1016.

Gylys, J.A. "Antitrust Violators—Hit 'em Where It Hurts." *Business* 29 (November-December 1979):2-9.

Hartz, H.L. "Combating Organized Crime." *Police Chief* 44 (September 1977):48-49.

Hauptley, Denis J. "The Proposed Federal Criminal Code and White-Collar Crime." *George Washington Law Review* 47 (March 1979): 523-549.

Henderson, T.W. "Product Liability Disease Litigation—Blueprint for Occupational Health and Safety," *Trial* 16 (April 1980):25-28.

Herschel, Federico J. "Tax Evasion and Its Measurement in Developing Countries." *Public Finance* 33 (1978):232-268.

Heymann, Philip B. "Introduction—Symposium on White-Collar Crime, Part I." *American Criminal Law Review* 17 (Winter 1980):271-274.

Husband, John M., and Powers, Albert Theodore. "Section 16(b) of the

Securities Exchange Act of 1934 and Insider Trading Involving Issuer-Granted Employee Stock Options." *Denver Law Journal* 57 (1979):71-102.

Jackson, Gary D. "White-Collar Crime in the United States." *Police Chief* 46 (May 1979):36-40.

Johnson, Philip S. "The First and Fastest Felony: Trading Futures Off the Exchange." *Business Lawyer* 35 (March 1980):711-714.

Karchmer, Clifford. "The Underworld Turns Fire into Profit." *Firehouse*, August 1977, pp. 22-27, 68-69.

———. "How to Fight the Arson Racketeer." *Journal of Insurance* 39 (March-April 1978):22-25.

Katz, Alfred. "Legality and Equality: Plea Bargaining in the Prosecution of White-Collar and Common Crimes." *Law and Society* 13 (Winter 1979):431-460.

Katz, Jack. "Concerted Ignorance: The Social Construction of Cover-up." *Urban Life* 8 (October 1979):295-316.

Kennedy, Kett. "Bribery and Political Crisis—Queensland, 1922." *Australian Journal of Politics and History* 25 (April 1979):66-76.

Kiechel, Walter. "Crime at the Top in Fruehauf Corporation." *Fortune* 29 January 1979, pp. 32-35.

Kirschner, Nancy M. "Criminal Consumer Fraud: Must the Goals of Deterrence and Compensation Be Mutually Exclusive?" *American Journal of Criminal Law* 7 (November 1979):355-384.

Kleinberg, Stanley S. "Criminal Justice and Private Enterprise." *Ethics* 90 (January 1980):270-281.

Kornblum, Guy O. "Punitive Damages on Parade: An Update of Recent California Appellate Decisions Affecting Punitive Damage Claims." *Insurance Law Journal* no. 676, May 1979, pp. 247-259.

Lacek, Michael J. "*Camara, See* and Their Progeny: Another Look at Administrative Inspections under the Fourth Amendment." *Columbia Journal of Law and Social Problems* 15 (1979):61-84.

Larson, William L. "Effective Enforcement of the Foreign Corrupt Practices Act." *Stanford Law Review* 32 (February 1980):561-580.

Lee, Li Way. "Some Models of Anti-Trust Enforcement." *Southern Economic Journal* 47 (July 1980):147-155.

Leuth, S. (pseudonym). "Wages of Fraud." *Journal of Accountancy* 147 (March 1979):43-44.

Lewis-Beck, Michael S. "Maintaining Economic Competition: The Causes and Consequences of Antitrust." *Journal of Politics* 41 (February 1979): 169-191.

Lindenberg-Woods, J. "The Smoking Revolver: Criminal Copyright Infringements." *Bulletin of the Copyright Society* 27 (December 1979): 63-87.

Liu, Ben-Chieh. "Costs of Air Pollution and Benefits of Its Control." *American Journal of Economics and Sociology* 38 (April 1979):187-194.

Loescher, Samuel M. "Limiting Corporate Power." *Journal of Economic Issues* 13 (June 1979):557-572.

Magarity, Gregory I. "RICO Investigations: A Case Study." *American Criminal Law Review* 17 (Winter 1980):367-378.

Majone, Giandomenico. "Process and Outcome in Regulatory Decision-Making." *American Behavioral Scientist* 22 (May-June 1979):561-584.

Mann, Kenneth; Wheeler, Stanton; and Sarat, Austin. "Sentencing the White-Collar Criminal." *American Criminal Law Review* 17 (Spring 1980):479-500.

Mann, R.A., and Gurol, M. "An Objective Approach to Detecting and Correcting Deceptive Advertising." *Notre Dame Lawyer* 54 (October 1978):73-101.

Marican, Y. Mansoor. "Combatting Corruption: The Malaysian Experience." *Asian Survey* 19 (June 1979):597-610.

Marris, Robin, and Mueller, Dennis C. "The Corporation, Competition, and the Invisible Hand." *Journal of Economic Literature* 18 (March 1980):32-63.

Mason, Robert, and Calvin, L.D. "A Study of Admitted Income Tax Evasion." *Law and Society Review* 13 (Fall 1978):73-89.

McCormick, Albert E., Jr. "Dominant Class Interests and the Emergence of Antitrust Legislation." *Contemporary Crises* 3 (October 1979): 399-418.

Meyer, Berhard F. "Swiss Banking Secrecy and Its Legal Implications in the United States." *New England Law Review* 14 (Summer 1978):18-81.

Mileti, D.S.; Gillespie, D.F.; and Eitzen, D.S. "Structure and Decision-Making in Corporate Organizations." *Sociology and Social Research* 63 (July 1979):723-744.

Miller, Samuel R. "Corporate Criminal Liability: A Principle Extended to Its Limits." *Federal Bar Journal* 38 (Winter 1979):49-68.

Morris, Christina Ortega. "Noise Pollution: Attempted Federal Controls of Airplane Noise." *Natural Resources Journal* 18 (July 1978):621-638.

Mueller, Gerhard O.W. "Offenses Against the Environment and Their Prevention: An International Appraisal." *Annals of the American Academy of Political and Social Sciences* 444 (July 1979):56-66.

Nathan, Richard E., and Spindel, Frederic. " 'I'm Guilty of What?': Emerging Concepts of Commodities Fraud." *Business Lawyer* 35(b) (March 1980):811-822.

Needleman, Martin L., and Needleman, Carolyn. "Organizational Crime: Two Models of Criminogenesis." *Sociological Quarterly* 20 (Autumn 1979):517-528.

Nielsen, Richard P. "Should Executives Be Jailed for Consumer and Health Safety Violations?" *Journal of Consumer Affairs* 13 (Summer 1979): 128-134.

Note. "Corporate Crime: Regulating Corporate Behavior Through Criminal Sanctions," *Harvard Law Review* 92 (April 1979):1227-1375.

Note. "The Foreign Corrupt Practices Act: A Transnational Analysis." *Journal of International Law and Economics* 13 (1979):367-402.

Note. "Institute Supports Wide-Ranging Inquiry into White-Collar Crime." *LEAA Newsletter* 8 (March 1979):12-13.

Note. "Marshall v. Barlow's (OSHA)." *University of Detroit Journal of Urban Law* 56 (Winter 1979):652-673.

Note. "The Securities Exchange Commission: An Introduction to the Enforcement of the Criminal Provision of the Federal Securities Laws." *American Criminal Law Review* 17 (Summer 1979):121-152.

Note. "Structural Crime and Institutional Rehabilitation: A New Approach to Corporate Sentencing." *Yale Law Journal* 89 (December 1979): 353-375.

Notes. "Compensating Victims of Occupational Disease." *Harvard Law Review* 93 (March 1980):916-937.

Orland, Leonard. "Reflections on Corporate Crime: Law in Search of Theory and Scholarship." *American Criminal Law Review* 17 (Spring 1980):501-520.

Ostermann, Peter; et al. *White-Collar Crime: A Selected Bibliography.* National Institute of Law Enforcement and Criminal Justice, LEAA, U.S. Department of Justice, July 1977.

Perlman, E. Elizabeth. "The Attorney-Client Privilege: A Look at Its Effect on the Corporate Client and the Corporate Executive." *Indiana Law Review* 55 (Winter 1980):407-416.

Peters, S. "Occupational Carcinogenesis and Statutes of Limitations—Resolving Relevant Policy Claims." *Trial* 16 (January 1980):46-55.

Phillips, Lynn W., and Phillips, Bobby J. "Educating Consumer Protection Programs, Part I: Weak but Commonly Used Research Designs." *Journal of Consumer Affairs* 13 (Winter 1979):157-185.

Posner, Richard A. "Optimal Sentences for White-Collar Criminals." *American Criminal Law Review* 17 (Spring 1980):409-418.

Richards, P.R. "Feasibility Study: A Rational Method of Choice in Selecting Crime Investigations." *Police Chief* 44 (September 1977):24-26.

Ritts, L.S. "Occupational Cancer and Limitation Periods on Occupational Disease Claims." *Trial* 16 (February 1980):44-48.

Rothstein, Mark A. "OSHA Inspections After *Marshal v. Barlow's, Inc.* *Duke Law Journal* no. 1, February 1979, pp. 63-104.

Rudelius, William, and Bucholz, Rogene A. "Ethical Problems of Purchasing Managers." *Harvard Business Review* 57 (March-April 1979):3-5.

Schrager, Laura Shill, and Short, James F., Jr. "Towards a Sociology of Organizational Crime." *Social Problems* 25 (April 1978):407-419.

Shapiro, Susan. "Thinking about White-Collar Crime: Matters of Conceptualization and Research." Unpublished monograph, Yale University, 1979.

Sherman, Lawrence W. "Three Models of Organizational Corruption in Agencies of Social Control." *Social Problems* 27 (April 1980):478-491.

Sinden, Peter G. "Perceptions of Crime in Capitalist America: The Question of Consciousness Manipulation." *Sociological Focus* 13 (January 1980):75-91.

Smith, Dwight C., Jr. "Paragons, Pariahs, and Pirates: A Spectrum-based Theory of Enterprise." *Crime and Delinquency* 26 (July 1980):358-386.

Smith, K. "Occupational Carcinogenesis and Statutes of Limitations— Competing Policy Goals." *Trial* 16 (March 1980):44-46.

Smith, R.S. "Impact of OSHA Inspections on Manufacturing Injury Rates." *Journal of Human Resources* 14 (Spring 1979):145-170.

Stein, Harry H. "American Muckrakers and Muckraking: The 50-Year Scholarship." *Journalism Quarterly* 56 (Spring 1979):9-17.

Storey, D.J., and McCabe, "The Criminal Waste Discharger." *Scottish Journal of Political Economy* 27 (February 1980):30-40.

"Study on the Impact and Incidence of White-Collar Crime in American Society." Proposal No. JYFRP-80-R-0031 to U.S. Department of Justice, 18 August 1980.

"Symposium: White-Collar Crime." *American Criminal Law Review* 17 (Winter 1980):271-408.

Taylor, William W., III. "Forfeiture under 18 U.S.C. §1963: RICO's Most Powerful Weapon." *American Criminal Law Review* 17 (Winter 1980):379-398.

Tettenborn, A.M. "Bribery, Corruption, and Restitution—Strange Case of Mr. Mahesan." *Law Quarterly Review* 95 (January 1979):68-77.

Tiefer, Charles. "OSHA's Toxics Program Faces a Supreme Court Test." *Labor Law Journal* 30 (November 1979):680-688.

"Too Many Executives Are Going to Jail: An Interview with Stanley S. Arkin." *Fortune* 17 December 1979, pp. 113-114.

Trowbridge, Thomas R. "Enforcement of Criminal Sanctions for Violation of the Federal Controls on the Prices of Crude Oil and Petroleum Products." *American Criminal Law Review* 17 (Autumn 1979):201-232.

Tuerkheimer, Frank M. "Corporate Violence Goes Unpublished." *National Law Journal* 2 (26 May 1980):21.

Useem, Michael. "Studying the Corporation and the Corporation Elite." *American Sociologist* 14 (May 1979):97-107.

———. "The Social Organization of the American Business Elite and Participation of Corporation Directors in the Governance of American

Institutions." *American Sociological Review* 44 (August 1979): 553-571.

Van Meter, D.S., and Van Horn, C.E. "The Policy Implementation Process: A Conceptual Framework." *Administration and Society* 6 (February 1975):445.

Vilanilam, J.V. "A Historical and Socioeconomic Analysis of Occupational Safety and Health in India." *International Journal of Health Services* 10 (1980):233-250.

Viscusi, W.K. "The Impact of Occupational Health and Safety Regulation." *Bell Journal of Economics* 10 (Spring 1979):117-140.

Weber, J.W. "Criminal Prosecutions for Income Tax Evasion." *Journal of Criminal Law and Criminology* 70 (Autumn 1979):355-359.

Webster, William H. "An Examination of FBI Theory and Methodology Regarding White-Collar Crime Investigation and Prevention," *American Criminal Law Review* 17 (Winter 1980):275-286.

Welborn, David M., and Brown, Anthony E. "Power and Politics in Federal Regulatory Commissions." *Administration and Society* 12 (May 1980):37-68.

"White Collar Crime Erodes Respect for Justice System." *LEAA Newsletter* 8 (January 1979):2ff.

Wilkes, Robert E. "Fraudulent Behavior by Consumers: The Other Side of Fraud in the Marketplace: Consumer Initiated Fraud Against Business." *Journal of Marketing* 42 (October 1978):67-75.

Zimmer, Troy A. "The Impact of Watergate on the Public's Trust in People and Confidence in the Mass Media." *Social Science Quarterly* 59 (March 1979):743-751.

Index

Index

List of Contributors

Simon Dinitz, Professor of Sociology, Ohio State University, Columbus, Ohio.

M. David Ermann, Associate Professor of Sociology, University of Delaware, Newark, Delaware.

Gilbert Geis, Professor, Program in Social Ecology, University of California, Irvine, California.

Richard J. Lundman, Associate Professor of Sociology, Ohio State University, Columbus, Ohio.

Robert F. Meier, Associate Professor, Social Research Center, Washington State University, Pullman, Washington.

James F. Short, Jr., Professor, Social Research Center, Washington State University, Pullman, Washington.

Edwin H. Stier, Director, Division of Criminal Justice, State of New Jersey, Princeton, New Jersey.

Ezra Stotland, Director, Society and Justice Program, University of Washington, Seattle, Washington.

John M. Thomas, Director, Center for Policy Studies, State University of New York, Buffalo, New York.

About the Editors

Herbert Edlehertz is a staff scientist in the Science and Government Center of the Battelle Human Affairs Research Centers in Seattle. He received the bachelor's degree in political science from the University of Michigan and the LL.B. from Harvard University.

Before coming to the Battelle Human Affairs Research Centers, Mr. Edelhertz was in the private practice of law in New York City. He directed nationwide federal prosecutions of a broad spectrum of white-collar-criminal activities as chief of the Fraud Section, Criminal Division, U.S. Department of Justice. His other activities in the public sector included direction of federal interdepartmental task forces examining compliance problems in the U.S. Department of Housing and Urban Development and the Agency for International Development and direction of research on courts, prosecution, and law revision in the Law Enforcement Assistance Administration.

Mr. Edelhertz has written or coauthored numerous works including *The Nature, Impact, and Prosecution of White-Collar Crime, Public Compensation to Victims of Crime, The Investigation of White-Collar Crime, The White-Collar Challenge to Nuclear Safeguards,* and *A National Strategy for Containing White-Collar Crime.*

Thomas D. Overcast, a lawyer and a psychologist, is a research scientist in the Law and Justice Study Center of the Battelle Human Affairs Research Centers. His primary research interests concern the relationship between the science and profession of psychology and the law, legal system, and legal process.